**RENEWALS 458-4574**
DATE DUE

# WITHDRAWN
UTSA LIBRARIES

# Syria's Kurds

This book is a decisive contribution to the study of Kurdish history in Syria since the Mandatory period (1920–1946) up to the present.

Avoiding an essentialist approach, Jordi Tejel provides fine, complex and sometimes paradoxical analysis of the articulation between tribal, local, regional, and national identities, on one hand, and the formation of a Kurdish minority awareness *vis-à-vis* the consolidation of Arab nationalism in Syria, on the other hand.

Using unpublished material, in particular concerning the Mandatory period (French records and Kurdish newspapers) and social movement theory, Tejel analyses the reasons behind the Syrian "exception" within the Kurdish political sphere. In spite of the exclusion of Kurdishness from the public sphere, especially since 1963, Kurds of Syria have avoided a direct confrontation with the central power, most Kurds opting for a strategy of 'dissimulation', cultivating internally the forms of identity that challenge the official ideology. The book explores the dynamics leading to the consolidation of Kurdish minority awareness in contemporary Syria; an ongoing process that could take the form of radicalization or even violence.

While the book offers a rigorous conceptual approach, the ethnographic material makes it a compelling read. It will not only appeal to scholars and students of the Middle East, but to those interested in history, ethnic conflicts, nationalism, social movement theories, and many other related issues.

**Jordi Tejel** is a Ph.D. in History (University of Fribourg, Switzerland) and Sociology (Ecole des Hautes Etudes en Sciences Sociales-EHESS, Paris). He is currently a Post-Doctoral Fellow at the EHESS, Paris. His research interests focus on nationalism in the Middle East, with a particular interest in Kurdish mobilizations in the interwar period. He is the author of several books and articles, including *Le mouvement kurde de Turquie en exil. Continuités et discontinuitées du nationalisme kurde sous le mandat français en Syrie et au Liban (1925–1946)*.

# Routledge Advances in Middle East and Islamic Studies

1. **Iraqi Kurdistan**
   Political development and emergent democracy
   *Gareth R. V. Stansfield*

2. **Egypt in the Twenty-First Century**
   Challenges for development
   *Edited by M. Riad El-Ghonemy*

3. **The Christian–Muslim Frontier**
   A zone of contact, conflict or cooperation
   *Mario Apostolov*

4. **The Islamic World-System**
   A study in polity–market interaction
   *Masudul Alam Choudhury*

5. **Regional Security in the Middle East**
   A critical perspective
   *Pinar Bilgin*

6. **Political Thought in Islam**
   A study in intellectual boundaries
   *Nelly Lahoud*

7. **Turkey's Kurds**
   A theoretical analysis of the PKK and Abdullah Ocalan
   *Ali Kemal Özcan*

8. **Beyond the Arab Disease**
   New perspectives in politics and culture
   *Riad Nourallah*

9. **The Arab Diaspora**
   Voices of an anguished scream
   *Zahia Smail Salhi and Ian Richard Netton*

10. **Gender and Self in Islam**
    *Etin Anwar*

11. **Nietzsche and Islam**
    *Roy Jackson*

12. **The Baha'is of Iran**
    Socio-historical studies
    *Dominic Parvis Brookshaw and Seena B. Fazel*

13. **Egypt's Culture Wars**
    Politics and practice
    *Samia Mehrez*

14. **Islam and Human Rights in Practice**
    Perspectives across the *ummah*
    *Edited by Shahram Akbarzadeh and Benjamin MacQueen*

15. **Family in the Middle East**
    Ideational change in Egypt, Iran and Tunisia
    *Edited by Kathryn M. Yount and Hoda Rashad*

16. **Syria's Kurds**
    History, politics and society
    *Jordi Tejel*

# Syria's Kurds
History, politics and society

**Jordi Tejel**

**Translated from the French by
Emily Welle and Jane Welle**

LONDON AND NEW YORK

First published 2009
by Routledge
2 Park Square, Milton Park, Abingdon, Oxon OX14 4RN

Simultaneously published in the USA and Canada
by Routledge
270 Madison Ave, New York, NY 10016

*Routledge is an imprint of the Taylor & Francis Group, an informa business*

© 2009 Jordi Tejel

Typeset in Times New Roman by
Book Now Ltd, London
Printed and bound in Great Britain by
TJI Digital, Padstow, Cornwall

All rights reserved. No part of this book may be reprinted or reproduced or utilized in any form or by any electronic, mechanical, or other means, now known or hereafter invented, including photocopying and recording, or in any information storage or retrieval system, without permission in writing from the publishers.

*British Library Cataloguing in Publication Data*
A catalogue record for this book is available from the British Library

*Library of Congress Cataloging in Publication Data*
Tejel, Jordi
Syria's Kurds: history, politics and society/Jordi Tejel.
    p. cm.
Includes bibliographical references and index.
1. Kurds—Syria—History—20th century. 2. Kurds—Civil rights—Syria.
3. Syria—Ethnic relations. 4. Nationalism—Syria. I. Title.
DS94.8.K8T452 2008
956.91′00491597—dc22                                   2008008013

ISBN10: 0-415-42440-2 (hbk)
ISBN10: 0-203-89211-9 (ebk)

ISBN13: 978-0-415-42440-0 (hbk)
ISBN13: 978-0-203-89211-4 (ebk)

Library
University of Texas
at San Antonio

# Contents

*Acknowledgements* vii
*A note on transliteration* ix
*List of abbreviations* xi
*Frontispiece map 1: Kurdish enclaves in northern Syria* xiii
*Frontispiece map 2: Areas inhabited by Kurds* xiv

**Introduction** 1

**1 The Kurds during the French Mandate** 8

*Kurdish populations under the French Mandate 8*
*The mandate system and the birth of the Syrian state 13*
*The Mandate and "colonial expertise" 15*
*The Kurdish cultural movement in Syria and Lebanon 21*
*Fragmentation of the Kurdish community: politics in Jazira 27*

**2 Syria in transition, 1946–63** 38

*Minorities under suspicion 40*
*Searching for new political horizons 42*
*The triumph of Arab nationalism and the United Arab Republic 47*

**3 The Ba'athist system and the Kurds** 53

*Ba'athism: an exception in Arab nationalism? 54*
*The years of ideological purity (1963–70) 59*
*The years of exploitation (1970–2000) 62*

**4 The Kurdish issue and its transnational dimension** 69

*The emergence of Hafiz al-As'ad's game 71*
*The fall of Saddam Husayn and the collapse*
*of Syrian strategy 79*

vi  Contents

5  **The Kurdish response and its margins: "dissimulation" of a hidden conflict**  82

*The Kurdish parties at the margins of the legal system 85*
*Kurdish identity at the margins of official Islam 95*
*The defense of Kurdish culture 102*

6  **The Qamishli revolt, 2004: the marker of a new era for the Kurds in Syria**  108

*The events preceding the Kurdish upheaval 110*
*The Qamishli revolt 114*
*Toward a radicalization of ethnic divisions? 126*

**Conclusion**  133

*Appendix*  139
*Notes*  141
*Bibliography*  169
*Index*  182

# Acknowledgements

After having studied Kurdish nationalism in Syria during the French Mandatory period (1920–46) I was interested in extending my reflection on strategies of integration utilized by "minorities" in new states and the shifting of collective identities in the former Ottoman territories up to the present. This book is the result of my attempt to examine these issues in the context of contemporary Syria.

I am indebted to Hamit Bozarslan who took the time to read and comment on all parts of the manuscript during its preparation. Nadine Méouchy and Elizabeth Picard shared with me their intellectual wisdom, thus helping me to formulate my own approach on the subject of Kurds in Syria. Conversations with Myriam Ababsa, Seda Altug, Julie Gauthier, Sirwan Hajji Husayn, Siamend Hajo, Paulo G. Pinto, Eva Savelsberg, and Stefan Winter also contributed to the development of the hypotheses presented herein. Between 2001 and 2007 I undertook research for this book in Syria, Iraq, Britain, France, Germany, and Switzerland, and I wish to thank those who facilitated my research in these places. In particular, I would like to extend my gratitude to those Kurds who consented to be interviewed, though sometimes under difficult circumstances.

It was a pleasure working with the Routledge staff. In particular, Natalja Mortensen, editorial assistant, was an enthusiastic supporter from the very start and saw the work through the various stages of production. Finally, Emily Welle and Jane Welle have showed a great understanding, thanks to which they endeavored to translate and polish my long French sentences.

I thank all of the above mentioned for their invaluable contribution and assistance. I alone am responsible for any and all flaws that remain.

One of the maps contained in this book has previously appeared in other sources. I would like to thank the editors of Peter Lang for granting me permission to draw from

- *Le mouvement kurde en exil. Continuités et discontinuités du nationalisme kurde sous le mandat français en Syrie et au Liban (1925–46)*. Map 1. Kurdish enclaves in Northern Syria, page 36. Copyright © Peter Lang, Bern, 2007.

# A note on transliteration

With as much consistency as possible, I have used the system of transliteration adopted by the *International Journal of Middle East Studies* for Arabic. Diacritics have been reduced to a minimum. The article "al-" has been omitted from last names belonging to Kurds from Turkey exiled in Syria during 1920–1930s. The Kurdish alphabet established by Jaladat Badirkhan in 1932 has been used in some cases in order to make certain well-known Kurdish names understandable.

# Abbreviations

| | |
|---|---|
| AIR | Air Ministry, National Archives, Kew, London |
| CADN | Archives diplomatiques, Nantes, France |
| CO | Colonial Office, National Archives, Kew, London |
| FO | Foreign Office, National Archives, Kew, London |
| FONDS RONDOT | Institut kurde de Paris, Paris |
| MAE | Ministère des affaires étrangères, Paris |
| SAULCHOIR | Archives dominicaines, Paris |
| SHAT | Service historique de l'armée de terre, Vincennes, France |

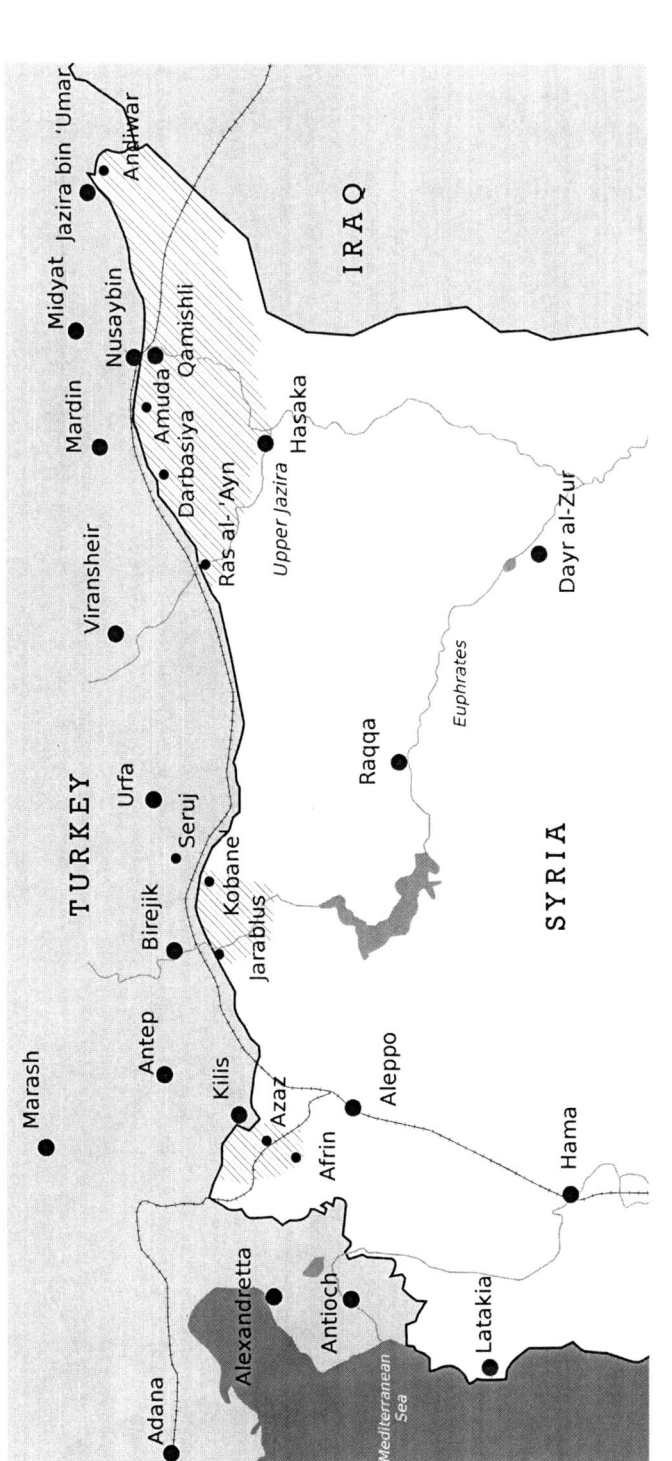

Frontispiece map 1 Kurdish enclaves in northern Syria

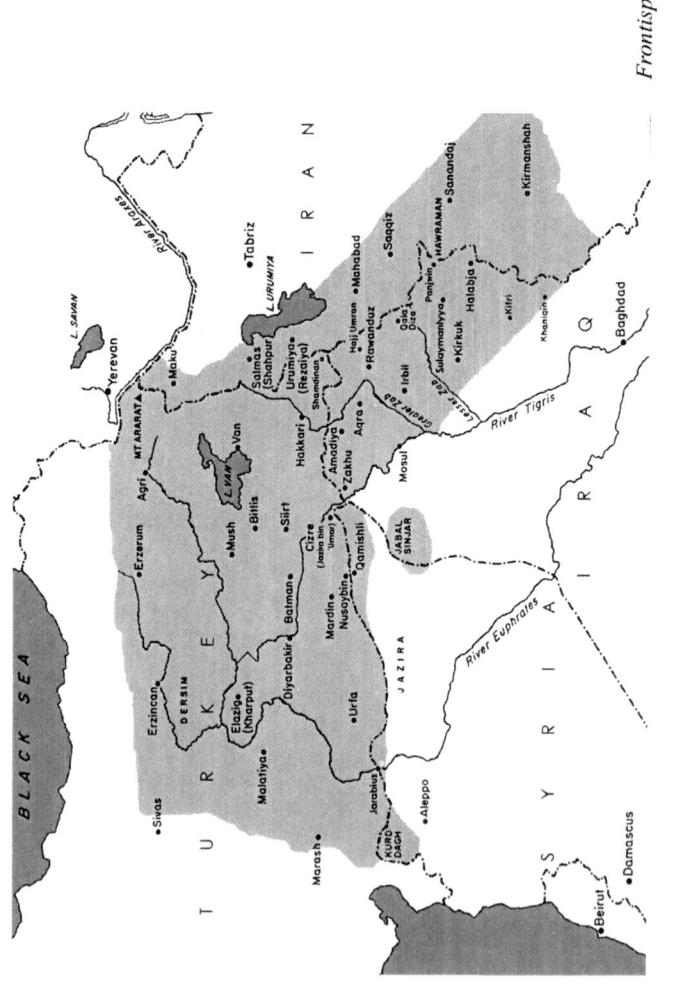

*Frontispiece map 2* Areas inhabited by Kurds

# Introduction

The Syrian Kurds are rarely featured in the media. This is also true of academic research dedicated to Syria, even research on the Kurdish question. Most works concentrate on the Kurdish regions of Turkey, Iraq, and to a lesser degree, Iran.[1] This is not only true for a specific period. The Kurdish factor in Syria has also been a marginal issue in classic works about the French Mandate (Longrigg 1958; Khoury 1987) and the period of independence (Raymond 1980) in the Levant. The only exceptions are the works of Ismet Sharif Vanly, which are generally biased in favor of the Kurds (Vanly 1968, 1978, 1992).

It is only since the 1990s, as a result of the increasing importance of human rights issues in all countries of the world, that the first complete and detailed studies of the Syrian Kurds have emerged (Human Rights Watch 1991, 1996; McDowall 1998). These studies offer some essential chronological reference points, but, even more so, they put particular emphasis on the Kurdish status as a "minority" with respect to the Syrian legal framework. Above all, the riots in Qamishli in March 2004 encouraged the publication of a series of works (Montgomery 2005; Yildiz 2005) and articles (Gambill 2004: 1–4; Gauthier 2005: 97–114, 2006: 217–31; Lowe 2006: 1–7; Tejel 2006: 117–33, 2007b: 269–76) on the Kurdish issue in Syria. Despite increasing interest in the Kurdish question in Syria, there remains a dearth of anthropological, historic, and political perspectives on the subject.

Many factors are responsible for these gaps in information. First, following contradictory logic, the Syrian Kurds were considered as either a group that could be easily assimilated into an Arab majority environment[2] or a peripheral population which played only a marginal role in the evolution of contemporary Syria in contrast to other, more "compact minorities" (Hourani 1947) such as the Druzes and the Alawites. Also, the lack of a strong political movement had been considered proof that Kurdish "identity demands" were only a resort of the elite (notables and landowners) due to their loss of power in the face of the socioeconomic transformations of the country.

On another level, the field of Kurdish studies, which is still meager, has only become a reality since the 1980s and 1990s.[3] From a more general perspective, the focus of historians and political scientists on the authoritative role of the state and the ruling family, Arab nationalism and the Arab–Israeli conflict, and the position

2  *Introduction*

of Syria in an international context marked by the Cold War (Van Dam 1979, 1996; Kienle 1990; Perthes 1995; Ehteshami and Hinnebusch 1997) had omitted all of the cross-cutting dynamics affecting all areas of Syrian society despite the official statements regarding "Arab" and "socialist" Syria. These dynamics include modes of consumption, ethnicity, Sufism, unofficial settlements in large cities, and a growing generational division. This book seeks to contribute to the new momentum given to contemporary studies on Syria by a new generation of researchers who take their investigations in many new directions, demonstrating an interest in the "margins" and giving priority to anthropological and sociological dimensions (Chiffoleau 2006; Dupret *et al*. 2007), without neglecting the historical dimensions.

In truth, field work in Syria has become more accessible since the end of the 1990s, giving way to valuable anthropological research about the Kurdish shaykhs in Damascus, Aleppo, and Kurd Dagh (Böttcher 1998; Christmann 1998; Pinto 2004). It remains extremely difficult, however, to conduct a field study[4] with Kurdish identity as its central subject, because Kurdishness continues to be considered, in spite of some perceptible changes, a sign of *fitna* (dividing of society) by the regime. Finally, our reflection has benefited from the revival since the end of the 1990s of studies of the mandatory period (Gelvin 1998; Méouchy 2002; Mizrahi 2003; Méouchy and Sluglett 2004; Provence 2005).

Rather than summarize each of the chapters that make up this work, we would like to highlight several themes which we think are important from a theoretical and empirical point of view. The first of these themes concerns the necessity of re-evaluating the role of the mandatory period (1918–46) in the emergence of certain political and social dynamics in Kurdish communities beginning at the time of the construction of contemporary Syria to the present and which belong to the *longue durée*. We also wish to emphasize the importance of the mandatory period in the establishment of a certain "political culture" of Kurdish civil and religious representatives, which were known for peaceful confrontation and the accommodation of an ambiguous political scene. Finally, we will briefly touch on the subject of "margins" in the Kurdish groups and the necessity of both establishing "bridges" between the Kurds and other Syrian populations and of articulating a detailed account of the history of the Kurds, which sometimes involves temporal differences from that of the rest of the Syrian population.

## The Kurds under the Mandate: between continuity and change

An analysis of the mandatory archives, Kurdish publications from the 1930s and the 1940s, and field studies done in Syria confirms that the mandatory period must be considered both a phase of continuity in relation to the Ottoman period and a time of change for the Levantine populations, including the Kurds. This period should be considered as a phase of continuity as the heritage of the ethnoreligious (*millet*) organization of the Ottoman Empire[5] was not eradicated and continued to shape notions of policy and community long after the decline of Istanbul as the political center of the region (Karpat 1988: 35–53).

The group which is known and recognized under the generic name of "Kurd" is far from being homogenous. It includes several dialects, religious denominations (Sunnism, Shi'ism, Alevism, and Yazidism), and various social and geographic identities (both tribal and nontribal). The anthropologist Martin van Bruinessen nevertheless affirms that the Kurds have been conscious of their distinctive identity for some centuries, despite internal divisions. The "borders" defining the Kurds have, however, changed during the course of the centuries. Before World War I, the opposition between Christians and Muslims, tribes and nontribes, proved to be the main determinants of divisions between the populations of the Ottoman Empire (Bruinessen 1994: 21–6).

Thus, ethnicity was not a predominant issue for the Kurdish populations before the creation of the new states in the Middle East. Belonging to an ethnic group[6] was only one component of their identity. Its importance fluctuated during the course of the reinvention of their identity and adjusted according to the whim of their relations with a multitude of actors. What is important are the personal networks of affiliation constructed by individuals, the ethnic network being only one among many. An individual or a community can also have more than one identifying characteristic, such as denominational, ethnic, or urban. Therefore, categories such as "ethnicity" and "community" are created, legitimized, and perpetuated in the context of a complex political equation. They do not exist as "primordial" categories (Geertz 1973), but as groups in a relational dynamic (Barth 1969). Under certain historic conditions, ethnic or national, even transnational identities, can be placed at the forefront and determine the economic, social, and political stakes, but it is, above all, longevity that indicates which identities are preeminent in a specific group (Gershoni and Jankowski 1997: xx).

The reason that ethnicity can serve as a political tool is that it can be perceived as a natural source of social and political cohesion (Berman and Lonsdale 1992: 317). The engagement of individuals and groups around an ethnic identity can only occur via an identity discourse (Vali 2003), a doctrine (Kedourie 1986), an ideology (Breuilly 1993), or even a leap of the imagination (Anderson 1983). Nationalism, with its vague contours, is able to draw together diverse assemblages which can be identified with an "ethnic group." In order to overcome the divisions which exist within the community, nationalism must integrate into its discourse diverse sensibilities (conservative, progressive, supporters of the west, etc.) and encourage "nationalist" actions which touch the entire Kurdish population and merges all aspects (social, religious, linguistic, tribal, and local) of group belonging.

The role of "political entrepreneurs" in the essentialization of relationships with other groups is critical (Smith 1981: 108). The elites set themselves up as spokesmen of the "imagined community" (Anderson 1983) and construct, thanks to their intellectual and organizational capacities, the "national" group. In order to exist, nationalism requires "objective" elements (race, language, kinship, etc.) upon which a consciousness of this distinction or difference (identity) can be based. This distinct identity may then be introduced by "political entrepreneurs" into the modern political field as a conscious and rational tool.

However, for anthropologist Olivier Roy, ethnic nationalism rarely involves political action. Forms of political action are most often created outside of a strictly ethnic logic, even when ethnicity is the discourse "par excellence" of the players. "Ethnicity is operative, but hardly explicative" (Roy 2004: 65). There would be other operative logistics in political mobilization such as infraethnics in the workings of 'asabiyya (group solidarity), supraethnics, in this case, in relation to religious references like the Shi'is in Iran, who founded a loyalty to the Iranian nation-state despite ethnic divisions.

Additionally, as asserted by Rashid Hamo, one of the founders of the Kurdish Democratic Party of Syria in 1957, the concept of a Kurdish community, defined as a group distinguished by one trait, linguistic or denominational, which the group considered as "specific" and a "border" of demarcation from the "others" during a period of conflict, was not a reality at the beginning of the 1920s.[7] On the other hand, patrilineal relationships, local, religious, and tribal ties determined the social practices and the mobilizations of the Kurdish populations of northern Syria. It was not until the arrival of the Kurdish nationalist intellectuals, formerly based in Istanbul, that the idea of a "national Kurdish group" took on a certain reality among a small minority of the Kurdish population in Syria. From that time, the perception of Kurds as a "community" endowed with a sense of solidarity among its diverse elements must be challenged at least as of the time of the French Mandate.

The mandatory period also perpetuated the triangular relationship between European powers, the local states, and "minorities" that had been in place since the nineteenth century[8] and which have continued up to the present day (Khoury and Méouchy 2007: 20–1). In effect, the establishment of the mandate system in the period following the World War I permitted France and Great Britain to remain in the Middle East. While France was focused on establishing the mandate in Syria and Lebanon, Great Britain implicated itself in the management of the new Iraqi state.

Socioeconomic projects to raise the status of Syrian Jazira and the disagreement between France and Turkey in regard to the establishment of the Turko-Syrian border favored the utilization of the "Kurdish card" by the French (Tatchjian 2004; Tejel 2007a). As a result, thousands of Kurdish refugees, including the instigators of the Kurdish movement in Turkey, moved to Syria. Although France did not always present a clear and consistent policy toward the Kurds, Kurdish "political entrepreneurs," intellectuals, and tribal chiefs could, to a certain extent, develop their community's strategies of formation and action, including the organization of a military revolt against the Kemalist regime, around Ararat in the northeast of Turkey in 1927–31 (Nouri Pacha 1986).

The price of this alliance between modernistic elites and tribal chiefs was the nationalist movement's dependence on infraethnic group solidarity and finally a progressive, mutual intermingling that permitted the formation of an "identity between 'asabiyya and the ethnic group" (Roy 2004: 47). Also, the involvement of the Kurdish movement in the Ararat revolt indicates that active Kurdish nationalists in Syria had their view turned toward other Kurdish regions, particularly in Turkey and Iraq. From then on, the orientation of the Kurdish demands toward these two countries, under the regime of Hafiz al-As'ad, was well established. It was inspired by the incontestable reality of the transborder character of the Kurdish question (Bozarslan 1997: 291–347) and the understanding, on the part of the Syrian Kurds, that the border was more a common space, in terms of language, tribal affiliation, ethnicity, and family, than a line of separation.

At the same time, the exploitation of the Kurds by France reinforced the existing dynamics by exacerbating the existing divisions between the already fragmented Kurdish groups. Thus, French officials of the mandatory administration prodded Kurdish nationalists (with the support of the tribal chiefs) to concentrate their political activities on Jazira (Terrier Plan). Each Kurdish enclave was treated as a separate territory, with no political ties between them. What is more, the poor state of the roads between various regions of northern Syria made relations between the Kurds and the creation of a unified Kurdish "space or envisioned community" (Deutsch 1962) very difficult.

## Politics and infrapolitics

The instrumentalist and "situational" approaches to ethnicity do not explain why non-elites clung to their ethnicity and why members of an "ethnic group" involve themselves in the "identity" movement. Certainly, groups of intraethnic solidarity, like certain tribes, may use ethnic discourse to disguise the "selfish" interests of the *'asabiyya,* but how could the militant involvement of nontribal elements, in the name of ethnic identity, be explained? If some tribes use the "ethnic" movement to advance their own situation, would this mean that for tribal members, ethnicity is superfluous and stripped of meaning? Finally, can the lack of political action around the issue of ethnic identity in a given state mean that there are no problems in areas where ethnicity play a predominant role?

The Syrian Kurdish movement has traditionally employed a strategy of peaceful action, coupled with a moderate political program. The Syrian parliament which emerged during the mandatory period had, despite its failings, permitted the political integration of civil representatives from the Kurdish communities. However, the opening of the Syrian political space during the mandate was not the only factor to explain the apparent accommodation of Kurdish nationalist leaders in the Syrian legal system.

As with other tribal chiefs and ethnoreligious community representatives of the Levant, Kurdish leaders were enlisted by the French authorities, creating dependency in regard to the administrative machine. Even though these preferential relationships opened ways for Kurdish ethnicity to establish its local power, the room for maneuverability of the Kurdish representatives was limited by the French. Kurdish elites were forced to navigate in a political arena with several other players (mandatory powers, officers of the Intelligence Services, local state, minority players, etc.) who often took opposing positions and had ambiguous attitudes toward Kurdish identity claims in Syria, attitudes which were maintained throughout the mandate and beyond.

In the postmandate era, Syrian political space became progressively less tolerant of ethnic pluralism. The "Arabness" of Syria, anti-imperialism (and as a corollary, the rejection of western democracy), enmity toward Israel, and for certain sectors, pan-Arab aspirations constituted elements of a "consensus" between the principal political and military forces in the country, excluding all other visions of the construction of the state and Syrian society. The steady progression of an ideological unanimism in Syria encouraged a strategy of "dissimulation" (Mardin 1977; Scott 1990) among the Kurdish communities. This strategic act shows that under certain conditions, social, ethnic, and religious groups may choose to cultivate their differences in order to challenge the official unanimous ideology. The "permeability of the disguise" depends on the degree of dominance in the relationship: "The greater the disparity in power between dominant and subordinate, and the more arbitrarily it is exercised, the more the public transcript[9] of subordinates will take on a stereotyped, ritualistic cast" (Scott 1990: 3).

Like all Syrian citizens, the Kurds had been coerced into acting as though they adhered to the regime, its leader, and its principles (Wedeen 1998, 1999). But the Kurds had also been encouraged, for two decades (1963–84), to cultivate their identity away from the public sphere. This fact guides our interest toward the actions and strategies of Kurdish players in the domain of infrapolitics, "the silent partner of a loud form of public resistance" (Scott 1990: 199). To affirm the importance of practices of infrapolitics is to also affirm that beyond the official unanimist façade in Syria, Kurdish society, and Syrian society in general, has not been hindered as much as has been suggested (Droz-Vincent 2004). To the contrary, somewhere between submission and revolt (Badie 1987: 226, 231–2), there exists a political terrain which is much more difficult to grasp than that of open political struggle.

The vivacity of the infrapolitics of subordinate elements can more easily be measured after the "mask" is removed. The road from "dissimulation" to "visibility" depends, in large measure, on political opportunities because "depending upon circumstances and political structures, even the most die-hard nationalists may choose to emphasize their socio-economic status, civic identity, or religious affiliation over their distinct ethno-nationalism" (Natali 2005: xxiii). However, as the massive mobilizations of the Syrian Kurds in 2004 confirmed, the perception of windows of opportunity by the "challengers" can also be influenced by subjectivity. It is then necessary to look not only at rational factors, but also at areas of subjectivity.

## Multivariant temporalities

The mandatory and postmandatory periods (1946–63) were witness to two parallel and nonexclusive dynamics: on the one hand, the progressive ethnicization of individuals and groups known as Kurds and, on the other, the formation of a "civil society"[10] which relied on the active participation of members of all the "communities" based not on communal solidarity but on ideological commitment and political factions (Syrian nationalism, pan-Arabism, communism, etc.).

The Kurds had been subjected to a large number of legal measures which had affected all Syrian populations, such as the establishment of a state of emergency since 1963. Aside from the emergence of a regime with an authoritative stance toward individual liberties, there were other actions promoted by the Ba'athist regime which did not only affect the Kurds, such as the Arabization of toponyms in Christian villages. Rural exodus had been another socioeconomic transformation touching all peripheral regions. There were clearly many possibilities for "bridging the gap" between the Kurds and mainstream Syrian society.

However, it is necessary to remember that the politics of the Syrian regimes has inadvertently but nevertheless directly contributed to the ethnicization of relations between the Kurds and the other populations. The Kurds, understood by the government as a "community" or "group" apart, have been the object of specifically discriminatory policies, such as being forbidden to teach their language, the "Arab belt" project in Jazira, revoking of Syrian citizenship for 120,000 people, as well as the institutionalized symbolic violence of having their ethnic identity excluded from the definition of Syrianness. Finally, the statement of the "exteriority" of the Kurds progressively nourished the sentiment among the Kurds that they constituted a "national minority."[11]

Furthermore, Kurdish groups have not only been affected by local and national sociopolitical transformations, but also by transborder dynamics,[12] in regard to their "macro-ethnicity" (Roy 1991: 22). These transborder dynamics include tribal, familial, and religious networks, armed Kurdish struggles in Turkey (1927–31; 1984–2007) and Iraq (1943–45; 1961–70; 1986–88), and the increasing independence of Iraqi Kurdistan since 1991. Therefore, a history alternating references common to all Syrians with a detailed chronology, carefully inscribed in the Kurds' own reality, has become a necessity.

We are aware that we have not exhausted all levels of analysis (Revel 1996), nor covered all relevant geographic areas or the broad range of themes – including gender issues, land distribution, mixed marriages, and so on – which exist in the margins not only of the Syrian political system, but also of Kurdish political parties, in bringing to light the complexity of Kurdish populations and their integration into the Syrian society. However, this task would require a much easier access to the field and a collective and interdisciplinary effort. We nevertheless hope to have introduced new questions and provided additional information, which will allow us to advance our knowledge and understanding of the Kurds of Syria.

# 1 The Kurds during the French Mandate

The Ottoman Empire's entry into the war directly affected the Levant by opening a front on the Suez Canal. During the same period, Middle Eastern countries were being affected by the ambitions of the European powers in the region. French ambitions began to take shape during a period when Syria and the Middle East in general were experiencing significant transformations, be it economically, by way of the region's integration into the world economy, or politically, by the policies of the *Tanzimat*[1] and the assertion of Arab nationalist ambitions, with the two developments being indirectly connected.[1]

Despite the continuity of local power during the French Mandate, the old elites of Syria were challenged during this period by a new generation of leaders and new ideologies, as a consequence of diverse social and institutional changes, including the declining significance of "vertical ties of dependency" within the broader context of social hierarchy. In their stead, "the organization of power relationships among the non-elites of Syria increasingly followed horizontal, associational and national lines" (Gelvin 1994: 646). The mandatory power was largely responsible for further transformations in the region. The French authorities were important agents in defining local ethnic and religious groups as minorities and in creating modern nation-states, namely Syria and Lebanon. Minorities became a constant source of friction between the local Sunni elites and the French Mandatory administration. The concept of specific social and cultural groups as "minorities" was a new construction, having been recently inherited from the Ottoman *millet* system[2] and having emerged from the creation of new, naturally homogenizing nation-states. Among the "minorities" the Kurds represented the largest non-Arab Muslim group in Syria from the 1920s onward.

## Kurdish populations under the French Mandate

The majority of Syrian Kurds speak Kurmanji (a Kurdish majority dialect spoken in Turkey and northeastern Iraq and Iran) and are Sunni Muslims with the exception of the Yazidis[3] who are dispersed between Jazira, the Jabal Siman region, the Afrin valley, and Kurd Dagh. The Kurdish populations placed under French Mandate occupy three narrow zones, isolated from one another, all along the Turkish frontier: Jazira, Jarablus, and Kurd Dagh. These three Kurdish enclaves constitute the natural extension of Kurdish territory into Turkey and Iraq. However, the Syrian Kurds, because of their geographic origins, their history, their lifestyle (nomadic/sedentary), and their settlement of diverse environments (e.g. Alexandretta, Hawran, Jazira) did not constitute a homogenous group at the beginning of the twentieth century. On the contrary, the populations designated as Kurds were characterized by their segmented nature, a trait that was further reinforced by the French during the mandate.

Subsequently, it became impossible to speak in terms of unique identifying characteristics of the Syrian Kurds during the first half of the twentieth century. For individuals and groups (e.g. clans, tribes, families), ethnic identity was more likely determined according to their social and political interests and constraints and less often in terms of their linguistic and historic identifying traits. Up until the advent of contemporary Syria, the natural reference point for Kurdish groups was not found in ethnic or linguistic terms, but it was defined in relational terms, including geographic origin (valley, village, quarter), family, clan, tribe, or sect (as for the Yazidis). In light of these factors, it is problematic to consider the Kurds as a "minority" in the prescriptive sense during the mandatory period.

Certain Kurdish tribes present in *Bilad al-Sham* (Syria Land) in the eighteenth century preserved their close endogenous structures or their connections with oriental Kurdistan, while others were assimilated into villages and Turkish and Arab confederations. Thus, while the Kurds of north Aleppo were being integrated into rural Ottoman society during this period, all the while maintaining their ethnic "frontiers" (Barth 1969), the Kurdish tribes established on the Qusayr Plateau were quickly being assimilated into the Arab populations. During the mandate, five large tribes were sharing Kurd Dagh: Amikan, Biyan, Sheikan, Shikakan, and Jums. Among the other, smaller tribes were the Robariya, Kharzan, Kochar, and Khastiyan. Most of the 26 Yazidi villages, with a total population of about 1,140 members, were subject to the Robariya leaders (Lescot 1975: 265–8).

Among the Kurdish tribal confederations deeply rooted in northern Syria, the Millis were distinguishable. The presence of the Millis is documented in Ottoman sources from the year 1518 onward. At the time of Diyarbakir's incorporation into the empire, they controlled the southern foothills of the Qaraja Dagh and were frequently assigned to the tribal district governorship of nearby Mardin.

Beginning in the late seventeenth century the Millis came under the purview of the empire's tribal settlement project and were forced to settle first around Diyarbakir and then in the *eyalet* of Raqqa. They frequently left the lands assigned to them to return north to better pastures. From the eighteenth century, the tribe was powerful enough to refuse to pay tribute and to fight against the Porte (1830–40). Internal struggles in the confederation and conflict with Arab tribes from the Shammars had a weakening effect until a new chief, Ibrahim Pasha, arrived, infusing the tribe with new life. However, Ibrahim Pasha never actively opposed the central government. On the contrary, he aided the sultan by providing men for the *Hamidiyye* regiments, created at the end of the nineteenth century. During the Young Turk revolution, he again sided with the sultan and tried to rouse Syrian support. Pursued by the Young Turks, he found refuge in Syria where he died under mysterious circumstances.[4] His heir,

10  *The Kurds during the French Mandate*

Mahmud Bey (aka Mahmud ibn Ibrahim Pasha), would never enjoy the same prestige as his predecessor (Rondot 1937: 34–9). Later, the new international boundary, established by the French and the Kemalist government at Ankara in October 1921, would cut straight through this region, leaving a large part of the Millis' ancestral lands within the mandated territory of Syria.

Besides the Millis, other seminomadic and sedentary tribes were present in Jazira: the Dakkuri, the Heverkan, the Hasenan, and the Mirans. The left bank of the Euphrates, around Jarablus and Seruj, as well as some strips of land on the right bank, had been settled by Kurds at the beginning of the seventeenth century following forced migrations provoked by the sultans. Thus was formed, in Jarablus, the Kurdish confederation of Barazi, which united its very heterogeneous members, some of whom claimed to be of Arab origin. Before the arrival of the French and the delimitation of the Turko-Syrian border, the Barazi wandered the hilly region between the plain of Seruj and the Jarablus. This 16,000-strong Kurdish group inhabiting Jarablus can be divided into five tribes: Alaedinan, Shedadan, Sheikan, Kitkan, and Pijan.

Kurdish–Arab relations were not defined entirely by any isolated series of interactions between these two groups. The Kurds had been deported in significant numbers deep into Arab countries as punishment or at the whim of sovereigns for administrative or military purposes. Consider the example of the long-standing Kurdish military colonies in Damascus, in the Hawran, in Upper Galilee and in Jordan, along the pilgrims' route (Zelter 1969: 18–19).

The Kurdish military colony in Damascus was made up of Kurdish regiments who, in the thirteenth century, had accompanied Salah al-Din al-Ayyubi (Saladin) who was of Kurdish origin himself, during the crusades. In the beginning, these first Kurdish regiments settled in the Suq al-Saruja quarter before subsequently migrating to Mount Qasyun. Under the Ottoman Empire, the Kurdish community's military role in Damascus was confirmed. Kurdish soldiers and police officers imposed order in the town and at the same time assured the protection of the pilgrims' route toward Mecca. Many Kurds from Syria's rural hinterland joined the local Janissary corps (*yerliyye*). Others, trained in Istanbul, arrived in Damascus as members of the Imperial Jannissaries (*qapi-qul*). For many Kurds in Damascus, identification with their mission contributed to a profound feeling of belonging to a distinct ethnic group.

Subsequently, Kurdish migrants of diverse origin (Diyarbakir, Mosul, Kirkuk) came to join these military elements causing the expansion of the Kurdish quarter. It was only under the French Mandate that *Hayy al-Akrad* or the Kurdish quarter, with an estimated 12,000 inhabitants during the 1930s, was entirely integrated into Damascene life thanks to the construction of a shaded boulevard which united the Kurdish quarter with the rest of the city. However, during the nineteenth century, before this overdue urban reconciliation, certain Kurdish notables had succeeded in gaining political and economic notoriety in the Syrian capital. In effect, the *Tanzimat* reforms, and in particular the land law, allowed local notables to acquire vast expanses of land in the countryside around Damascus. Likewise the administrative reorganization of the city between 1840 and 1860 permitted the new landowning aristocracy of Damascus to fortify its position at the expense of the traditional power of religious leaders (Khoury 1987: 26–46).

Among the Kurdish notables settled in the Kurdish quarter, two families, the Yusufis and the Shemdinis, distinguished themselves from the rest. The Yusufis, cattle merchants, could be traced back to Diyarbakir, while the Shamdinis' origins are not clear. Although the two families decided to settle in the Suq Saruja, a move which indicated their upward social mobility, they maintained their client network in the Kurdish quarter in Damascus. The other family of Kurdish notables of Damascene origin was the Abids, who were, however, not as well established in *Hayy al-Akrad* and had considerably less power (Khoury 1983: 37–40). The Kurdish elites were perfectly integrated into the economic and political life of the city and their neighborhoods,[5] unlike a large part of the quarter's other inhabitants. The local leaders maintained ethnicity not so much as a political resource by which to defend their "specific rights" as a minority, but rather as a tool to assure clientelist relations between its members.

Finally, since the nineteenth century Aleppo also had a Kurdish quarter, whose population was bolstered by the constant arrival of immigrants from Kurd Dagh and Jazira or by commercial exchanges between the Aleppine town and the countryside to the northeast.

## *Kurds, Arabs, and the colonial state*

The agreements and treaties signed by the Allies after the collapse of the Ottoman Empire considerably diminished the area of French influence in the Middle East. The Kurdish regions entrusted to the French by the mandate of 1920 were reduced to an area bounded by Antep, Birejik, Mardin, and Jazira bin 'Umar. The Franco-Turkish agreement of October 20, 1921 limited French influence even further in the Kurdish regions to where they were bounded by the line drawn by Payas, Meidan Ekbes, to the south of Kilis, Tchoban Bey, to the railway line connecting Baghdad and Nusaybin, to the old route between Nusaybin and Jazira bin 'Umar, the last two of which were located outside of the new boundaries of French authority. Finally, France lost Sinjar, another piece of Kurdish territory, inhabited by Kurdish Yazidis and conceded to Iraq by the Syrian–Iraqi agreement of July 3, 1933. The mandatory power only came to incorporate the Syrian Kurds as French troops progressively took over territories inhabited by Kurdish tribes. This colonization process lasted a full decade, which is rather unusual under a mandate system.

The first Kurdish populations encountered by the French in Syria were those of Kurd Dagh toward the end of 1919, when French troops penetrated this mountainous region with relative ease. The Damascene Kurds proved themselves to be immediately loyal to the French after the fall of Faysal's cabinet in July 1920.[6] The great Kurdish families of al-Yusuf and Shemdin, although steadily "Arabized" over the course of the nineteenth century, were never particularly well disposed toward Arab nationalism, which threatened to erode the ethnic and clan loyalties on which their influence was partly based. Furthermore, according to Philip S. Khoury, "the role that Kurdish auxiliary troops had played in suppressing the Great Revolt [in 1925] strained relations between [Arab] nationalists and the Kurds of Damascus for the duration of the mandate" (Khoury 1984: 526).

The Kurdish tribes from the Jarablus region expressed diverse attitudes toward French presence in the region. The Kitkan submitted immediately to the French troops on their arrival in 1920, and the Millis cooperated with the French in the Urfa region. However, several Kurdish bands, among them clans connected to the Millis, encouraged by pan-Islamic propaganda joined the Turks in combat between the French troops and those regiments loyal to Mustafa Kemal around Marash, Antep, and Urfa. However, it was in Upper Jazira that the mandatory authorities encountered the greatest resistance up until 1926. Once again, Kemalist (pro-Turkish) propaganda in Jazira, targeting Kurdish and Arab tribes, proved to be extremely effective in hindering the advance of French troops. The result of the progressive and fragmented integration of Kurdish populations in mandatory Syria was a redefinition of Kurdish identity at the local level, "in the face of universalist representations of Kurdish ethnicity suggested both by nationalist historians and state-centered historical interpretations" (Fuccaro 2004: 595).

In this sense, the Kurdish case is not exceptional, since every ethnic and religious group in Syria followed a parallel evolution. The Syrian political landscape during the 1920s was characterized by great ambiguity. Various communities and their leaders were trying to adapt to or gain an advantage in a confused and changing environment which was marked by many issues such as the ending of the Ottoman Empire, pan-Islamic propaganda, the establishment of the French Mandate, and international attempts to protect "minorities," among others.

The anti-French revolts in the southwest of Aleppo in 1919 were a good example of this scenario. Most studies of these uprisings assume that they represented a local expression of an embryonic Arab nationalist movement with a primary aim of preventing France from overthrowing the government established in Damascus by Amir Faysal bin al-Husayn and his allies. However, there is ample evidence to challenge this view. The guerrillas who took part in the revolts belie the claim that the movement's primary objective was to promote a return to a decentralized Ottoman polity dominated by Muslims, which would protect the local elite's hegemony as landowning rural notables or ascending bureaucrats (Lawson 2004: 257–74). Furthermore, those who joined the uprisings in the north tended to express their reasons for taking up arms against the French as based in Islamic ideology, through the use of Islamic terms and symbols (e.g. in terms of "holy war" and "anti-infidel" discourse).[7]

Such use of religious rhetoric and symbols does not necessarily rule out the possibility that some of the rebels' underlying motivations were more likely related to local patriotism (Mizrahi 2003b: 23), the protection of a lifestyle, and other cultural values (Méouchy 2004: 286). In other regions of Syria, particularly in the Hawran, Arab nationalism could be seen as an underlying motivation combining strong local identity with a broader ethnic consciousness (Provence 2005: 20–2).

In summary, a study of political mobilization during the mandatory period is impossible if its interpretation hinges on a binary minority/majority opposition (Kurd/Arab) when each of the two groups constitutes a hybrid sociopolitical entity. In other words, if the Syrian state was in a construction phase during the French Mandate, the Kurdish "group" was experiencing a transition in its own right (Fuccaro 2004: 595).

The ambiguity of the Syrian political scene, coupled with the segmented nature of the Kurdish population and the mandatory policy which was committed to the fragmentation of the Kurdish sphere, impeded all attempts to mobilize the Kurdish enclaves behind a nationalist ideal. The rare mobilizations of the Syrian Kurds during the mandatory period – the autonomist movement in Jazira and the Murud movement in Kurd Dagh,[8] for example – had an eminently local impact. The socioeconomic development of the majority of Kurdish areas favored the continuation of a politic of primordialism (primordial links and networks like tribe, village, or even family) that defined popular and elite movements, as well as the experience of communal belonging for most individuals.

Yet after more than 20 years of the French Mandate, primordial attachments among the Kurds were finally being challenged by notions of national and transnational communities. The result of this process was an increasing conflict of loyalties among Kurdish communities. The growing awareness of a separate Kurdish identity raised great suspicion among the Arab political elites who identified the Kurdish population as an obstacle to Syrian national construction, which was increasingly identified with Arabism. This emerging identity was little appreciated by Jamil Mardam (leader of the National Bloc), who declared that "since the arrival of the Badirkhan brothers, the Kurds of Damascus have gone back fifty years."[9]

The continuity of the old patron–client (clientelist) networks based on tribal loyalties or the re-emergence of Kurdish tribal politics in different forms did not prevent Kurdish nationalism from emerging in the Kurdish enclaves. Quite the contrary, tribal and religious dynamics served to cultivate Kurdish nationalism.

## The mandate system and the birth of the Syrian state

After the arrival of Anglo-Arab forces in Damascus, all promises to respect the independence of the local populations were forgotten. France pursued a policy consistent with its interests in the region, which it considered by all rights its own area of influence. Britain's position in the region was more delicate due to its commitments to the Sharifians.[10] Despite secret compromises between London and Paris, particularly the Sykes–Picot agreement,[11] which outlined France's "exclusive influence" over Syria, Britain attempted to persuade Faysal, the son of Husayn, to abandon his claims on Palestine in exchange for Syria. Faysal was aware of French ambitions in the Levant and looked to the United States and the participants of the Peace Conference to support his ambition to remain in Syria as king. The most important outcome of this diplomatic activity was the creation of an allied commission whose purpose was to study the attitudes of the Levantine population. As a result, faced with French and British reticence, the

King–Crane commission (from the names of the two men leading the inquest) was made up entirely of American representatives.

While waiting for the commission's conclusions, and always with the hope that Britain would honor its promises, the Sharifians immediately organized an Arab government on their arrival in Damascus. In its resolutions, the parliament made a unanimous declaration for Syria's total political independence from Taurus to Aqaba and from the Euphrates to the Mediterranean. The King–Crane commission report, finished in July 1919, advocated Syrian unity under the supervision of a single, clearly defined mandatory power, to ensure, at least for a limited period, the development of a healthy national consciousness (Corm 1989: 135).

Confronted by pressure from the two European powers, Faysal was compelled to negotiate an agreement with Paris by which Syria would recognize French privilege in military, administrative, and educational matters. Moreover, France received permission to remain in Lebanon and the coastal region of Syria, while the Biqa valley was considered a neutral zone. In exchange, France recognized Syrian and Lebanese independence, the establishment of a democratic government, and the right of Syrians to representation abroad (Bokova 1990: 35). However, in Damascus on March 7, 1920, the parliament declared Syrian independence (including Palestine and Lebanon) and rejected all foreign tutelage. Faysal was concurrently crowned "constitutional" king of the new Arab state.

France and Great Britain subsequently invited Faysal to Europe in order to renegotiate conditions to ensure the survival of an Arab state, even a drastically reduced one, in Syria. But in view of the two powers' categorical refusal to ratify the Syrian parliament's decisions, Faysal was refused permission to accept the invitation. It was therefore in the total absence of Arab representation that Syria's fate was decided at San Remo. France again found itself officially invested with an international mandate over the zone stipulated by the Sykes–Picot agreement. The mandate and the division of the country were thus imposed by force. As for Faysal, he fled to Iraq where, with British consent, he received the Iraqi throne, while his brother, 'Abdallah, became the king of Transjordan.

## *The origins of the mandates*

During the period following the end of World War I, the classic system of colonies and protectorates received bad press not only in the United States but also in Europe. Negative memories of the colonial wars persisted. Moreover, neither Bolshevik Russia nor the United States recognized the validity of the secret Sykes–Picot agreements. From this time onward, the idea of mandates, consisting of placing territories far removed from defunct empires under the tutelage of the League of Nations, appeared to constitute a compromise between advocates of annexation and advocates of placing these territories under the control of an international administration (Northedge 1986: 193).

While the old system of colonization and protectorates assumes only two parties (colonial state and colony or protector and protectorate), the new mandate system anticipated a third actor, namely, the League of Nations. Under the new mandate system, a new precedent was set, by which the protection of people who were perceived as yet unable to organize and govern themselves would be conferred to the "developed nations" who would exercise this tutelage in a mandatory role in the name of the League of Nations.

However, the Allied Supreme Council decided, on April 25, 1920, to grant France the Syrian mandate and Great Britain that of Palestine and Mesopotamia without consulting the League of Nations, contrary to their expectations. Subsequently, the mandate charter promulgated on July 24, 1922 set out the essentials of the task imparted to France: draw up an organic statute for Syria and Lebanon in agreement with the indigenous authorities which favored local autonomous structures; support public education in the indigenous languages; ensure the security of the territories, and access to relations outside the territories; and guarantee the privileges, immunity, and undifferentiated treatment of foreigners (Fournié and Riccioli 1996: 19).

France, as the mandatory power, was in turn subject to the direction of the League of Nations, and in particular the permanent commission for mandates. This commission, in addition to receiving petitions from the local administrations of each territory under mandate, would also receive the annual report drafted by France outlining the situation of the countries of the Levant and the measures taken to encourage progress toward autonomy.

The High Commissioner, established in the Serail, Beirut, was the first representative of the mandatory power in the Levantine countries and acted as intermediary between the French minister of foreign affairs and the states placed under the French Mandate. It enjoyed almost total power in the legislative and executive domains. Furthermore, by virtue of Article 3 of the Act of Mandate, mandatory representatives superseded Syrian authorities in all relations with foreign countries.

Directly under the High Commissioner's control were the Secretary General and the Special Services (with specialized branches dealing with intelligence, the press, propaganda, and national security) who were broadly responsible for the development and application of French policy in Syria. Among the latter, the most important branch was the Intelligence Service, which was the "cornerstone of French administration in Syria serving as the link between the civilian regime and the military" (Khoury 1987: 78).[12]

## The Mandate and "colonial expertise"

French interests in the Levant were based on a "secular tradition" of protecting Christian communities, which was reinforced during the nineteenth century by a vigorous effort to develop religious missions and teaching institutions. Although French public opinion did not appear to be particularly supportive of the nation taking control of Syria, some businessmen from Lyon succeeded in imposing their point of view (thanks to the joint efforts of commercial, church, and university representatives) in favor of a colonial policy in the Levant (Seurat 1989: 173–220). Finally, France, swayed more by nationalism than by the logic of capitalist expansion, elected to consolidate its possession of "Muslim power" in the

Mediterranean from the Levant (Palestine, Syria, and Lebanon) to the vilayat of Mosul. All of these dynamics were connected to the old concept of a *civilizing mission* and to the French perception of "France's moral duty to extend the benefits of her civilization and language to a wider world, which was also tied to ideas of assimilation and association" (Sluglett 2004: 111).

While the civilization project was accepted by the westernized Syrian elite, the political project of the mandate was rejected by all strata of Syrian society. Confronted with the diverse oppositional issues of Syrian society, the French authorities applied a policy of divide and rule by playing on the rivalry between the rural elites (tribal leaders and shaykhs) and the urban elites, between ethnic and religious minorities (local autonomy) and Sunni Arabs. At the same time, France relied on support from certain urban elites (Christian bourgeoisie and traditional elites) in order to reinforce the Arab nationalists isolation following, in part, the so-called "Lyautey system"[13] (Longrigg 1958; Khoury 1987; Bokova 1990).

French policy in the Levant went completely in the opposite direction to that of the British in Iraq. Instead of looking for support from unified Sunni–Arab nationalism, the French policy was based on the defense of non-Sunni communities, notably the Druzes, the Alawites, and the Christians. The French administration presented itself simply as being the arbitrator between the ethnic and religious minorities and the Sunni Muslim majority. The mandate charter only served to reinforce this argument, one of its aims being to protect the autonomy of certain religious and ethnic minorities. For France, Syrian unity was nothing more than an Arab nationalist invention perceived as an artificial creation of the British to harm French interests in the Middle East and the result of Muslim fanaticism.[14]

The French authorities did not employ the same political strategy when faced with diverse ethnic and religious groups (which were often comprised of internal sects) in the Levant. For this reason, the mandatory state cannot be analyzed as a simple model with one independent agent, given that its different sectors (civil and military administration) were competing with one another and contributing either directly or indirectly in many different ways to the inception of various social movements.

## *The rise of Kurdish nationalism in Syria*

Under the Ottoman Empire, Kurdish identity was not directly threatened. Within the Ottoman context, repression of Kurdish principalities and revolts lead by the Kurdish shaykhs did not respond to a wish to "Turkify" the region, but to a desire to put an end to vague, irredentist desires or concerns related to the emergence of a rival authority that challenged centralized power. Power was shared between the state and tribes alike, and confrontation resulted from the struggle for its redistribution. If certain notables aspired to greater independence, the state exercised enough pressure to recuperate lost power and, as a last recourse, granted a degree of autonomy in exchange for loyalty (Lapidus 1990: 42–3). Certainly, the unionist period witnessed the beginning of change, particularly with the consolidation of

Turkish ideology, to the detriment of that of other nationalist ideologies. However, most intellectuals, notables, and tribal and religious leaders from the prewar period remained attached to the ideal of Ottoman unity guaranteed by the caliphate.

Nevertheless, the beginning of the twentieth century saw the emergence of a Kurdish movement, a predecessor of political nationalism proper, which was growing around Kurdish history and literature. Formed alongside the elites from the other ethnic groups (Turks, Armenians, Arabs) active in the unionist clubs of Istanbul,[15] the trail-blazing Kurdish elites progressively embraced the nationalist ideal, partly in reaction to other nationalisms, first Armenian and later Turkish.[16]

In Syria, Kurdish nationalist sentiment emerged in connection with regional events. After the crushing of the Shaykh Sa'id Insurrection (1925)[17] in Turkish Kurdistan, the Ankara government envisaged the deportation of Kurdish tribes toward the west of the country as a means of clearing the Kurdish provinces of its more dangerous elements. At the same time, members of Istanbul's Kurdish clubs found themselves forced into exile due to repression by the new Turkish regime. While some of them found refuge in Iraq, others looked to France for protection in the Levant.[18]

In exile, certain Kurdish intellectuals worked for the reformation of Kurdish associations into one "national" organization, the Khoybun League (literally translated as "Be yourself"). This committee was the basis for the conceptualization, in Kurmanji dialect, of modern Kurdish nationalism, and by consequence, for the widespread doctrine in Turkey and Syria. The Khoybun League made deliberate efforts to create diplomatic contact, for the most part unofficial, with state players (Iran, France, Great Britain, Italy, the Soviet Union) and nonstate actors of the region (Armenians and the Turkish opposition). In so doing, the Khoybun succeeded in establishing itself as part of the network of politicomilitary alliances, to such a degree that it became an essential regional actor, for example, at the time of the Ararat revolt (1927–31).

The Khoybun also played a role in the creation of various Kurdish committees and associations in northern Syria and in the larger cities of the Levant including Aleppo, Damascus, and Beirut and as such could be considered a "school" of Kurdish nationalism in the Levant. Furthermore, the Khoybun leaders, in particular the brothers Jaladat and Kamuran Badirkhan, played a determining role in the movement toward cultural renaissance in the Kurmanji dialect.

*The formation of the Khoybun in Lebanon*

The Khoybun League embodied a sort of "unnatural marriage" between a westernized intelligentsia and representatives of the traditional Kurdish world. Some intellectuals, ex-officers, aghas, shaykhs, and tribal leaders came together within the Khoybun to work out a new, common, nationalist syntax in order to oppose the Kemalist regime.[19] The leaders of the refugee Kurdish tribes of Turkish origin in Syria were the main targets for the Khoybun leader's propaganda efforts, believing them to be particularly susceptible to anti-Kemalist arguments. However, this alliance in itself was not enough. A considerable effort on the part of Kurdish intellectuals was needed to adapt the westernized nationalist discourse to the mentality of the representatives of the traditional Kurdish world. The following sermon of loyalty to the Kurdish cause, formulated by the Khoybun, constitutes an apt example of this attempt to adapt national ethos to the particularities of a tribal environment:

> I do hereby swear on my honor and religion that from the date of my signing this promise for a period of two years, I will not use arms against any Kurd unless an attack is made by him on my life and honor or upon the lives and honor of those for whose safety I am responsible by family or national obligation. I will postpone until the expiration of these two years, all blood feuds and other disputes, and do my utmost to prevent bloodshed among two Kurds on private matters. Any Kurd who attempts to contravene this undertaking is regarded a traitor of his nation, and the murder of every traitor is a duty.[20]

Despite the mixed character ("traditionalist/modernist") of the Kurdish committee, the geographic origin of its members was limited to the Karput–Bitlis–Botan triangle. In regard to religion, there were no Alevis Kurds in the Khoybun League with the exception of Nuri Dersimi, who arrived in Syria in 1937. From then on, it can be said that the Khoybun became, in spite of itself, the cradle of Kurdish nationalism mainly representing regions inhabited by Sunni Kurds and Kurds of Kurmanji dialect.

The Khoybun attempted to establish itself in other countries, notably Iraq, creating contacts in towns and cities such as Sulaymaniyya and Baghdad.[21] Moreover, it is known that Sureya Badirkhan went to the United States in order to mobilize the Kurdish community in Detroit in favor of the Ararat revolt.[22] However, confronted with difficulties, the Khoybun was able to strengthen its position in the Levant territories thanks to an unexpected coalition which formed between Kurds and Armenians. During the first congress held at Bihamdun (Lebanon), Vahan Papazian, the leader of the Armenian Tachnak party, was present. He also participated, along with Ador Levonian, in the congress at Aleppo on March 29, 1928. Other Tachnak members also worked in close cooperation with the Kurdish committee. This collaboration was sealed when the treaty of October 1927 was signed in Beirut between the Tachnak and the Khoybun, advocating the liberation of the two brother states. According to the text of the treaty, the two parties would each recognize the right to independence of Kurdistan and United Armenia, while the delimitation of the border between the two nations would be decided according to the number of prewar indigenous Kurdish and Armenian populations and the ethnic and judicial principles established by the Treaty of Sevres (Bozarslan 1995: 55–76).

It is clear that the French authorities could have prevented, from the very beginning, all activity by the Khoybun League if it had so wished. According to available documentation, the French Intelligence Services were well aware of the Kurdish committee's subversive activities. The movements and contacts of its members were under surveillance. Additionally, these very services had "official" informers in the Khoybun League itself, notably Memduh Selim and Jaladat Badirkhan, as well as spies in the Kurdish and Armenian communities. The mandatory power in the Levant followed, with regard to the Khoybun League, a highly erratic policy. The Serail was aware of the potential usefulness, under certain circumstances, of the Kurdish opposition groups in the Kemalist regime. Thus, during Franco-Turkish negotiations on the delimitation of the Turko-Syrian border, the "Kurdish card" was *discovered* by those highly placed in the mandate.

Furthermore, France was obliged to take into account the "susceptibility" of the Kurds in the Levant, given their essential importance in colonization projects and the economic development of Syrian Jazira. Nevertheless, during times of high Franco-Turkish tension, France always sided with Ankara, to the detriment of the Kurdish nationalists.

## *The program and doctrine of the Khoybun*

The Khoybun's objectives were disseminated through propaganda brochures. These objectives included: to fight the Turks in order to create, on their territory, a center for Kurdish nationalism; collaborating with the Armenians; refusing to comply with the anti-Kemalist Califat partisans (as a successful collaboration with this group offered no sufficient guarantee of Kurdish independence); amicable relations with the USSR, Persia, and Iraq, with a view to maintaining their neutrality; and seeking support from a large power (France or, if necessary, Great Britain).

The members of the Khoybun League did not systematically defend pro-independence stances. Engaging in a kind of cultural *continuum,* the Kurdish leaders demonstrated, on several occasions, a willingness to renegotiate a tacit agreement with more moderate political actors. This illustrated that the possibility of conforming to autonomy within Turkey's frontiers by the Kurdish elite was not out of the question, as was suggested in Jaladat Badirkhan's *Open Letter* to Mustafa Kemal, president of the Turkish Republic (Badirkhan 1973: 61).

The continuity of the Kurdish discourse also manifested itself in themes dear to the Kurdish elite, educated in Ottoman associations in Istanbul. Following the example of Arab intellectuals, the leaders of the Khoybun expressed their wish to lead the Kurds toward western civilization and the declared necessity of modernizing Kurdish society "from the top-down." But the Khoybun insisted on this aspect as a reaction to Kemalist propaganda, which claimed to have brought "civilization" to Kurdistan. While the official Turkish view regarded Kurdish nationalism, and by extension, any sign of Kurdishness, as "reactionary" and "resistant to civilization," the Kurdish intelligentsia deemed it necessary to counter this Turkish nationalist discourse, indeed, to reverse the roles by demonstrating to the "civilized world" that it was the Turks and not the Kurds who were uncivilized. Henceforth, the Turks became the "enemy," "barbarians" of "Mongol race," while the Kurds, under the Kemalist yoke, were cast as victims, declaring themselves the new "martyr nation." It is important to note, however, that the Kurdish nationalist movement in Syria did not, in the beginning, define Arabs as the enemy.

Confronted by the failure of the revolt in Ararat (1927–31),[23] the alliance of regional actors who were hostile to sympathizers with Kurdish independence movements, and internal struggles in the Kurdish camp, the Khoybun entered a waiting phase in 1933, due to its inability to set itself new objectives and a new course of action.[24] However, the uncertainty created by the evolution of World War II and the French Mandate favored the revival of the Khoybun League. It entered into secret diplomatic relations with agents from several countries. In so doing, Kurdish nationalists came into contact with world powers representing the three great ideologies of the era: liberalism (Great Britain, United States, France), fascism (Germany, Italy), and communism (Soviet Union). The primary concern of the Kurdish nationalists was not the ideology professed by warring factions, but the search for political and/or military support for the creation of an autonomous Kurdish state in Turkey.

According to allied intelligence, German agents exposed the Kurds to propaganda insisting on the fact that, Turkey being allied by a treaty to Great Britain and France, they could expect nothing from the Allies, and that it would be in their best interests to follow the policy of the Axis powers. After the decline of French power in the region the German commission in Syria, presided over by W.O. Von Hentig, made contact with Khalil ibn Ibrahim Pasha[25] and Kamuran Badirkhan. At this point, German projects demanded a new reconciliation between the Kurds and the Armenians, further to which the Germans would assure the independence of Kurdistan and Armenia after German victory, on the condition that the Kurds and the Armenians conformed to Nazi directives and provoked trouble in Turkey.

Although no documents confirming the signing of an official agreement between Kurds and Germans have been found, according to French Special Services, certain Kurdish and Armenian representatives were placed at Germany's disposal to provoke a Kurdish rebellion in Turkey in 1942.[26] However, the first significant defeats of Hitler's army, along with the germanophile orientation of Turkey and the effects of British propaganda on the Kurdish leaders, compelled the Khoybun to cut contact with Germany while trying to reconcile relations with the Free French Forces on one hand and forming an alliance with Great Britain on the other.

An anglophile tendency asserted itself within the Khoybun League, albeit due to influence from British agents who professed that the British government in London supported the creation of a Kurdish autonomous entity, regrouping certain regions of Turkey, Syria, and Iraq. However, British hesitation served to discredit its latest promises and alienated a large number of the Kurdish leaders in Syria who were also being courted by Moscow.

Soviet propaganda targeting the Kurds intensified at the end of 1944. Slogans proclaiming the Soviet Union as a protector of oppressed national minorities and future liberator of the Kurds and the Armenians became more and more frequent. A service especially dedicated to the affairs of minorities and linked to the Soviet legation established in Syria since September 1944 (Ter Minassian 1997: 291) was behind these activities. The importance of this office increased when the

Turkish ambassador to Moscow was informed in 1945 that good Turkish–Soviet relations, in the framework of the renewed friendship treaty of 1925, presupposed the transfer of Kars and Ardahan to Soviet Armenia.

Kurdish nationalist sympathy in Syria for the USSR grew considerably as a result of the contacts established with Soviet representatives at the beginning of 1945.[27] The result of these initiatives was a political document endorsed by Molotov, who was committed, in the name of his government, to diplomatic support for any Kurdish nationalist movement tending toward the resuscitation of the "old Independent State of Kurdistan."[28] However, this support was subject to certain conditions, notably, the military engagement of the Kurds in Turkey. The Kurdish delegates, conscious of the lack of a clandestine organization in Turkey capable of organizing a revolt, failed to give a clear response to the Soviet legation, preferring instead to wait for more precise details from Moscow. The events that followed destroyed any hope of an eventual Kurdo-Soviet pact.

Contact with agents from the USSR left its mark on both the Kurdish nationalist movement and Kurdish nationalism itself. There is evidence, de facto, of a changing paradigm, which translates as a division between the "old" and "new" generations of Kurdish nationalists. The latter were no longer inspired by the west but, following the example of the new generation of Syrian nationalists, by populism mingled with certain socialist references and the rhetoric of national liberation movements.

Thus, in 1945, the Kurdish nationalists created a new association, the Kurdish League (*Yekbûn û Azadî*: "Unity and Freedom"), to replace the Khoybun without dissolving it. Despite the Kurdish League's determination to break with the past, the new committee came very quickly to resemble the Khoybun in its composition as well as its agenda. Without outside support, the Kurdish League, as with the Khoybun, ceased little by little to attract interest.

## The Kurdish cultural movement in Syria and Lebanon

Although the Khoybun made strides in the cultural domain with the petitioning of the mandatory authorities in favor of the teaching of Kurdish in schools and the creation of a boarding school to form the Kurdish elite, the committee, roused by Jaladet and Kamuran Badirkhan, favored propaganda activities and support for the Ararat revolt. The urgency of the moment and the limited number of members of the Khoybun League obliged the Kurdish leaders to choose between fighting with the "sword" and fighting with the "pen," tending more toward the latter.

However, the failure of the Ararat revolt in 1930 set the stage for the reformation of Kurdish military strategy. All these events together demonstrated the pointlessness of sporadic revolts against Turkey without the support of a great power. On the other hand, the Kurdish cultural entrepreneurs believed that a particularly urgent task – the task of strengthening feelings of belonging to the Kurdish community by restoring the language, developing education in the Kurdish language, and reviving popular Kurdish literature – could be accomplished despite their present difficulties.

Abandoning the sword for the pen signified, up to a point, a return to intellectual activities of the Ottoman period. In the scenario proposed by Miroslav Hroch concerning the development of nationalist movements, this approach implied passing from phase C (general insurrection embodied by the revolt of Ararat) to phase A (a period of interest in intellectual research) while hoping that after this initial step would follow phase B (national agitation) ending once more with the final phase of military revolt (Hroch 1985: 22–4). This change of heart was also mirrored by some of the scholarly works of the period, whose subjects included the importance of the language, the cause of Kurdish backwardness, aspiration to modernity, the founding myths of Kurdishness, the search for unity among the Kurds.

The small circle of intellectuals reunited around the Badirkhan brothers took their inspiration from the Armenian model to launch a cultural Kurdish renaissance. If the Kurdish experiment in Iraq and Soviet Armenia both served as examples to the Syrian Kurds, their situation showed a greater resemblance, notably in their weak numbers and in their exile, to the situation of the exiled Armenians in the Levant. In effect, from the second half of the 1920s, the Tachnak committee enacted a lively cultural policy among the Armenian refugees of the Levant, in order to safeguard Armenian identity, by campaigning against Arab and Turkish cultural influences. Hence, the party became the instigator of various cultural initiatives such as the creation of libraries, literary societies, and schools. For the Tachnak, it was a question of creating "true Armenians," men and women who could master their language and who possessed a strong feeling of nationality (*hai tade*) to resist the peril of assimilation (Suny 1993: 220).

The Kurdish cultural renaissance movement also looked to avoid the division of the "group" by increasing the consciousness of national identity among the Kurds, in other words to create a group of "real Kurds," who were knowledgeable of both their language and their history. In order to do so, the by now dormant Khoybun gave its support to the Badirkhan brothers by creating around them a network of philanthropic societies serving as economic and social support for the publication of revues and school manuals. The first initiative in this sense was launched in Hasaka in 1932 in the form of a foundation of a charity society to help the poor Kurds of Jazira. This project was realized in 1932 with the appearance of the revue *Hawar* ("The Calling," 1932–43). This periodic journal (twice monthly, sometimes monthly) was published in two languages, Kurdish and French. The chief editor and owner was Jaladat Badirkhan.

Given the declared objectives of its editor, *Hawar* aimed to make the following contribution to Kurdish culture and identity: the propagation of the Kurdish alphabet; the classification and publication of grammar in Kurdish and later in French; the comparative study of the different dialects of the Kurdish language; the publication of the Kurdish classics and folklore; the definition of the characteristics of traditional Kurdish music; the publication of ethnographic studies on Kurdish habits and customs; the publication of studies on the history and geography of Kurdistan (Badirkhan 1932: 29–30). The widespread instruction of the Kurds in the Kurdish language and in Latin characters remained the principal objective. "We know that our independence lies in our language and that only through learning to read and write our language and by protecting it can we live independently and with pride like other countries of the world" (Badirkhan 1943: 1).

The distribution of literary classics was coupled with the publication of contemporary Kurdish poets (Cigerxwîn, Qadri Jan, Kamuran Badirkhan, etc.), inspired either lyrically or nationalistically and appeared along with prose, theater, and opinion pieces in the columns of *Hawar*[29].

While the revue *Hawar* was associated with work produced by Jaladat Badirkhan, *Roja Nû* ("New day," 1943–46) was closely linked to the personage of Kamuran Badirkhan. Among the Kurdish collaborators, Jaladat Badirkhan, Qadri Jan, 'Uthman Sabri, and Cigerxwîn were so closely involved that the basis of the periodical was the same as that of *Hawar*. *Roja Nû*[30] displayed, nevertheless, an important difference compared to *Hawar*. While the French language section of *Hawar* was composed of articles translated from Kurd, the revue edited by Kamuran Badirkhan was to be found under different titles (*Roja Nû/Le Jour Nouveau*), with often differing contents.

The Levantine Kurds still availed themselves of other means of expression during the French Mandate. Radio emissions in Kurdish began on March 5, 1941 and consisted of 30-minute broadcasts twice a week. Kamuran Badirkhan was responsible for these informative programs broadcast by Radio Levant from Beirut. Although the broadcasts were not very long, news read by Kamuran Badirkhan in Kurmanji dialect reached Turkey, giving both real and symbolic importance to Kurdish language broadcasts from Radio Levant.

The Kurdish associations founded in the Levant and the Koranic schools were important staging posts for the spreading of ideas expressed by the revues and the radio. In Jazira, the Kurdish Charitable Society, counting about 230 members in 1932, subscribed to *Hawar*. Also in Jazira, *Ciwanên kurd* ("Young Kurds") and the Sharaf al-Din Bitlisi Club, driven respectively by Cigerxwîn and Qadri Jan, both of whom were authors of diverse revues edited in Damascus and Beirut, together established the means of expression for the Kurdish cultural movement. In Damascus, finally, the Salah al-Din Club organized conferences and evening classes to teach the Kurdish alphabet in Latin characters following the model established by Jaladat Badirkhan.

## The Kurdish–French connection

The actors in the Kurdish cultural movement found collaborators in the mandatory administration. Among the French officers and administrators in Syria, there were a number with scholarly interests in Kurdish affairs, most importantly, Pierre Rondot[31] and Roger Lescot.[32]

Today, we know that Rondot and Lescot went beyond the parameters of their missions (scientific and military) giving precious assistance to the intellectuals behind the Kurdish nationalist movement, namely the Badirkhan brothers (Tejel 2007a). In the beginning this collaboration rested on two principles. On one hand, the "Kurdish–French connection" was only possible between like-minded parties. The French Kurdologists established bonds of friendship with the enlightened and more cultivated Kurdish elite, with whom it would be possible to establish relations that were viable and mutually beneficial. On the other hand, for the westernized Kurdish elite, as well as for the French Kurdologists, the political, moral, and material salvation of the Kurdish people could only come from the west.

Toward the end of the Ottoman Empire, the Kurdish associations hoped to obtain British aid in order to create an autonomous Kurdistan, and the hopes of the Kurdish intellectuals exiled in the Levant still depended on support from a western power (especially France or Great Britain, the situation permitting). Henceforth, the leaders of the Kurdish nationalist movement showed themselves ready to collaborate with the French orientalists in order to create a wave of sympathy, or Kurdophilia, among the high ranks of French diplomacy and also among the French public.

Relations between Kurdologists and Kurdish intellectuals evolved eventually, though not without ambiguity, toward cordiality[33] and intellectual complicity. This collaboration between French orientalists and Kurdish intellectuals was integral to a new phase of creative nation building. By absorbing the findings and attitudes of European scholars and agents on folk traditions, Kurdish nationalists adopted a strategy that compensated for the lack of high culture with an equally respectable "low" or folk culture, as well as a code for favorably presenting the Kurds to the world.

Attempts to define a Kurdish identity underwent a change in focus as these scholars overhauled and replenished the arsenal of cultural markers, seeking to map the terrain of the Kurdish soul as it was supposedly manifested in their traditional culture. The romantic glorification of the "Volk" which had been the basis of German nationalism from its inception offered the possibility of viewing Kurdish "primitiveness" differently, by seeing it as containing all the unadulterated, authentic, and noble qualities which had been lost in cosmopolitan culture.

Roger Lescot's enquiries provided the editors of *Hawar* and *Roja Nû* important ethnographic material, notably, stories and proverbs, offering Kurdish intellectuals a "calling card" from the Kurdish people to foreigners, but primarily to the western public. Similarly, Pierre Rondot used the proverbs, elsewhere provided by the Badirkhan brothers, to assert the individuality of the "Kurdish people" (Rondot 1937: 27–8). In this way, the Kurds could claim a kind of universality, since by these projections they would discover themselves, thanks to the richness of their folklore, to be equal to those of the Europeans and other eastern peoples.

What is important is that the discourse around Kurdish identity would be legitimized and spread, first by Kurdologists and then by journalists and sympathizers with the "Kurdish cause." Thus, Thomas Bois[34] took up the works of colonial British agents who had worked closely with the Kurds to reject the negative stereotypes present in western thinking concerning the "Kurdish type." According to the image depicted by these authors, the Kurds had many virtues, such as honesty, affection for their elders, a literary sense and the love of poetry, pride in their country, a sense of humor, a strong work ethic, and hospitality. Moreover, according to these authors, Kurds were not fanatics and possessed "virile" qualities (Bois 1962: 639).

By the same token, while the Kurdish periodicals of the Ottoman Empire lamented over the backwardness of the Kurds, deploring in particular the plight of Kurdish women (Klein 2001), the revues edited by the Badirkhan brothers in the Levant claimed that Kurdish women had more freedom than their female counterparts in the Middle East. The privileged position enjoyed by Kurdish women, although the product of myth, was perceived as a hopeful sign for the Kurdish people and as "one of the elements of the eastern renaissance" (Badirkhan 1933: 390).

This discourse was destined for not only for a western public but also for the westernized oriental elite was assimilated progressively by the Kurds themselves allowing them to enrich the Kurdish identity under construction and to enter into the "universal" (ever-present) west. Paradoxically, the so-called Kurdish "national character" that resulted was not so different from that of the Turks. This similarity can be explained by the wish of both elites to construct an image that was compatible with western values, inscribed within a shared framework, resulting in a "mirror image effect." In other words, the opposition between Turkish and Kurdish nationalism compelled both elites to continually adapt their discourse in contrast to their opposite, the enemy. Hence, a kind of mimicry, in a double sense, was established between the "dominant" and the "oppressed." However, this making of the Kurdish identity, marked by an extreme process of social closure, had a significant consequence in that the "westernizing Kurdish elites" had to come to inhabit a social and symbolic community that differed dramatically from the community inhabited by the traditional elites (shaykhs and tribal leaders) and nonelites.

The intellectual relationship between Kurdish elites and French Kurdologists brought about a sort of *consensual* nationalist doctrine. In this sense, it becomes difficult to know who was at the source of this new ethnic discourse that sought to legitimize Kurdish aspirations to establish a state since 1919 in order to give the Kurds a place among the modern nations. Thus, the active role of Kurdish elites in the construction of the "hommus kurdicus," albeit according to western standards, leads us to move beyond the perspective described by Edward Sa'id in his book *Orientalism* (Said 1978). To modify his famous expression, it is clear that the west alone has not constructed the east. In other words, eastern elites have actively participated in this ideological construction. In this sense, Badirkhan's doctrine must be understood as both a program for modern innovation and an indigenous culture of invented tradition.

## *Opportunities and constraints for the standardization of the Kurdish language in Syria*

The Badirkhan brothers were instrumental in the development of Kurdish as a normative and standardized language. First, they opted for the spoken Kurmanji and in particular for the dialectal variant *Botani*, and later they fixed the norm by working on the Latin alphabet, handwriting, and grammar. Following Haugen's explanatory model, one could say that they succeeded in completing and stabilizing the first two phases of development toward the standardization of a language (Haugen 1983), namely, the selection and codification of the norm. However, for the work of the linguistic planners to be successful, the process of standardization implied two other equally determinant phases: the elaboration and popular acceptance of the norm.[35] These two final phases depended on the political and social conditions in which they took place.

The sociopolitical context in the Levant was of a unique character in many respects. As previously discussed, the actors behind the Kurdish cultural expansion had been exiled, not only in sociocultural terms, but also to a political environment different from what they had known before. The liberty of action granted by the French authorities in the cultural arena offered, to a certain extent, a context favorable to the emergence of a Kurdish culture. But given that the French Mandate in the Levant was by definition limited, this intellectual undertaking was very strongly linked to the presence of the French in the region. This gave Arab nationalists all the more reason to oppose the granting of certain linguistic and political rights to the Kurdish minority.

If the Kurdish periodicals published between 1930 and 1940 were principally the work of Jaladat and Kamuran Badirkhan, then the mandatory authority's actions largely influenced internal functioning and the resources at their disposal (photographic material, printing characters, periodicity, etc.). The High Commission's economic support was transferred to the intermediary of the French Institute in Damascus (F.I.D), and more specifically to Commandant Robert Montagne. But for "reasons of political opportunism" the Serail decided to bestow the responsibility upon the delegation from the High Commission in Damascus. Badirkhan's financial dependence on the Serail allowed the French authorities to also influence the contents and orientation of Kurdish publications. Despite the reduced readership of *Hawar*, the Serail took great interest in Kurdish cultural activities, asserting that "we must avoid, as judiciously noted by the Commandant Montagne (director of the French Institute in Damascus), a situation wherein Kurdish studies only succeed in creating a movement whose direction eludes us entirely."[36]

Regarding linguistics, the program for public education in Syria was comprised only of Arabic and French, to the exclusion of all other languages except Turkish in the Sanjak of Alexandretta. The Kurdish language was therefore considered relevant only to the private sector. The mandatory authority's reticence in recognizing the Kurdish language was affected by two complimentary factors.

First of all, we must recall that one of the principles of mandatory policy in the Levant was to avoid compromising relations between France and Turkey, except under exceptional circumstances. In keeping with this principal, after the signing of the Franco-Syrian Treaty in 1936, the High Commission displayed extreme sensitivity with regard to criticism of Arab nationalists. Time dedicated to supporting local autonomies and ethnic minorities was no longer the order of the day, at least not officially. The Arab nationalists, for their part, had no desire to support widespread teaching in Kurdish. Faced with limits imposed by the High Commission, the actors in the cultural revival devised diverse strategies to fill the void, such as night classes,[37] the teaching of Kurdish in the Koranic schools,[38] and various individual efforts.[39]

Political conditions aside, successful standardization of a language also depends on opportune social conditions, and it must be said, during the mandatory period, the towns of northern Syria could not be regarded as important cultural centers. Also, the meager Kurdish "public readership" turned out to be a major obstacle to the development of Kurmanji as the standardized language. Even the urbanization of Jazira during the mandatory period could not hide the fact that the peasant populations, Kurds for the most part, survived in difficult living conditions.[40] Agricultural smallholdings were rare, whilst the aghas kept control of the large farms and in so doing were guaranteed social control of the villagers. Public services, like hospitals and schools, were nonexistent in the rural zones. Furthermore, Syria and Jazira were not unaffected by the worldwide economic crisis. In this context, it seems obvious that the development of the Kurdish language would not be a priority during the 1920s and 1930s for Kurds. Material survival became an all-consuming task.

The small number of societal circles educated in Kurdish also had a limiting effect on the spread of the language. Although the revues edited by the Badirkhan brothers strove to cultivate diverse forms of literature and journalism (translation, political and scientific chronicles, novels, fables, etc.) there were no public or private institutions that could continue their work on the language. Therefore, the task of finishing the work fell on the Kurds exiled in Europe, who became involved during the 1970s. Especially active in Sweden, where political conditions were extremely favorable, Kurds of Turkish and Syrian origin created Kurdish writers associations, which made great strides toward the complete standardization of Kurmanji Kurdish. However, acceptance of the norm proved to be limited to the Kurdish community in exile, since the teaching of Kurdish in official Turkish and Syrian schools is forbidden. As a result, the standardization of the Kurdish language remains unfinished to this day.

## Fragmentation of the Kurdish community: politics in Jazira

Given the late occupation of Upper Jazira, if the French had envisaged a law of autonomy for the Kurds, it would only have been possible from 1927, when this region fell entirely under the control of French troops. However, after 1925, the High Commission put into practice a regressive policy of autonomy aiming to integrate the minorities progressively into the Syrian state, in such a way that no law of autonomy for the Kurds was envisaged. They could, however, benefit from the individual rights accorded to the entire population by the constitution promulgated by the High Commission in 1930 and by the mandate charter.

The first demands came from Kurdish circles which had been advocates of autonomy since May 1924. The deputy Nuri Kandy, from Kurd Dagh, submitted to the mandatory authorities a memorandum demanding administrative autonomy for all regions with a Kurdish majority, that is to say, the whole length of the border region separating Turkey from Syria. Nuri Kandy had a clear idea of the role that the Kurds could play in favor of the French Mandate, such as fending off the Arab nationalists who, left to their own devices, would "influence the Arab Union and bring down the mandatory administration." A second petition in favor of Kurdish autonomy came from the tribes allied to the Alaedinan leaders from the Barazi Confederation, Bozan and Muhammad Shahin. It contained the same considerations of strategic order. The last petition coming from the Jarablus leaders demanded autonomy exclusively for their area.[41]

Nevertheless, these three petitions revealed more the wish of its signatories to become the local support for the French administration than a desire to obtain specific cultural or political rights that would be to the benefit of the Kurdish population. The character of Kurdish demands changed after the establishment in Syria of Kurdish intellectuals of Turkish origin. The former leaders of the Kurdish clubs in Istanbul, now settled in Syria, succeeded in winning over a large part of the Kurdish tribes, notably those having found refuge in Syria since 1920, whom generally backed their political and cultural demands. Thus, in August 1928, a memorandum, based on the mandate charter and on the stipulations relative to the mandatory power's obligations to favor local autonomy, was submitted to the French authorities demanding, most notably, the introduction of teaching in the Kurdish language in the schools of regions with a Kurdish majority; the replacement of all functionaries in these regions by Kurds; the constitution of a Kurdish regiment charged exclusively with the guarding of the northern frontier; French aid to facilitate the settling of Kurdish refugees in the Hasaka region where they would practice agriculture and raise livestock.[42]

In compensation, the petitioners would commit themselves to supporting the mandatory power's policy and to encourage the enrollment of Kurds (already initiated in Kurd Dagh) in the French army. However, the French eventually rejected the petition. Afterward, it was out of the question to create a Kurdish autonomy that could provoke protests from Syrian nationalists or Turkish authorities.[43] However, not all sectors of the mandatory administration in the Levant agreed with this approach taken by the High Commission. Thus, part of the military, working in particular for the Intelligence Services, did not accept the provisional character of the mandate, with the result that some officers from far-lying regions put into practice policies that were sometimes contradictory to the directives from Beirut (Thomas 2002: 3–4).

The independence of the French Intelligence Service in the mandatory administration produced some surprising results in Upper Jazira. Its officers became *conquistadors* in a way, granted freedom of action, "carte blanche," in a region previously little known to the French. Among these officers, Captain Pierre Terrier distinguished himself by the realization of his projects in Upper Jazira. In the region since 1924, Terrier was cognizant of the potential of the Kurds in the colonization project of Jazira and in the resolution of frontier disputes with Turkey. He immediately proved to be amenable to the welcoming of Kurdish refugees and to cultivating good relations with their leaders. He was also responsible for the conception of the project that bears his name, the Terrier Plan. After leaving Jazira in 1927, Pierre Terrier was attaché to the Political Cabinet of the High Commission where he centralized all the affairs affecting Franco-Kurdish relations in Syria. Faced with increasingly pressing demands for independence from the three Kurdish enclaves in northern Syria, Terrier launched a counter-proposition. For Captain Terrier, the geographical disposition of the Kurdish territories rendered the constitution of an autonomous province across these regions untenable. He proposed therefore that the Kurdish leaders and notables concentrate all their attention on Jazira, where "one could hope to see the evolution of an autonomous Kurdish center. As for the Kurd Dagh and Jarablus districts, one must be content with certain prerogatives."[44] The implementation of this plan established the effective division between different Kurdish enclaves and their political and social evolution for years to come.

According to the Terrier Plan, the French authorities could authorize the leaders of the Kurdish National Movement to establish their residences in the town of Hasaka, the capital of Jazira. According to an official report elaborated in 1943, some of the measures envisioned by the Terrier Plan were realized between 1928 and 1936. The foremost among these were the nomination of Kurdish functionaries in Jazira; the constitution of a battalion of the Levantine army comprised of Kurds and Kurdophone Christians; the opening of a course in Kurdish at the Arab college for higher education in Damascus; the creation of Kurdish night classes in Beirut; the obtaining of permission for the appearance of the Kurdish revue *Hawar*; and the Intelligence Service's intervention obliging the Syrian government to grant identity cards to Kurdish refugees having lived in the country for several years.[45]

Franco-Kurdish collaboration ended in 1936, the year of the signing of the Franco-Syrian Treaty, which foreshadowed the independence of Syria and the withdrawal of French troops from its territories. At the same time, thanks to a border agreement with Turkey, the need to use the Kurds to oppose their "northern neighbor" had diminished.

Following Ronald Robinson's model (Robinson *et al.* 1981), the emergence of a "Kurdish policy" under French Mandate was an attempt to influence local intermediary groups supposedly defending French interests. However, Franco-Kurdish collaboration, ongoing since 1925, was not without its weaknesses, given that neither local support nor that of the mandatory authorities was guaranteed definitively.

### *The autonomist movement in Jazira*

The autonomous movement in Jazira, often referred to as the Kurdish–Christian bloc, was partly the result of the Terrier Plan. This movement aspired to obtain administrative autonomy similar to that granted to the Druzes and the Alawites. The alliance between urban Christian notables and influential Kurdish notables in the Jazira countryside resulted in the creation of new social relations and in the learning of the inner workings of the policy of the new elite.

These new political actors were endowed with an arsenal of demands which ranged in form from popular demonstrations over the closure of suqs, to numerous memos and petitions, from the creation of identity symbols like the autonomist flag, to the creation of local festivals. The French policy of forced relocation of urban Kurdish leaders followed a distinctive pattern.[46] Kurdish resistance against central power in Syria was not based in the countryside, as was the case in Turkish and Iranian Kurdistan, but in the cities with outposts in the rural areas. The effect of this was that the mobilizations of Jazira resembled, in a way, other regional experiments in Syria where the active role of the cities, particularly in rural resistance, and the determination of the urban elite to profit from these movements turned out to be a common denominator (Méouchy 2002: 31).

The expression "Kurdish–Christian bloc" was created by French officers to impress upon the Serail the existence of the local alliance between certain Kurdish leaders and Christian notables from 1936, though it did not necessarily reflect the complexity of the ties or the internal divisions between the different groups engaged in the autonomist movement. In fact, more obvious oppositions between center/periphery, Kurd/Arab, Christian/Muslim, and town/countryside obscured the internal divisions between minority groups. A look toward the actors in the autonomist movement helps provide a better understanding of the true motivation behind their championing of regionalist demands.

The driving force[47] behind the autonomist movement was supplied by Hajo Agha, Kaddur Bey, and Khalil Bey Ibrahim Pasha.[48] Hajo Agha established himself as the representative of the Kurds in Jazira maintaining the coalition with the Christian notables. In the autonomist movement, he also occupied important posts, such as the presidency of a local administration, the Supreme Committee of Jazira in 1938, charged with the drafting of provisional regional statutes.

An old *qaymaqan* from Nusaybin, Kaddur Bey enjoyed a certain notoriety in Qamishli, a town built on land belonging to him. He ran in the legislative elections in 1936 and found himself elected deputy for Jazira alongside Khalil Bey Ibrahim Pasha and Sa'id Ishaq, but from the outset he was regarded as too moderate by the partisans of autonomy.

According to Christian Velud, Khalil Bey must be considered as a representative of the "legalist tendency." He hoped for the emergence of an autonomous region under French protection and to proceed toward elections so that the population could choose its "true" representatives (Velud 1991: 574). The sons of Ibrahim Pasha had always claimed authority over all the Kurds because of the supposed superiority of the Milli tribe, placing themselves in opposition to other tribal leaders like Hajo Agha. Confronted with Hajo Agha's power in Upper Jazira in the late 1930s, the Millis changed their strategy and rallied to the National Bloc government providing, with the Barazis, another leading Kurdish family from Hama, several key figures in the national government and the military in independent Syria during the 1940s and 1950s. The autonomist movement was also supported by the Kurdish nationalist intellectuals like Jaladat Badirkhan, who collaborated with the autonomists, drafting manifestos that were later forwarded to the government and the High Commissioner by delegations from Jazira.

For Kurdish leaders, the alliance with the Christian notables allowed them to broaden their influence in cities as well as in the countryside. For the Christians, this allowed them to maintain control over local affairs and also guaranteed the future of Syria's Christian minority surrounded as it was by other minority groups (Kurds).

*The Kurds during the French Mandate* 31

The Christian bloc counted on the support of the religious leaders and notables from the different churches present in Jazira. The most active of these were the members of the churches of Catholic origin, Msgr. Hanna Hebbé, general vicar of the Syriac Catholic Patriarch for Jazira, and Michel Dome, mayor of Qamishli. This pair constituted the driving force behind the *radicals* in the autonomist movement. On the other hand, the Orthodox Syriacs and the Apostolic Armenians chose a neutral position in the conflict between the autonomists and the central government.

Most of the Arab tribes in Jazira found themselves divided between the two camps. The origins of these divisions are found principally in the struggle for power within the tribes and for the control of land. The most symbolic case is undoubtedly that of the Shammars. While Daham al-Hadi[49] took the Damascene side, presenting a candidature opposed to that of the autonomists, the Shammars Sinjara clan had Shaykh 'Abd al-Karim Muhammad, a regionalist leader, as a contender.

The actions of outside actors, notably officers from the Special Services, formerly the Intelligence Service, and French Dominican missionaries, toppled this fragile equilibrium. In fact, the announcement of the Franco-Syrian Treaty in 1936 and the clauses that it contained constituted a threat to the Special Services, inciting certain officers to do everything in their power to prevent or at least delay the ratification of the Franco-Syrian Treaty by France. They also committed themselves to the regionalist movement in Jazira, and they instigated a series of events, such as the "Revolt of 1937," the most virulent episode of autonomist protests, and the influx of autonomist *mazbatas* to the League of Nations.

The French Dominicans, settled in Jazira since 1936, also played an important role in the development of the regionalist movement. Their experience in northern Iraq, their considerable economic resources, and support from French Catholics and the Vatican gave them an advantage over the other Christian communities. Their schools had an excellent reputation in the eyes of the various communities regardless of religious affiliation, and both Christian and Muslim notables sent their children to boarding schools run by the Dominican fathers.

The Catholic clergy had their own interests and strategy, the maintaining of the Syrian mission, in particular, which were sometimes in conflict with those of the mandatory authorities. Certain Dominican Fathers worked side by side with officers from the Special Services who spread rumors among the autonomists suggesting that the creation of a special administration was still possible, thereby disorientating the regional leaders. The frustration of these regional leaders is illustrated in the passage below:

> The High Commission received a visit from Hajo Agha, a Kurdish leader who along with Msgr. Hebbé constituted the other pillar of the Kurdo-Christian bloc in Jazira. Hajo Agha was accompanied on his visit by Jaladat Badirkhan who, hailing from Damascus, drove the whole Kurdish movement. These two leaders categorically posed the following question: "What does France really want? You lavish advice of prudence and moderation on us and invite us to seek grounds for an alliance with Damascus while giving us contrary signals. Who must we believe?" We can assume

that Hajo Agha and Jaladat Badirkhan were alluding to the Dominican Fathers in Qamishli who, with their strong French connections, and the signals that they seem to be receiving, maintained very close relations with the regional leaders. The High Commissioner could only reiterate its advice to Hajo Agha, that he remain calm [...][50]

This look at the autonomist camp illustrates the number of actors implicated and, consequently, the diversity of motives found in the autonomous movement. Moreover, the Syrian nationalists, as well as the officers from the Special Services, had "bought" several leaders, which provoked "the switching of sides" in both directions. As such, Sa'id Agha, Kurdish leader of the Dakkuri from the Amuda region, figured among the partisans of the autonomist movement from the very beginning, only to rapidly become a *fervent* defender of the Damascus alliance. Moreover, the cooptation of a few tribal leaders by the mandatory authorities created jealousy among tribal leaders excluded from French tribal policy. Elsewhere, the turnarounds and inconsistencies of the mandatory policy provoked an anti-French reaction or the search for neutrality among those disappointed with the mandate.

Turkish propaganda also had a notable effect on the Kurdish tribes. Turkish agents tried, particularly during times of high tension, to convince the Kurds to turn their back on France before France turned its back on the Kurds. The Muslim brotherhood between Turks and Kurds was also played upon to rally the tribes from northern Syria behind Ankara's policy. Additionally, Arab propaganda, besides tapping into religious sentiments, exploited the arrival of Assyrian refugees in Jazira in 1933 and the requests of numerous Jews wanting to settle in Syria. This propagated the idea that France planned to create a haven for foreigners in the country, much like the Zionist projects in Palestine. The Arabs and Kurds of Jazira who had been excluded from progress in the region very naturally understood this warning.

*Demands from Jazira*

The principle demands of the autonomist movement from Jazira can be summarized as follows: (1) a special statute with guarantees from the League of Nations comparable to that of the Alawites, the Druzes, or even that of Alexandretta; (2) the support of French troops to guarantee the security of the minorities; and (3) the nomination of a French governor under the control of the League of Nations.

In the most elaborate of the regionalist's documents, they avow that in exchange for this special statute they would agree "to be Syrian citizens," that they would contribute to the "economy of the country," and that they would defend "Syria's frontiers with all their might."[51] Secondary demands could be divided into the following categories: economic (e.g. the granting of credits for the improvement of Jazira's infrastructure, as well as subventions for the pro-mandate tribal leaders); cultural (e.g. the teaching of the Kurdish language); administrative (e.g. the choice of functionaries and police officers from among the native population); and judiciary (e.g. the return to Jazira of all the autonomist leaders exiled by the mandatory authorities).

It seems obvious that the Christian notables and Kurdish tribal leaders engaged in the autonomist movement looked primarily to safeguard their privileged positions in Jazira. As protégés of the mandatory authorities, they were granted land and the statute of intermediaries for the local populations, who had become useful to the High Commission's projects of economic development of this steppe-like region. In close collaboration with Special Service officers, Kurds and Christians alike assured the security of this peripheral province, which escaped de facto Damascene control.

The demands of the autonomist movement were highlighted by an identifying discourse that will be described here as "Steppe nationalism," which should not be ignored. This expression encompasses the diverse elements that shaped this vague new identity, confronted with unionist pretensions from Damascus.

First of all, Jazira was considered by some of the Kurdish tribes to be an "ex-imperial space," much like an extension of Kurdistan under the control of the mandatory power. This explains why, both before and after the formation of the Kurdo-Christian bloc, certain autonomist leaders claimed the *Kurdishness* of the region.[52] This discourse changed slightly during the formation of the Kurdo-Christian bloc. Although the Kurdish and Christian autonomists were newcomers to Jazira, the economic development of this desert-like territory conferred rights on the new inhabitants who considered themselves the true creators of modern Jazira: "They believed that they had, by consequence, the right to self rule" (Tatchjian 2004: 404).

Furthermore, the collapse of the Ottoman Empire initiated the formation of new identities within the framework of political entities, which were themselves defined by the break up of the empire. The presence of the Syrian state in Jazira was practically nonexistent, and thus, apart from a few police officers and Arab functionaries, France remained the principal reference for the Kurdish and Christian populations. The effect of this was that Syrian identity in Jazira became an abstract concept, which had no relevance to the daily lives of its people. From then on, a feeling of alienation toward the government in Damascus was perceptible in the autonomist's discourse. In 1937, during a conversation with the Count of Martel, High Commissioner, Michel Dome, the mayor of Qamishli, explained this phenomenon in the following manner: "[Upper Jazira] was never a part of Syria under the Turks. Their customs, traditions, populations, all differ from those of the Syrian interior. Jazira formerly belonged to the *vilayat* of Diyarbakir."[53]

Finally, the inhabitants of Jazira felt themselves "abandoned" by the political center. Roads were in poor condition. There were no hospitals and few public schools. This peripheral region loyal to the mandatory power was looked upon with suspicion from Damascus. The solution to these problems was the creation of an autonomous administration, managed by the indigenous population. Thus, upon contact with the nationalist culture established between the wars and the "mandatory framework"[54] came the emergence of a kind of rural patriotism, transformed into an autonomist message. The leaders of the movement had the difficult task of winning over the members of this group so that the autonomist discourse could be accessible and succeed in imposing a unique vision of its identity and unity.

In order to win over the largest number of partisans, the regionalist discourse of Jazira tried to reflect the plurality in the extremely heterogeneous nature of even the base of the autonomist movement. Besides the autonomist texts, whose influence cannot be overestimated, there was also a whole series of initiatives encouraging other means of expression. Thus, the autonomist leaders created a flag,[55] which contained symbolic elements from each community, while the people wore banderoles bearing slogans common to Arab nationalists, for example: "Religion belongs to God, Patriotism to all" (La Religion à Dieu, la Patrie à tous).[56]

The autonomist leaders also invented local festivals showing the traditions of the inhabitants of the region, thus initiating a multiethnic and multidenominational sociability in the public domain. The assassination of Christians by Damascene partisans during the events known as the "Amuda affair"[57] in August 1937, was commemorated by the autonomist leaders a year later to reaffirm the bond between the various communities of Jazira in opposition to Damascus and its collaborators. According to the newspaper *Al-Bashir*, these public acts included multidenominational religious celebrations, speeches in Kurdish and in Arab, the composition of the regional hymn ("Jazira is Ours"), and the singing of Kurdish "national" songs.[58]

"Steppe nationalism" also fed on a certain apprehension, perceptible among the non-Arab populations of Jazira who feared that with the creation of an Arab nation state would come an aggressive policy toward minority elements, as happened in Turkey and Iraq. The fate of the Assyro-Chaldeans in Iraq and the threats proffered by high-ranking officials in Damascus toward the Christian populations of the region fueled the anxieties of these communities which had been "protected" by the French up until that point. For the Kurds, particularly those who fled Turkey because of the Kemalist regime's coercive measures, the demands for direct protection addressed to France in Jazira can be explained by the cross-border nature of the "Kurdish problem." In effect, despite the agreements between France and Turkey concerning the delineation of the Turko-Syrian border, the government in Ankara leaked rumors suggesting that in addition to the desired annexation of Alexandretta, other parts of Syria including Kurdish enclaves in the north, could suffer the same fate. For Ankara, the occupation of these colonies appeared the best way of resolving definitively the "Kurdish problem" subjacent in the diplomatic conflict with France.

*From "revolution" to accommodation*

The factor that triggered the autonomist's political offensive was the negotiation of the Franco-Syrian Treaty, according to which Syria had to be recognized as an independent and sovereign state within 3 years from the ratification of the treaty, in order to join into the League of Nations. France and Syria signed this treaty of alliance to last for a period of 25 years. As far as the Druze and Alawite territories, they would be annexed to Syria while conserving a special administrative regime. The treaty failed to include special measures for Jazira despite the petitions sent by the autonomists from the beginning of negotiations between the nationalists and the French. The legislative elections of 1936 provided another reason for discontent among the autonomist leaders. The National Bloc decided to present an alternative list to the one created by the notables of Jazira, marked as it was by regionalism and support from the mandatory authorities. However, the autonomist candidates from Jazira, and also from Jarablus, won all the available seats. The National Bloc, winner of the elections in the rest of Syria, reacted badly to this news, its leaders threatening to invalidate the results.

Under pressure from the French, who feared that invalidation might provoke Turkish interference in the zones inhabited by Kurds, the National Bloc finally validated the results. However, once in government the National Bloc pursued an aggressive policy toward the regions demanding administrative autonomy. The Muhafiz of Jazira, Amir Bhajat Shibabi, intended to disarm the population, encourage the settling of Arab peasants from Aleppo, Homs and Hama in Jazira, and dismiss functionaries suspected of autonomist sympathies (Khoury 1987: 529).

Consequently, the "Revolt of 1937" began. A few gunshots were exchanged and the suqs in the principle towns of Jazira were closed. The Muhafiz chosen by Damascus left, and the Syrian police officers submitted to the insurgents. The importance of the summer uprising of 1937 resides not in the facts themselves but rather in their consequences. In the first place, positions became more entrenched in Jazira, in particularly after the seizure by insurgents of a letter from Fakhri Barudi, leader of the National Bloc, to the Muhafiz of Jazira stating "When we have an army, we will do to the Christians of Jazira what the Iraqis did to the Assyrians [...]."[59] While the National Bloc provoked the fall of the Muhafiz, the High Commissioner Ostrorog named a replacement as well as a new *qaymaqan* who was welcomed by jeers from the crowd. At the same time, the regionalists acquired an alternative local administration in Jazira.

Secondly, the "Revolt of 1937" marked the high point of direct interference in the autonomist movement by officers of the Special Services and of competition between agents in the High Commission in Jazira. If the uprising in Qamishli could be linked to explicit encouragement by Special Service officers, the aggressive attitude of certain Arab and Kurdish tribes toward the Christians was, according to Msgr Hebbé, the result of propaganda issuing from the Contrôle Bedouin.[60] Henceforth, Jazira became a battleground between the two institutions, while the two established camps, autonomist and nationalist, became pawns in a power struggle, rendering peaceful cohabitation between the ethnic and religious groups more and more fragile.

In Damascus, the National Bloc policy was increasingly contested by Arab nationalist elements that considered government policy too conciliatory with regard to the High Commission. Thus, pressures brought to bear on the nationalist sectors drove Jamil Mardam to resign. A double crisis ensued in Syria. The conflict between Damascus and the French authorities went hand in hand with the conflict between Damascus and the minorities. Faced with these two fronts, the National Bloc showed itself incapable of guaranteeing the authority of the governments of Damascus and Jazira. The new High Commissioner, Gabriel Puaux, suspended the Syrian constitution in 1939, dissolved the parliament, and created autonomous administrations (with governors and territorial advice) for the Jabal Druze, the territory of Latakia and Jazira. France's entry into the war put an end to the smooth functioning of the mandate in the Levant. The collapse of France in May and June of 1940 drove the Vichy government to take the reins of power in the Levant and to oust those elements suspected of being pro-Gaullist. With the evacuation of Vichy forces in France, General de Gaulle's followers reclaimed power. In order to guarantee popular support, Free France accepted the principal of independence for Syria and Lebanon and, under British pressure, prepared the ground for the normalization of political life in the Levant, particularly by the convoking of legislative elections in 1943.

One cannot speak of the formation of an autonomist Kurdish–Christian bloc between 1943 and 1944 in the same way as that which was formed in 1936. The opposition to Syrian nationalism by some of the Christian communities and Kurdish tribes led to the rediscovery of the specificity of each group engaged in the autonomist camp. On one hand, the Christians felt threatened by their Muslim neighbors, especially after the Amuda affair and the rallying of certain Kurdish tribes toward the unionist camp in the name of Muslim brotherhood between Arabs and Kurds. Pressure from the French officers (formerly party to the autonomist movement) on the Christian notables to silence Jazira demands in 1938 only reinforced the feeling of isolation among the autonomist Christians. Leading up to the French departure, the Christian notables looked increasingly to accommodate, indeed, to take sides with the government in Damascus.

On the other hand, Kurdish actors brought to the forefront the Kurdishness of the majority of the population of Jazira, thus strengthening the cohesion of its people and highlighting the differences between them and the rest of the country. The claimed identity of Kurds living in Upper Jazira aroused suspicion among some Christian notables who believed they had discovered the true aims of the Kurdish nationalists concerning the future of Jazira. According to Msgr. Hebbé,

> since the incidents of 1937, [...] the Kurdish leaders, the majority of which came from Turkey, took advantage of this situation to launch a propaganda campaign among their co-regionalists of Jazira, claiming that this region was destined to become a Kurdish center incorporated into Kurdistan and which would be proclaimed an independent state.

The report returned by Msgr. Hebbé to the mandatory authorities is telling for a number of reasons. First of all, it underlined the different identity strategies of the Levantine Kurds. While Kurdish refugees paid attention to the nationalist slogans, the Kurds established in Syria for several generations were, in principal, less responsive to the call of Kurdishness. Secondly, it revealed the existence of collaborative projects with the Kurds across the border in order to create an autonomous entity.[61]

The Kurdish nationalists appeared to be playing two cards at once. On one hand, they kept hoping to see the reunification of Jazira with an autonomous

Kurdistan under the patronage of a power or under international protection. On the other hand, they had no wish for open confrontation with the government in Damascus, because if the Kurds were obliged to remain in Syria after the war, it was better not to create a conflict whose consequences would be unpredictable.

It was in this spirit that in 1945, Kurdish deputies from Jazira presented their demands to the president of the Republic, Shukri al-Quwwatli. They expressed very moderate grievances of the habitants of the region,[62] but despite the government's promises, the mandatory period ended without the Kurdish demands being met.

# 2 Syria in transition, 1946–63

The departure of French troops from Syria in 1946 opened the way to a period of social, economic, and political upheaval, which would continue unchecked for nearly two decades. Certain of these upheavals (e.g. political radicalization, expansion of the education system, the agricultural development in Jazira, etc.) originated during the mandatory period or near the end of the Ottoman Empire (e.g. the settling of nomadic populations and the emergence of "middle-class" urbanites). Others, such as military dictatorships and the Arab–Israeli conflict, were the products of regional and new internal dynamics. The Kurds, like the other populations present in the country, played a role in these changes.

On a socioeconomic level, the Kurds were especially affected by the agricultural "miracle" in Jazira during the 1950s. This economic success was based in part on the unique conditions created by World War II. With imports stopped since the onset of hostilities, the provisioning of French and allied troops and of Syrian, Lebanese, and neighboring populations necessitated the creation of a collection and distribution mechanism. Hence, in 1939 a Grain Office was founded, which would eventually become the Mira. To the small farmers who used it, the system proved to be advantageous, as the sale of their goods was virtually guaranteed. Prices increased steadily and profits could then be used to acquire additional materials and arable land. In spite of the economic crisis of 1949, a certain economic momentum was sustained by this system.

The urbanites of Aleppo, Hama, and Damascus, armed with capital, obtained the rights over unclaimed land or acquired land at low cost that had been abandoned by ruined proprietors. In the year 1951 alone, the number of water pumps in the country doubled to 5,068, permitting the irrigation of thousands of hectares, half of which were situated around the Euphrates and in northeastern Syria. Thus, Jazira entered into an era of large-scale mechanized grain culture that would soon be dominated by cotton production. After a period of economic decline at the end of the 1940s Ras al-'Ayn witnessed a resurgence of activity due to the development of large agricultural companies, Asfar and Najjar.[1] Thanks to its commercial railway station, Qamishli attracted many newcomers, reaching a population of 30,000 at the beginning of the 1950s, confirming its status as the economic capital of Upper Jazira.

The economic development that came with increased agricultural production, however, sparked tensions between competing tribal chiefs, known as "cotton shaykhs." The members of this emerging social class quickly established their social status and insured their local power by occupying important political and economic positions and becoming the intermediaries between local communities and the national system.

The rapid development of Jazira also led to the marginalization of certain groups. By practicing an increasingly mechanized agriculture, the large landowners[2] had inadvertently forced a large portion of their farm and agricultural workers, the majority of which were Kurds, to relocate to cities. Some became porters, others became builders or mechanics or tried their hands at business and other lucrative activities (Zaza 1982: 137–8). Rural exodus and abuses by large landowners created fertile ground for the growth of communism among the Kurdish populations. In a new urban setting, Kurds would discover another important sociological transformation of that time, that of the mobilization of the lower class, particularly laborers, by way of the union movement.

This socioeconomic transformation leads us to the second great upheaval of postmandatory Syria, the decline of the "politics of notables,"[3] and the transition from a mandatory or colonial state to a postcolonial independent state. Following the example of Iraq (Owen 1991: 157) as a state which drew its organization and its sense of power from an external authority (France), it became essential after 1946 to find new foundations to secure Syria's unity and, if possible, to secure a legitimacy based on internal resources such as the development of a common Syrian patriotism. The energy spent in the struggle against the French had to be channeled from 1946 toward the resolution of the economic, social, and political challenges that were appearing.

No single social class possessed the strength necessary to monopolize power and play a dominant role by universalizing its own interests and demands. The result was the constant challenging of the authority of the heirs of mandatory order, that is to say, of the notables who first came to power in the National Bloc. They were finally replaced by a coalition of military and civil actors who worked together temporarily to create a powerful and united state apparatus, under the banner of independence, anti-imperialism, and social justice.

In effect, a new generation of players with different (lower and middle-class) social origins and different training, carriers of new political messages, and organized into new parties (SCP,[4] SPP,[5] Ba'ath,[6] Muslim Brotherhood[7]) contested the power of the heirs of the Republic of Syria. These heirs were the *haute bourgeoisie* and deeply rooted landowners who, moreover, were seen to be concerned with personal rivalries and alliances which had little to do with national interests. In 1947 the primary player in the struggle for Syrian independence, the National Bloc, fell apart. The result was the formation of smaller organizations (the National Party, People's Party, Arab Republican Party) which revolved around the notables (Shukri al-Quwwatli, Jamil Mardam, etc.) or "za'ims" (leaders) who were local to Aleppo, Hama, and Homs. These parties did not inspire the allegiance of minorities because they were perceived as being closely tied to Sunni Islam, until recently when they became marginalized in the political arena. In order to escape their marginal position, minorities (Druzes, Alawites, Isma'ilis, etc.) had already opted during the mandatory period for alternative organizations and more radical ideologies advocating, for example, pan-Arabism (represented most prominently by the Ba'ath party) and the Syrian Popular Party (SPP) by contrast, which was perceived by minority groups as a protective shield from pan-Arab ambitions (Watenpaugh 2003: 257–86). This investment in modern alternative parties by the "minorities" contributed to the ethnicizing of politics following the logic of identity solidarity (Van Dam 1996).

Moreover, urban notables during the 1950s found themselves challenged by militants from modest social circles, who attempted to oust them from decision-making positions. This process confirmed the increase in power of networks composed of Alawites or other rural minorities who had entered in large numbers into the administration and the army. New elites were ascending to positions of power by first gaining control of political resources (as in the case of Arab nationalism), or by other means, such as the *coup d'état*. This third upheaval prepared the way for continued authoritarianism in Syria.

In postmandatory Syria, as in other Arab countries, the army played an increasingly central role in the political life of the country. In the space of a few years, most recently independent Arab countries had changed from a monarchical regime or parliamentarian republic to a military dictatorship. The first Syrian dictators (1949–54), Husni Za'im (Kurd), Sami al-Hinnawi (Druze), and Adib al-Shishakli (Kurd), justified their intervention as a desire to "bring order" to a traditional political system in crisis. Influenced by the Kemalist model, the three colonels wanted to initiate a rapid transformation of society, around the central figure of an absolute leader.

The three officers also sought to improve the military institution after the fiasco of the Arab armies against Israeli forces in Palestine in 1948. Although during this period the Syrian army numbered around 18,000 soldiers, the effect of successive *coup d'états* was a considerable increase in the army's numbers – from 31,700 in 1949 to 43,000 in 1951 – which was reflected in the growing size of the national defense budget. In addition, the Syrian army progressively became more professional and was eventually endowed with a functional military arsenal (Picard 1993: 553–6) with a view towards eventual armed conflict with Israel.

## Minorities under suspicion

The fourth upheaval to take place in independent Syria was caused by the significant intermingling of internal and external politics in the context of the struggle against Zionism and Imperialism. The fragility of the Syrian system inherited from the French Mandate and the lack of a unified strategy made Syria a country vulnerable to pressure and intervention from external powers. For this reason, politicians had to rely on regional events (e.g. Arab–Israeli conflict, the pan-Arab movement, Kurdish and Iraqi revolts, etc.) and global events (e.g. the bipolar Cold War) to shape their sometimes volatile alliances with outside players (Seale 1965, 1988). The ideological debate between conservatives and progressives intensified in Syria where it allowed the success of pan-Arabism and Arab socialism, as evident in the formation of the United Arab Republic (UAR, 1958–61[8]) and the first Ba'ath cabinet (1963), which were in turn defended by a new generation, more radical and anti-west than its predecessor.

The old debate between Syrian nationalists and pan-Arabists intensified in Syria where it resulted in a distrust of ethnic and/or religious minorities. If Syrian nationalists and pan-Arabists had different political aspirations the two camps aspired to make their specific differences disappear in order to move towards either consolidation of a unified Syrian state or a larger entity encompassing all of the Arab countries. The French policy of reinforcement of the "structural pluralism" (Chabry and Chabry 1984: 57) of the Levant, which was a continuation of Ottoman policy, had deeply affected Syrian society and left a heavy political heritage marked by local divisions and alliances that were difficult to channel into a national plan.

Of the three colonels who succeeded in 1949, al-Shishakli was the only one of time (1949–54) and will to forcibly integrate minorities into the national Syrian social structure. The task turned out to be difficult because the Alawites and Druzes did not want to lose their local autonomy, so much so that the "Syrianization" of Alawite and Druze territories had to be accomplished in part using violence. Adib al-Shishakli believed that among his many opponents in Syria, the Druzes were the most potentially dangerous, and he was determined to crush them. He frequently declared: "My enemies are like a serpent. The head is the Jabal Druze, the stomach Homs, and the tail Aleppo. If I crush the head the serpent will die" (Seale 1965: 132).

To this end, al-Shishakli encouraged the stigmatization of minorities in the political debate in Syria. He saw minority demands for special privileges as tantamount to treason. His increasingly chauvinistic notions of Arab nationalism were predicated on the denial that "minorities" existed in Syria. Shishakli launched a brutal campaign to defame the Druzes for their religion and politics. He accused the entire community of treason, going so far as to claim that they were agents of the British and Hashimites, and that they were fighting for Israel against the Arabs (Landis 1998: 369–96).

But like neighboring countries, the Syrian elites would not be forced to conform solely by way of strong government territorial controls. The general population became the target of nationalist political projects which claimed that the state and the nation were indivisible. Thus, in 1953, Armenian associations were subject to a first wave of restrictions aiming to discourage all activities based on denominational or racial solidarity (Migliorino 2006: 105–6). At the time of the United Arab Republic, emphasis was placed on the pan-Arab discourse of the state, and spaces of autonomy for culturally diverse groups were further restricted.

The Kurds became the other major scapegoat of Arab nationalism and became part of the "shu'ubiyyun" or, in other words, people who would not allow themselves to be "Arabized." They were considered as hired agents in the service of powerful foreign enemies of Arabism. It was a definitive return to the tensions previously seen during the final years of the Ottoman Empire, and later during the mandatory period, between the state and minority groups. The fear that minority groups would be used by foreign powers became the leitmotiv of Middle-Eastern regimes that had only recently achieved independence, and if for a while the Cold war obscured this dynamic of conflict, it has nonetheless constituted one of the constant and undeniable features of the region's modern history.

## Searching for new political horizons

Towards the end of the French Mandate in Syria, the political engagement of the Kurds could be classified into three camps: Arab nationalism, Communism, and Kurdish nationalism. The latter proved to be especially active during World War II. The principles stated by the Allies during various conferences and the aggressive policies of the USSR toward Turkey since 1945 fuelled Kurdish hopes for the formation of an autonomous Kurdish state following the war. Most notably, the Atlantic Charter constituted for the Kurds a promise of future autonomy similar to that of the Wilsonian Principles announced following World War I.[9]

In vain, the Kurdish rulers asked that the San Francisco Conference admit a ruling that would allow people who had not yet gained their independence the right to express their demands at the international assemblies. In this sense, as Hamit Bozarslan remarked, Kurdish nationalism represented a new type of nationalism in which the people "demand the right to independence not against an empire or a colonial power, but against the States themselves that were created in the process of de-colonization or from a war for independence" (Bozarslan 1997: 16). Without any political sponsors among the members of the United Nations and powerless to influence the agenda created by international bodies, the Kurds were excluded from the United Nation's debates for four decades.

The defeat of diplomatic initiatives by the Kurdish committees led to a new crisis in the Kurdish nationalist movement in Syria. The agenda of the westernized elites to create a Kurdish state with the assistance of a foreign power proved to be entirely infeasible. Faced with this fact, the old members of the Khoybun slowly withdrew from the Kurdish political scene. Memduh Selim and Akram Jamil Pasha lived a sort of internal exile. Qadri Jamil Pasha remained in the Kurdish circles of Damascus without having any influence on the Kurdish nationalist movement. Jaladat Badirkhan remained in contact with the foreign legations established in Damascus, but he was prevented from playing a more central role in the Kurdish movement.[10] Instead, he continued to pursue his research on the Kurdish language.

Kamuran Badirkhan moved to Paris where he envisioned continuing his political activities in favor of Kurdish autonomy. In charge of the Kurdish language course at the National Institute of Oriental Languages and Civilizations (INALCO), he created the Center of Kurdish Studies in Paris and became a sort of Kurdish ambassador in France. He spearheaded diplomatic initiatives and solidarity campaigns with the different Kurdish movements.[11] He also obtained study scholarships from France for young Syrian Kurds[12] who could organize political activities in Europe under his patronage.[13]

Kurdish deputies to the Syrian Parliament abandoned all autonomist demands for their respective regions, in a new effort to maintain the status quo. Some did this voluntarily and some under pressure. The Shahin brothers of Jarablus, for example, still considered their return to Turkey as a possibility. The death of Mustafa Kemal and the assent to the presidency of Ismet Inönü, originally from Diyarbakir in Turkey, was viewed in the Syrian and Iraqi Kurdish populations as a chance for improvement in the situation of Kurds in Turkey. With this in mind, the Shahin brothers requested British representatives to intervene on their behalf with the Turkish government, asking that certain rights be granted to Kurds under Turkish jurisdiction, after which they could return to Turkey.[14]

However, the past activities of the Kurdish chiefs of the Khoybun committee weighed heavily on their present situation. As a result of this, in 1948, the director general of Syrian Tribal Kurdish leaders, Fuad Bey al-Halabi, explained that the principal Kurdish leaders were under a death sentence in Turkey, almost without exception. Should they be seen as asserting too much independence or disregarding the wishes of the Syrian Government on any important matter "they would have been conveniently disposed of by arranging to have them fall into Turkish hands" (Landis 1998: 373).

The consequence of all of these dynamics throughout the Kurdish movement at the end of the 1940s was that they lacked both a leader and a plan to bring together their diverse political factions. Faced with this void, some of the politically engaged Kurds, following the example of the old members of Kurdish Nationalist committees, like the poets Cigerxwîn (Cigerxwîn 1995: 283–91) and Qadri Jan (Zengi 2000: 19), sympathized with the Syrian Communist Party (SCP).

Young, politically active Kurds perceived the Kurdish nationalist elite (westernized intellectuals, shaykhs, and aghas) to be enemies of the people and vestiges of a bygone era. The involvement of Kurds in the SCP took on such proportions that it was known in the north of Syria as the "Kurdish Party." From 1933 the Syrian Communist Party was under the direction of a Kurd from *Hayy al-Akrad*, Khalid Bakdash.[15] The secretary general of the SCP used this "Kurdish" resource to spread the party's propaganda and gained its deputy seat in 1954, in large part thanks to the mobilization of this electoral stronghold.

This phenomenon was explained, on the one hand, by the privileged relationship between Bakdash and certain Kurdish notables of the area, such as 'Ali Agha Zilfu,[16] and, on the other hand, by the widely held perception among minorities of the Middle East (Ter Minassian 1997) that Communism might be their only bulwark against the pan-Arabist plan which was gaining strength at that time. The SCP was viewed as a guarantee of an exclusively Syrian national plan.[17] Furthermore, according to British reports, the SCP took full advantage of Soviet propaganda, broadcasted from Yerevan radio, in favor of Kurdish independence. Consequently, the principal aim of the SCP leaders was not so much to enlist members for the SCP as to create a large body of Soviet sympathizers in the area. In pursuance of this policy they had succeeded in convincing the majority of the younger Kurds that their best hope of furthering their nationalist aspirations was through the "communist movement and close collaboration with the USSR."[18]

According to the same sources, the local authorities did not make great efforts to check the spread of communist activity among the Kurds because of the strong presence of Kurds in high positions in the Surete and the Ministry of the Interior.[19] But the SCP also gained an audience amongst simple Kurdish peasants in Jazira willing to protest against forced labor and unfair taxes. Thus, in 1952, a peasant organization, supported mainly by the Kurdish peasants of the Jazira, "began to stand up to tribal-feudal despotism and published a newspaper to agitate on the peasant's behalf" (Hanna 2007: 329).

The Kurds in the ranks of the Syrian army in 1946 chose to stay there because a military career was seen as one of the rare opportunities for members of the working classes and the petite bourgeoisie to improve their social status. It must be remembered that despite the imminently Arab character of the Syrian Republic, the Damascene government had not automatically brought a systematic anti-Kurdish policy to this era. Thanks to the electoral system inherited from the French Mandate, Kurdish candidates were elected to the Syrian Parliament in 1947, in 1949, and between 1954 and 1958, while 'Abd al-Baki Nizam al-Din[20] held several ministerial posts between 1949 and 1957. However, the so-called politics as usual did not allow for the inclusion of "special interest" issues on the political agenda, and Kurdish demands therefore remained absent from discussions.

*The Kurdish dictators*

The Kurdish origins of two of the three dictators who succeeded each other in 1949 have often been held up as a sign of the "perfect" integration of the Kurds in postmandatory Syria. This rather surprising phenomenon can be explained by some correlative factors.

Each of these three dictators, Husni Za'im (1894–1949), Adib al-Shiskakli (1909–64), and Sami al-Hinnawi (1898–1950), had served in the French Mandatory troops where Kurds were well represented. As N.E. Bou-Nacklie suggests, the French balanced representation in one institutional branch of government against others:

> If one group was dominant in politics, other groups had to be placed in position of dominance in the military. In 1944, for instance, Sunni Arabs were dominant in Syria's politics, the officer corps, law enforcement agencies, and the police, but were underrepresented in the military's rank and file." (Bou-Nacklie 1993: 656)

By contrast, the Kurds were slightly overrepresented in the army and in the law enforcement agencies but poorly represented in Parliament.

Influenced by a "republican" model, Za'im and Shishakli were both supporters of an authoritative and modernizing plan, granting the right to vote to literate women, forbidding the wearing of the veil, eliminating Islamic opposition, revalorization of the army, government reforms, etc. In addition, both were sympathetic to the Syrian Popular Party (SPP),[21] of which Shishakli was a member in Damascus. As we have seen, the SPP of Antoun Sa'da attracted mostly minorities, partisans unified by the common belief in the territorial concept of the "great state of Syria" rather than ethnicity or religion. As a result of this, Za'im and Shishakli developed a neutral strategy, in spite of some early flirting with Iraq, with regard to the emerging debates surrounding unitarist projects in the region.

Another point that these two men had in common was that the cabinets formed by Za'im and Shishakli were reliant on members from Hama. The Adib al-Shishakli Party, the Arab Liberation Movement (created in 1953), was supported by Sunni officers from Hama and had strong social support in this region. It attracted young men from well-known middle-class Arab families, such as the Mulqi, Sabbagh, or Barudi. In addition, the right-hand men of Za'im and Shishakli, Muhsen Barazi (1904–49) and Fawzi Selo[22] (1905–72), were from Hama, though of Kurdish origin themselves. Even in light of these facts, the question remains as to whether this constituted a plot to establish "Kurdish power" in Syria.

The Kurdish origins of the dictators and their second in command could perhaps be construed as a simple coincidence due to a shared ideology, camaraderie forged in institutions like the army, and to personal affinities or social ties. Whatever the case, Adib al-Shishakli never acknowledged his Kurdish origins and demonstrated a rather uncompromising attitude toward Kurdish cultural activities.

The strategy followed by Za'im was just as ambiguous. Following Syria's independence, Husni Za'im became the chief of state and led the Syrian army during the Israeli–Arab war in 1948. Upon his return from the Palestinian Front, Za'im instigated a *coup d'état* on April 11, 1949, the first that Syria had ever experienced. Za'im did not resort to violence in order to establish himself in the country. Perhaps significantly, Syria's first dictator proved to be very selective in choosing his close collaborators. His personal guard was formed exclusively of Kurdish soldiers and Circassians.

Husni Za'im chose Muhsen al-Barazi[23] to be the prime minister of his cabinet. Other political figures of Kurdish origin, including Nuri Ibesh, who was closely allied to Kurdist circles,[24] were present in the government directed by Husni Za'im or in high positions in the Syrian administration at the time,[25] so much so that the duo of Za'im–Barazi provoked a reaction among Arab nationals who saw this as the forming of a "Kurdish military regime." Contrary to the secular reforms introduced by Za'im, the Muslim Brotherhood went on to accuse him of wanting to create a sort of "Kurdish Republic" and of favoring Circassians and Kurdish units of the army to the detriment of Arab units (Teitelbaum 2004: 140). Amicable relations with the United States and a determination to arrive at a peace agreement with Israel only increased doubts as to the "Arabness" of Za'im. When Sami al-Hinnawi instigated the second *coup d'état* and had Za'im and Barazi executed, the Syrian press spoke of the end of the "Kurdish government" (Cigerxwîn 1995: 280).

This view was also held in Kurdist nationalist circles, which circulated rumors claiming that Za'im "will do something" for the Syrian Kurds. In this hopeful context, Jaladat Badirkhan met Za'im to convey his willingness to invest himself in Syrian politics. Za'im apparently retorted, "I don't want two leaders (*za'ims*) in Syria."[26] Since Jaladat Badirkhan, clearly identified as a Kurdish nationalist and could not expect to become the leader of an Arab nation, one could deduce that Husni Za'im was expressing his wish to act out the role of Syrian national leader by relying on the network of Kurdish solidarity. In other words, Za'im envisioned maintaining power by using both Kurdish community channels or group solidarity – *'asabiyya* – and an ideology or *dawa*, in this case, Syrian nationalism.

The Za'im–Barazi cabinet was responsible for another ambiguous political movement concerning the Kurds in Syria. Muhsen al-Barazi contacted representatives of the Kurdish movement and old members of the Khoybun in order to convince them to go before the Turkish Consulate of Aleppo to beg for pardon and obtain amnesty from the government of Ankara. According to 'Uthman Sabri (Mela Ehmed 2003: 28) and Cigerxwîn (Cigerxwîn 1995: 278–9), certain Kurdish leaders[27] would have submitted to the Turkish government in 1949, in exchange for being able to stay in Syria without the constant fear of being delivered to the Ankara government because of their past political activities.[28] Sabri, who refused the amnesty that was offered to him, thought that it was an action by the Syrian cabinet to improve diplomatic relations with Turkey, which was allied with the United States. It remained to be seen if behind this initiative Za'im did not also have a hidden desire to use the Kurdish leaders and their network of patronage in his political favor, once they had gained a free hand.

In spite of these indications, the Husni Za'im regime was too short-lived to reveal exactly what its plans were as to the utilization of ethnic and geographical bonds. It seems that Za'im's intention immediately after the coup was to set up a predominantly People's Party government with the backing of a number of prominent Arab family groups with Faidi al-Atasi as Prime Minister, and himself as Minister of Defense. He was unable to do so and then began to seek support among different networks. Given that the Syrian army was marked by personal rivalries based on ethnodenominational divisions, Za'im would have sought to exploit the Kurdish component. The patronage relationship between, for example, Muhammad Sa'id al-Yusuf and Kurdish soldiers from Damascus were called upon to pledge a certain allegiance to the Husni Za'im regime. While there was theoretically an attempt to mobilize a Kurdish *'asabiyya* in 1949, the failure of this effort is apparent in that this is only a theory[29]. Be that as it may, from the end of the 1950s, the Syrian army would experience several purges during which Kurdish officers were expelled from it, and the military academies and the police force both closed their doors to young Kurds.

After the experience of the UAR and the period of insecurity during the rupture (1961–63) between Syria and Egypt, the accession to power in March 1963 of a military coalition claiming to represent the Ba'ath Party marked the end of the predominance of elite urban Sunnis in Syria. First, Druze officers, then the Alawites, would hold key positions in the army and in civil institutions in the name of pan-Arabism. Subversive plots, assassinations, the Arab foundations of the military, and the strong mobilization of the *'asabiyya* in the name of a compelling ideology succeeded during the 1960s and 1970s where Husni Za'im had failed.

## The triumph of Arab nationalism and the United Arab Republic

The Syrian political community sought an institutional response to the challenges posed by the economic, political, and ideological transformations occurring between 1946 and 1958. This search was accompanied by a lively discussion around the question not only of national identity, definitions of the fatherland and the nation, but also of social and religious orientation. These debates did not take place in isolation from current events. The active participants from the Syrian scene were influenced by events that were occurring at the regional level, such as the Arab–Israeli conflict, and the global level, such as the Cold War.

The legislative elections of 1954 marked a high point of Syrian participation and political activity. The four bodies representing an innovative plan in the Syrian political system – SCP, SPP, Ba'ath, and Muslim Brotherhood – confronted the powerful electoral machines of the conservative parties, which maintained a strong foothold in Syrian politics, and sparked robust public debate between the political right (pro-Soviet and religious) and the political left (pro-west and secular). For the first time, ideology seemed to prevail over political maneuvering. This relative "freedom" of speech and choice was reflected in the many different positions represented in Parliament after the results of the election.

These debates also resonated within the army. Indeed, more than 70 percent of the graduates from the military school belonged to or had close ties to one party since before their entry into the academy. From 1956, the rifts within the military establishment revolved around rival officers. In this way, the army largely reflected the crumbling and the radicalization that the Syrian political system was experiencing (Picard 1980: 156).

Following the elections of 1954, the Syrian Parliament was a mirror for the struggles between political parties, and between the political community and the army. Alliances and counteralliances with Iraq and Egypt increased from 1954 to 1957. It was as a result of this impasse that the Ba'ath, using the army, led Syria to integrate itself in February 1958 into the United Arab Republic (UAR) led by Gamal Nasser.[30] In so doing, the Ba'ath realized two long-standing aspirations of Arab unity and the consolidation of its party in Syria as a dominating force (Hopwood 1988: 39; Kaylani 1972: 21).

The UAR was a strongly unified state because the executive counsels of each province and their parliamentary assemblies had a field of expertise that was generally limited to local affairs. It was also a centralized state whose ministers and National Assembly were located in Cairo and whose powers were primarily concentrated in the hands of Nasser and two Syrian vice presidents. The authoritarian nature of the regime became more pronounced over time as provincial councils were suppressed, and the Syrian Assembly was displaced to Cairo, while Syrian representation in the government diminished.

Nasser imposed draconian conditions in order to unite the two countries, abolishing all political parties in Syria, including the Ba'ath, and putting the Syrian army under Egyptian command. The agrarian reform of 1958 elicited reactions from the notables and landowners, most conspicuously in the Ghouta oasis of Damascus.[31] Ba'ath opponents to Nasser began to organize into secret committees aiming to put an end to this experiment (Le Gac 1991: 93–4). In addition, militants of the Communist Party were harshly repressed by UAR authorities, and the political, cultural, and religious activities of ethnic and religious minorities of Syria were closely monitored.

Among these minorities, the Kurds had two "faults" in the eyes of the authorities. First, they were a non-Arab "minority" and, thus, a threat to plans for Arab unity, and second, they were associated with the "feudal chiefs" and the world of the "notables" which the authorities wished to eliminate. The last moderate representatives, including the Kurd Tawfiq Nizam al-Din, the brother of 'Abd al-Baki Nizam al-Din, were removed from their government positions. The destiny of the Kurdish "notables" was thus tied to the general decline of Syrian notability issued from prominent families since the Ottoman and mandatory periods.

Under the UAR, recordings of Kurdish music were smashed in cafés. The publication and even the possession of books written in Kurdish language were offenses punishable by imprisonment. Egyptian teachers were sent into Kurdish regions (Nemir 1992: 151). Local tragedies fanned the fires of discontent in northern Syria. For instance, although the facts were never established, the authorities were accused in November 1960 by the inhabitants of Amuda of causing a fire in a movie house that caused the death of 283 Kurdish children.[32] Those responsible for this act were presumably motivated by anti-Kurdish sentiments, the fruits of official propaganda in opposition to Kurdish nationalism associated with Zionism and American imperialism.

*The creation of the Kurdish Democratic Party of Syria (KDPS)*

Although they were represented in Parliament by independent candidates and in spite of the fact that they constituted 10 percent of the entire population of the country, between 1946 and 1957, the Syrian Kurds had no political organization to defend their rights (e.g. cultural rights). However, several factors converged during the 1950s, leading to the official creation of the KDPS, with the aim of inspiring a mass social movement. First, the ascent of an increasingly aggressive and chauvinistic Arab nationalism created uneasiness among the Kurds in Syria. Additionally, Kurdish figures close to the SCP, Cigerxwîn, 'Uthman Sabri (Mela Ehmed 2003: 31–2), and communist militants of Kurdish origin (including Rashid Hamo, Muhammad 'Ali Khoja, Khalil Muhammad, and Shewket Nezan) concluded that the party of Khalid Bakdash would not defend Kurdish rights. By consequence, it was necessary to create an organization that was both left wing and nationalist.

As with all Syrian political groups, Kurdish circles were influenced by regional events. Syrian Kurds watched the evolution of the Kurdish problem in Iraq with great interest. In this context, Jalal Talabani, a member of the political office of the KDP (Kurdistan Democratic Party of Iraq), then taking refuge in Syria, played a decisive role in the building up of the KDPS program. Consequently, the

KDPS served as a platform of propaganda for the KDP, which later served as a link between the KDPS and the "Iraqi" Party.

The party, like all political organizations during the time under the UAR, engaged in clandestine activities, such as the recruitment of new members and the publication of written works in both Kurdish and Arabic, in order to alert Kurds and the world in general to the specific problems of Syria. The objectives of founding party members were eventually dramatically reduced to merely seeking recognition of Syrian Kurds as an ethnic group with the right to their own culture. They sought to raise the Syrian public's awareness of the myriad obstacles to economic growth in Kurdish regions, and they implored the Syrian government to nominate non-Arabs to administrative positions in Kurdish areas.

The exact conditions of the founding of the party organization remain rather obscure. According to 'Uthman Sabri, the party was created in 1956 by himself, 'Abd al-Hamid Hajj Darwish, who was studying law at the time, Rashid Hamo (a teacher), and Shaykh Muhammad Isa Mahmud under the name Democratic Party of Kurds in Syria. One year later, the founding members chose Nur al-Din Zaza, who had returned from Europe in 1956, as president. At the insistence of Jalal Talabani, the name of the party was changed at the beginning of 1960 to Democratic Party of Kurdistan in Syria (Jemo 1990: 33–4).

This name change, to which 'Uthman Sabri was opposed because it could become dangerous to the party members, was significant because it implied that the Kurdish enclaves of northern Syria were also part of Kurdistan. Kurdish aspirations included the potential annexation of these Syrian territories to an autonomous or independent Kurdistan. In his memoir, Nur al-Din Zaza claimed a central role in the founding of the party in 1957, but did not touch upon the question of the organization's name change (Zaza 1982: 139–40). The most probable reason for this omission is that the basis for the party had been established in 1956 but the official founding, with a plan and a definite direction, was accomplished in 1957.[33] It is also probable that the name change of the party in 1960 and the continuing contacts with leaders of the KDP of Iraq, who had become allied with the cabinet of General 'Abd al-Karim Qasim,[34] triggered the widespread campaign against Nur al-Din Zaza and other directors of the KDPS. Thus, after several months of surveillance, on August 5, 1960, the leaders of the executive committee of Aleppo were arrested and tortured. The party organization was discovered and within a few days more than 5,000 people were arrested and interrogated. The leaders of the KDPS were accused of separatism and finally condemned to prison.[35]

### The "non-citizen" Kurds

The dissatisfaction of diverse sectors of Syrian society caused by the measures imposed by Cairo grew incrementally until the peoples' common discontentment erupted in the "separatist" movement of September 1961. Syria rapidly reclaimed its independence through nonviolent means on September 28. Two months later, the traditional parties, restored the country's institutions with the assistance of the army. Nazim al-Qudsi became the head of state and Ma'ruf al-Dawalibi directed the new civil government. The organization of free elections in December of 1961 revived the atmosphere of the 1950s. However, political instability was not entirely eliminated from the Syrian scene. Colonel 'Abd al-Karim Nahalawi led an attempted *coup d'etat* on March 28, 1962, which failed, as the army proved to be divided and hesitated to directly intervene. The step was eventually taken on March 8, 1963, with the cooperation of the Ba'ath Party, opening a new page in Syrian history.

During the 18 months of the "secessionist period," representatives of traditional sectors of the Syrian political community, reunited around the People's Party, hastened to abolish the nationalization measures taken during the time of the UAR and to remove all evidence of agrarian reform. The conservative party leaders sought to run the country as if no sociopolitical change had taken place during the 1950s. However, a return to the "good old days" of the notables and large landowners was impossible. According to Hinnebusch, the postmandatory regime collapsed because the Ottoman model had been upended. In this case, an overtly dominant state had been replaced by one that was intensely fragile. The Syrian state had left a dubious legacy in that civil society had a chance to develop under the liberal state, particularly in the new middle class, but the regime's lack of control over the dominant classes prevented the democratic inclusion of the middle and lower classes. The consequence of that lack of control was that the regime was extremely vulnerable in the face of emerging populist movements which adopted authoritarian means to gain power (Hinnebusch 1995: 218–19).

Despite the end of the UAR and a resulting brief period of hope for the Syrian Kurds,[36] their political, economic, and cultural demands were not taken into consideration by the new government. For the first time, Syria was proclaimed an Arab Syrian republic. Repressive measures were applied to the Kurds, notably in Jazira. On August 23, 1962, the Damascus government issued a decree (no. 93) authorizing a special census of the population in Jazira, which was conducted in November of the same year. Following its results, a large number of Kurds, as many as 120,000 according to several estimations, were stripped of their Syrian nationality.

The regional context is of great importance for this particular issue. The year 1962 was one of significant progress for the Iraqi Kurds who held all of the north of Kurdistan, from Zakho to the Iranian border. At the end of 1962, the Iraqi army operated only in the plains and depended primarily on the air force to defend the nerve center of the north, particularly the petroleum zones of Kirkuk. Large contingents of the Iraqi army were deployed to the south of the country as a result of the crisis in Kuwait.[37] The inability of the Qasim regime to crush the Barzani revolt gave rise to deep discontentment within the army and among Arab nationalists. Those opposed to the regime contacted the KDP in April of 1962 and promised them, verbally, Kurdistan's autonomy (Chaliand 1992: 116). From that time, for the Kurds, anything seemed possible.

Since the mandatory period, Syria suffered a succession of losses of territories which gave rise to fears in Damascus that the territorial integrity of the country was once again in danger. Faced with this possibility, the Syrian government opted to take drastic measures in order to avoid Syria's contamination by Kurdish nationalist sentiments by way of Jazira, the only territory inhabited by the Kurds and concomitant with the Kurdish regions of Iraq.

The census of 1962 had serious consequences for the 120,000 Kurds – or 20 percent of Syrian Kurds – who lost their citizenship. The reasoning put forth for this action by the Damascus government was that only 60 percent of the Kurds found in Syria were "true" Syrians. The others, they claimed, had illegally infiltrated Syria, coming from Turkey or Iraq[38] with the support of American imperialism, in order to destroy the Arab character of Jazira and to create a Kurdish state. The administration prepared lists of those who were considered Syrian, and the non-Arab elements of the population were invited to get new identity cards as their old ones had been "nullified." Only those whose names were on the list (the 60 percent found to be 'true' Syrians) could get the new cards. To retain their citizenship, Kurds had to prove residence in Syria dating from 1945 or before. However, implementation of this directive went awry, and even Kurds with proof of residence lost their nationality, while others were forced to pay large bribes to retain it (Lynch and Perveen 2006: 1). In some cases, families found out that some members were nationals and others were not. Some fathers, for instance, had nationality, while their children did not; one child could have nationality while his brother or sister could not.

Kurds who had their Syrian citizenship revoked were registered by the Syrian authorities as "alien" *(ajnabi,* plural: *ajanib)*. The Kurds who were stripped of their citizenship in 1962 were provided with a simple white piece of paper that read "His name was not on the registration lists of Syrian Arabs specific to Hasaka" (HRW 1996: 15). Kurds who did not take part in the census became *maktumin*, meaning "unregistered" or literally "concealed/hidden." The lack of nationality and identity documents meant that the stateless Kurds, for all practical purposes, were rendered nonexistent. Their basic rights to education, employment, property ownership, political participation, and legal marriage were severely limited, relegating them to the outermost margins of Syrian civil society. *Maktumin* Kurds, being completely unregistered, had even lower status that the *ajanib* and had no opportunities in Syria.

Many persons who lost their nationality later also lost the rights to their property, which was seized by the government and used for the resettlement of displaced Arabs. The Kurds whose lands were seized were not compensated for their losses. Since the Syrian Kurds did not have citizenship in another country, they were defined as stateless under international law.

These measures did not only affect Kurdish peasants but family members of notables and officers in the Kurdish army, like General Tawfiq Nizam al-Din, who were also relieved of their nationality. As Harriet Montgomery puts it, the Hasaka census of 1962 was a landmark event in Kurdish history in Syria, the effects of which have had continuing and worsening repercussions for those affected (Montgomery 2005: 77). In addition to that legal action, symbolic violence against Kurds took on worrisome proportions. A campaign launched by the Arab media sported slogans such as "Save Arabism from Jazira" or "Fight the Kurdish Menace." Certain houses of *Hayy al-Akrad* were covered with anti-Kurdish graffiti (Vanly 1992: 151). The foundation had been laid for a more coercive policy against the Kurds, as a "foreign group."

# 3 The Ba'athist system and the Kurds

On March 8, 1963, a coalition of officers put an end to the conservative regime in the name of pan-Arabism via a *coup d'état*, one month after the Iraqi Ba'athists had done the same in Baghdad. The new government, directed by Salah Bitar, reunited the unionist forces, including the Ba'athists, representatives of the Arab National Movement, members of the Unionist Movement, and other Nasserist organizations, which were opposed to the separatist regime. Meanwhile, even as a minority, the Ba'athist officers sought to expand their presence in the National Council of the Revolutionary Command and thereby gain exclusive control over the military sector of the party.

Until the *coup d'état* of February 23, 1966, conflicts between factions and people close to the Ba'athists were so intense that they systematically paralyzed decision making, most notably, the massive nationalizations decreed in 1965 by Damascus.[1] As a result, the rise of the "regionalists," which included army officers and active Marxist Ba'athists in the peripheral provinces, such as the Hawran, the country of the Alawites, and the Euphrates Valley, and the revival of the socialist movement, gave a new momentum to the rapid and spectacular growth of economic reserves and led to the nationalization of mines and large industries, and petroleum resources in particular.

As a result, the Ba'ath definitively ended the leading role of the urban notable families in the political and economic life of Syria. Moreover, the struggle for control of the state, which began in the 1950s, became the real political stake after the *coup d'état* of 1963. The construction of the state allowed the establishment of a nucleus of power by giving it access to administrative functions and by establishing clientelist relationships through redistribution of resources to the larger segments of society. The construction of the modern state in Syria, and everywhere in the Middle East, marked a significant increase in the opportunities for ruling groups to accumulate available resources.

Between 1966 and 1970 Syria experienced a period of significant economic investment that prepared the country for its entry into the industrial era and for the radicalization of foreign policy, in particular in matters concerning the Arab–Israeli conflict, in which the Syrian regime suffered costly defeats. Tensions in the ranks of the Ba'athists culminated in an aggressive coup led by General Hafiz al-As'ad on November 13, 1970 and the establishment of the Corrective

Movement a year later. The new leader of the Ba'athists aimed to shift and broaden the regime's foundation, by means of an open economic policy and a practical foreign policy, contributing to the creation of the constitution of the informal axis of Damascus–Riyadh–Cairo. Inside the country, al-As'ad created a façade of democratic dialogue by forming the Progressive National Front (PNF) in 1972, integrating the "progressive" forces[2] into the government without ceding anything in the way of political liberties and fundamental rights.

The Syrian Constitution of 1973, which is still in effect, proclaimed that Syria was a popular democracy directed by the Ba'athist Party with the help of other member organizations of the PNF, without, however, allowing any means of control on the part of citizens. The constitution tried to resolve this contradiction by supporting two overlapping institutional systems. The institutions inherited from the 1963 *coup d'état* (e.g. martial law, Director of State Security) were maintained, as were the new institutions (the constitution, People's Council, PNF, etc.). The power extended to the president of the republic was intended to ensure a liaison between the two systems and, consequently, the cohesion of the whole regime.

During the 30 years of the Ba'ath under Hafiz al-As'ad, the paradoxes and contradictions of Syria deepened. These contradictions included the simultaneous socialist ideology of the Ba'athists and Syria's dependence on the regard of the capitalist world; the theoretical functioning of the democratic parliament and the reality of the military regime; the aspiration to Arab unity and the pragmatic sense of Syrian interests; and the development of a real national consciousness and persistent community attachments (Picard 1980: 183).

The policy of the Ba'athists towards the Kurds followed the trajectory of the regime, with its internal disputes, its changing orientation, and its paradoxes. However, the principles of the Ba'athists are of interest because, in spite of the contradictions and the ideological treachery which occurred along the way, they would determine the official nationalism of modern day Syria, and, as a result, they would determine the state's relationship with Kurdish nationalism, the only nationalist doctrine to challenge them.

## Ba'athism: an exception in Arab nationalism?

The Ba'ath Party's access to power in Syria was neither a random occurrence nor an inevitability of the contemporary history of the country. Other modern political views, like Nasserism or the Populism of Antoun Sa'da, would have asserted themselves if the Ba'athists had not, giving rise to different regimes. However, the vision of Arab nationalism taken by the Ba'ath with respect to minorities emerged from a certain logical evolution of an older organicist thought.

Traditionally, the emergence of Arab nationalism has been analyzed either in the context of a struggle against European imperialism, according to the premise of the Islamic intellectual and reformist Jamal al-Din al-Afghani (1839–97), or as an idea articulated essentially by intellectuals and notables engaged in a movement of Arab cultural renaissance (Hourani 1962; Dawn 1973; Tibi 1991). From this perspective, nationalism is the doctrine of eastern elites[3] who were ready to adopt western ideas, such as "division of labour" (Gellner 1999: 35–61), in order to lead their respective groups into a state of civilization (western), which could only occur via the creation of a nation-state. In keeping with this idea, it was not an accident that Arab nationalism as a political doctrine appeared after the deconstruction of the Ottoman Empire. The western principles of human self-determination furnished it with a justification for its plan and actions.[4]

In the 1990s, new studies emphasized other aspects of nationalism and nationalist movements, two subjects of sociological study which are complimentary but distinct, such as the social and psychological bases of nationalism, the dissemination of new identities in society, or the non-elitist dimensions of nationalism (Chatterjee 1986; Gelvin 1994, 1998; Jankowski and Gershoni 1997; Provence 2005).

To this effect, the works of James L. Gelvin and Michael Provence have demonstrated very well that from the perspective of nationalism taken by the westernized elite Arabs, mandatory Syria was witness to the affirmation of a radical variant of Arab nationalism, which was populist in nature. In celebrating the actions of armed bands (*ishabat*) and tribes, the Arab populist organizations[5] not only rejected the civilizing model of the "Arab Kingdom" (1918–20), but, in defending social subversion, threatened the power of the local elites, including the nationalists.

For Gelvin, the differences between the populist nationalists and the westernized nationalists were not only centered on the power relations, the acceptance of western "civilization," or the degree of integration of the country in the world economy (the populist committees being against economic capitalism), but also revolved around the Syrian political community. For the populist committees, the connection between individuals was not political or contractual. Syrians, with ancestors and contemporaneous relations, were a "family," an organic body composed of discrete but interdependent members united by ties of kinship. So too, Syria was comprised of interdependent *tabaqat* (estates) "united by ties of mutual obligation" (Gelvin 1994: 653).

The consolidation of Arab nationalism during the mandatory period did not mean that all members of the nationalist committees shared identical concepts of their national identity. The exact sense of the "imagined community" (Anderson 1983) could differ from one individual to another, but "it was the common notion of membership that was important, not the common understanding of what membership meant" (Provence 2005: 152). In fact, the bitter competition between the representatives of the two variants allowed the expansion of the Syrian national ideal to larger segments of the population under the mandate (Khoury 1997: 287).

This situation, however, warrants a more nuanced analysis. It implied a rift separating the two concepts of the nation: the first would be the result of a free association of citizens, of a rational and willful construction, represented by the westernized elites; the second would be the consolidation of a historic community and the expression of a sense of identity, the organic and inherited cultural nation, represented by the populist committees.

But, as Alain Dieckhoff asserts, this division was revealed to be problematic because politics and culture are never separate in the process of nationalist mobilization, even if the temporal sequences and the modes of expression differ with each case. For Dieckhoff, the self-proclaimed cultural concept of the nation was not as detached from politics as was indicated (Dieckhoff 1996: 43–55). The interaction of politics and culture is in fact essential to all modern nationalism. What is more, this fusion is indispensable to the success of the process of "nationalizing the masses."

It is important to remember that a large portion of Arab intellectuals, as with the Kurdish and Turkish intellectuals, were not convinced by the "enlightenment," but by positivist and organicist theories in vogue in Europe at the end of the nineteenth century.[6] Thus, for the modernist elites, national emancipation was considered the condition *sine qua non* for the integrating of civilization and for survival in the "jungle" of nations. This Darwinist social thought left the conviction that the organic body that is the nation was always at war with other organic bodies (nations). Consequently its very survival might necessitate reorganization under the form of the modern state, endowed with military structures with a dual purpose: to defend the group from the outside and to ensure, even by force, internal cohesion.

## The nation according to the Ba'ath

The success of organicist ideas in Syrian political discourse from the 1920s, but mostly in the 1950s, cannot be reduced to a populist "victory" over the "enlightened" elites. Nor can it be reduced to a simple transition between two generations, the first made up of "traditional" notables, a second dominated by the middle and lower classes, but above all, as a consolidation of a sort of consensual doctrine. The organicist concept of the nation was laying the groundwork for the emergence of a much more radical and aggressive nationalism, which was part of the atmosphere in Syria as in other countries in Europe and the Middle East.

The creation of the face of the "enemy within" seemed to be part of that unanimist political culture in the first half of the twentieth century. According to the logic of organicist thought, the nation could also be endangered by internal threats, thought of as its sick members. Hence, it became essential to identify interior enemies (Schmitt 1972), that is to say, "otherness" (in terms of ethnicity, politics, etc.) which defied the unanimist definition of the nation. Disrespected and occasionally dehumanized, this enemy and perceived traitor could at any moment become the object of coercion from the state in order to "save" the nation.

Ba'athism is a variant of pan-Arab nationalism, with which it shared the central notion of the existence of the "Arab nation" declared as an unquestionable historical fact, though one which had never been proved. Despite some constitutional articles dedicated to the economic sector, most of the constitution of the Ba'ath puts the emphasis on Arab nationalism. The Ba'ath was supposed to be the "avant-garde" which was going to accomplish Arab unity. Its main slogan was and remains "an Arab nation with an eternal mission." According to Michel Aflaq, nations only appear on the historic scene by atavistically invoking their positive and negative missions (Bozarslan 2005: 323).

*The Ba'athist system and the Kurds* 57

It was also a matter of exclusive nationalism. The constitution of the party – articles 10, 11, 15, and 20 – was explicit in this sense: All political and social groups established in the Arab fatherland which did not actively share the Arab national ideal were illegal. As for the policy regarding language, general principles determined that the Arab language be the official language of the future unified state.

Despite the virulence of the Ba'athist position against all "schizmatic" tendencies on the part of any ethnic or religious group, Michel Aflaq recognized the existence of ethnic minorities within the "Arab nation." For Aflaq, the Kurds were a group easily assimilated into the Arab nation, if they were considered in a cultural and historic sense and not racially. Indeed, he argued that since the Kurds, as with the other members of non-Arab ethnic groups, wanted nothing more than to live a dignified life, they would "naturally" want to remain within the Arab fold because then they would not be a small group but would be part of a vast nation which would guarantee their power and "happiness." From then on, all resistance was attributed either to selfish interests from certain conservative sectors of Kurdish society, such as the tribal chiefs, or enemy plots from the outside.

Aflaq's ideas in reference to minorities were fraught with contradictions. While the Ba'ath ideology considered international communism artificial because it disguised each nation's national character, it proposed Arabism as a national horizon for the Kurds. What is more, although Aflaq denounced racial chauvinism, he affirmed the opposition of his party to *shu'ubiyya*. In the end, the recognition of Kurdishness was conditional on the Kurdish acceptance of the Arab nationalist ideal (Aflaq 1977).[7]

At the time of the sixth National Party Congress in 1963, the "Theoretical Starting Points" avoided all mention of the existence of minorities in Syria and referred to the country as an "Arab homeland" inhabited by "Arab masses from the Arabian Gulf to the Atlantic Ocean" (Carré 1996: 58–9).[8] After 1963, the directors of the Ba'ath defined the Kurds as a "foreign" group, which was a menace to the nation. The constitution of the Ba'ath Party continued to threaten all ethnic and religious groups in Syria who challenged the notion of the unity of the Arab nation.

*The Ba'ath: a regime under tension*

Like its Iraqi counterpart, the Ba'athist regime of Damascus progressively distanced itself from all ideological engagement with pan-Arabism and socialism – with the exception of a unanimist concept of Arab nationalism – in order to transform itself into a tyrannical power or *sulta*. This power would be defined as the personal property of Hafiz al-As'ad, and his family. "Arab nationalism" became, in this sense, a *dawa* or ideology which served as a façade to legitimatize the usurpation of the state by a clan or *'asabiyya*.[9]

This *dawa* was on an equal footing with *'asabiyya*, in the sense that "Ba'athist power, which boasted Arab nationalism was not Arab; it was founded on group belonging and solidarity "which allowed it to be maintained by internal cohesion" (Bozarslan 2003: 37).

The victory of the al-As'ad clan was the result of a process which lasted many years. Towards the end of the mandate, some ethnic minority and religious sectors as well as regions that had been "forgotten" by Damascus undertook a struggle to take their place in the new Syria. It was in this way that the Alawite leaders, for example, followed a strategy aimed at erasing their religious "particularism" by adopting maximalist positions on all of the regional and international issues concerning the national Arab and Muslim problems in order to assure their presence in and their control of the Syrian state (Chouet 1995: 98). From 1963 to 1966, the members of the Alawite, Druze, and Isma'ili minorities occupied the majority of the managing posts in the military, the regional and national office of the Ba'ath party, the government, and the administration.[10] From 1966, with the "neo-Ba'ath" dictator, Salah Jadid, the Alawites slowly ousted the Druzes (1966) and the Isma'ilis (1968–69) from key positions. In the end, the struggle was contained within the Alawite community, between rival clans, as symbolized by a duel between the generals Salah al-Jadid and Hafiz al-As'ad, until al-As'ad's victory in November of 1970.

Between 1970 and 1972 several Alawite Ba'athists were physically eliminated by al-As'ad's supporters. As Nikolaos Van Dam puts it, since challenges to al-As'ad's regime came mainly from within the Alawite community, he placed increasing trust on persons with whom he had a close personal relationship, such as members of his own family, tribe, or village and its surroundings, "in order to secure his position even against people from his own religious community" (Van Dam 1996: 70). In consequence, although the Ba'ath had been dominated by officers and politicians of Alawite descent, in practice, active participation in the regime had been limited to a fairly small section of the Alawite community, the Kalbiyya tribe.

The absolute power of Hafiz al-As'ad did not, however, ignore the importance of hierarchy, and several "secondary *'asabiyya*" were created and given their own leaders. These newly created units included a Department of Defense, Special Units, and Intelligence Services or *mukhabarat* (Seurat 1989: 85). In the absence of a strong and unified hierarchy, the Syrian system relied on the fragmentation of power between military chiefs (collectively referred to as *muasasa* or the "institution"), where power depended on blood relations – *nasab* – and on local patronage sometimes with the counterproductive side effect of competition, including violent competition between opposing sides of a decision,[11] emerging into what Charles Tilly called a "fragmented tyranny."[12]

The Syrian regime knew, however, how to create a certain stability and managed to expand its foundation. The *'asabiyya* had, in its plan to control power, condemned itself to an isolated and closed existence which was not conducive to the perpetuation of the regime. The Syrian regime was thus forced to search for openings in other sectors of society, in other words, to attempt to ally other groups with the founding *'asabiyya*, in order to perpetuate its hegemony of this last on society (Droz-Vincent 2004: 185). If the *'asabiyya* of al-As'ad, the Alawite community, and the army constituted the three concentric circles of the major network which managed current-day Syria, this *'asabiyya* also maintained relationships with other

Syrian networks, such as the capitalist Sunni and Christian bourgeoisie, both of which had some degree of economic power, as well as with networks outside of Syria, such as money-lending oil monarchies, with whom collaboration was vital for the survival of the regime (Balanche 2006: 147–8).

Furthermore, larger segments of the Syrian society have used the system created by the Ba'ath for the support of private interests. The party became a privileged conduit of access to positions of power and social advancement of families, clans, and even ethnic and religious communities (Kienle 1990). The unrestricted expansion of the bureaucracy had benefited the followers of the new hierarchy.[13] The true motivation of the regime had been the desire to form for itself a "clientele," thus, to create a dependence (Droz-Vincent 2004: 124).

At the same time, it had allowed the clique in power to monopolize the national patrimony by legitimizing its financial and economic practices, first the "socialization," and, later, the "liberalization" of the economy. Elizabeth Picard concludes that the explanation for this can be found by considering the Ba'athists as a "system" of domination and corruption rather than as a political party whose functionality explains, in part, its longevity (Picard 1996: 218).

Taking into consideration the tension between the *dawa* and the *'asabiyya*, between purity of their original doctrine and pragmatism, there are two distinct phases of Ba'ath policy towards the Kurds. The first phase, from 1963 to 1970, which can be described as the years of "ideological purity," was marked by a preponderance of coercion as a method of managing the Kurdish problem. A second period from 1970 to 2000 was much more pragmatic, combining coercion and the redistribution of goods as methods of managing the Kurdish problem.

## The years of ideological purity (1963–70)

After the revolution of 1963, "conservative" parties were prohibited in Syria, either because they represented "exploitative" classes or the bourgeoisie, who the Ba'ath were systematically attempting to ruin economically by imposing agricultural reform and nationalization of commerce and agriculture, or because they aspired to a religious ideology, as in the case of the Muslim Brotherhood. The Kurdish Democratic Party of Syria (KDPS) was in the first category because, for the regime, Kurdish nationalism was exclusively an affair of some notables and aghas representing "exploitative" classes. Thus, the authorities envisioned the application of agrarian reform in northern Syria not only as an act of "social justice" but also as a means of undermining the power of the Kurdish large landowners.

Farm workers periodically requested advances on their future harvests from their proprietors or village negotiators, in order to make ends meet or to mitigate the consequences of a poor harvest. The rate of interest was extremely high. The chronic debt of the farm laborer allowed the holder of capital, usually large landowners, to buy the harvests at low prices and to seize the lands of the insolvent. Furthermore, the debtors formed an obligated clientele which reinforced political domination, both because of their lack of social status and by their votes in favor of their "patrons." The fact is, from the epoch of the French Mandate to the *coup d'état* of 1963, the majority of Syrian deputies were large landed property owners.

For the Ba'athist regime, destroying this mechanism by which farmers land was so easily seized removed the means by which large ownerships were built up, and above all, broke the patrimonial ties between the farm laborer and the citizen bourgeoisie and their ilk. However, the Ba'ath did not so much have an interest in the liberation of the laborers as in providing a substitution for the patronizing network between the great landowners and the state. In spite of the restructuring of agricultural production at the time of the agrarian reforms of 1958, 1963, and 1966, the public sector of state farms and production cooperatives never fulfilled its economic and ideological objectives of the social transformation of rural populations (Ababsa 2006: 212).

The application of reforms was reliant on both political factors and technical factors, such as absence of surveying and land registry, lack of land agents, and division of lands among heirs. Thus, the Ba'ath created favorable conditions in Jazira for the emergence of a class of middle-sized property owners, *chawi*, who were loyal to the party. An amendment to the agrarian reform law was made in 1966, which banned the expropriation of recently irrigated lands. This amendment was inspired by the neo-Ba'athist militants originating in Dayr al-Zur, who were themselves middle-sized landowners, afraid to go against the bourgeoisie of the large towns, relying not on the laborer masses, but on their counterparts, other middle-sized landowners. On the other hand, the creation of vast state farms especially affected the Kurdish regions of northeast Syria and the area of Raqqa. As one example, of the 140,000 ha allocated in all of Syria by the setting up of state farms, 36,000 ha destined for the production of grains and cotton were expropriated from the area surrounding Qamishli (Ababsa 2006: 215).

*Dealing with the "Kurdish peril"*

On November 12, 1963, Lieutenant Muhammad Talab al-Hilal, former chief of the Secret Services in Hasaka, published a study of Jazira. It was a sort of security report that he had been asked to present to the authorities who accepted it as a guide to action and a source of inspiration in the management of the Kurdish issue.[14] In this report Muhammad Talab al-Hilal depended on references to "history" to deny the existence of the Kurdish people and deferred Kurdish demands to Arab territories. According to the report's author, the Kurdish people did not exist because they possessed neither "history nor civilization; language nor ethnic origin."

In flagrant contradiction with his previous affirmation, he called for an increase in repressive policies in all domains in order to expunge from Jazira all signs of Kurdish identity because the Kurds were "our enemies," and, in spite of the nexus of union existing between Kurds and Arabs through Islam, "there is no difference between them and Israelis, for Judistan and Kurdistan, so to speak, are of the same species." Loyal to the organicist thought which had first emerged in the

Middle East at the beginning of the twentieth century, he considered the Kurdish problem "simply a malignant tumor which had developed in a part of the body of the Arab nation." The only remedy "which we can properly apply thereto is excision" (Vanly 1992: 153–4). Aware of the transborder dimension of the Kurdish question, he explained the necessity of coordinating with the other concerned states in order to adopt a common step in the struggles against the alleged "Kurdish danger" which was a threat to all.[15]

Inside of Syria, the report suggested a dozen measures to eliminate the "Kurdish danger": (1) the displacement of Kurds from their lands to the interior; (2) the denial of education; (3) the handing over of "wanted" Kurds to Turkey; (4) the denial of employment possibilities; (5) an anti-Kurdish propaganda campaign; (6) deportation of Kurdish religious 'ulama (clerics) who would be replaced by Arabs; (7) the implementation of a "divide-and-rule" policy against the Kurds; (8) the colonization of Kurdish lands by Arabs; (9) the militarization of the "northern Arab belt" and the deportation of Kurds from this area; (10) the creation of "collective farms" for the new Arab settlers; (11) the denial of the right to vote or hold office to anyone lacking knowledge of Arabic; and (12) the denial of citizenship to any non-Arab wishing to live in the area (Vanly 1992: 156).

When the report was publicly revealed in 1968, the authorities assured the people that this was only a personal and not a government opinion. All the same, it is difficult not to place this type of document in the more global perspective of an "unanimist will" nationalism[16]. As we have seen, the "Kurdish group" had been designated as the internal enemy since the 1950s. During the UAR, Kurdish activities had been hounded and, in 1962, Syrian authorities had conducted the census under exceptional circumstances in the Hasaka province, depriving 120,000 Kurds of their citizenship. Taking these events into consideration, the adoption of the Hilal plan in 1965 by the government and the Ba'ath Syrian Regional leadership was but a logical consequence of the evolution of the latter's perception of the Kurdish problem.

Of all the points proposed by Muhammad Talab al-Hilal, Damascus was focused on the creation of an "Arab belt,"[17] a long band of arable, well-cultivated land that would extend 280 km along the Turkish border, from Ras al-'Ayn in the west, to the Iraqi border on the east, which was roughly between 10 and 15 km wide. The plan anticipated the massive deportation of 140,000 Kurds, most of whom had been deprived of their Syrian citizenship in 1962 and who were living in 332 villages situated inside this band. They would be replaced by Arabs. The objective, according to the Arab press, was to "save Arabism in Jazira." (Vanly 1968: 11).

However, the plan was not put into place until 1973. The reasons for this delay in creating the "Arab belt" seemed to be related to technical constraints. The "colonization" of Jazira depended upon certain favorable conditions, such as the construction of the Tabqa dam on the Euphrates basin. Thus, after the filling of the Tabqa dam in 1975, around 4,000 Arab families of the Walda tribe, whose own lands had been submerged, were settled (and armed) in forty-one of the "model" farms[18] in Jazira, in the very heart of the Kurdish region, as well as in fifteen "model" farms north of Raqqa. From the time of their arrival in Jazira, the Arab families received rights of proprietorship and the former proprietors of these lands received no economic or material compensation at all. In exchange for this "generous" government policy, the Arab colonists were expected to become loyal subjects of the regime.[19] Irrigation projects forced the displacement of the Arab population of Aleppo, Manjib, and al-Bab all along the Turkish borders, a location perceived by the Syrian Kurds as chosen to disrupt their physical links with the Turkish Kurds. The Arabization campaign of Jazira was halted by Hafiz al-As'ad in 1976, but the status quo remained unchanged (Meyer 1990: 245–78).

The Kurds were victims of the other policies which aimed to render the Kurdish identity invisible in Syria during this period. In 1967, all mention of the existence of the Kurds in this country was stricken from school books, while Kurdish parents began to receive strong pressure from functionaries to impede them from registering Kurdish names for their children in the state birth registry. Finally, police harassment, including house raids and arrests, even among peasants, became a common practice of the local authorities against the Kurds (Resho 1968: 14–16).

## The years of exploitation (1970–2000)

Arab nationalism not only established itself as a central element of Syrian political culture, but was also written into the constitution of 1973, and therefore became a compulsory aspect of Syrian civic life.[20] Similarly, the exclusion of Kurdishness became part of the official doctrine of the state. However, the Syrian regime, in its management of the Kurdish problem, as in other domains, had to tone down its official ideology in order for it to be socially viable. In fact, the functional alliances with the Kurds followed a time of fluctuation in the power relationships of the Alawites with other sectors of Syrian society.[21] Thus, the years of confrontation between the regime and the Muslim Brotherhood led al-As'ad to withdraw into his Alawite and Kurdish networks. Then, having stabilized his power and assured his position in the region, he conducted new overtures, most notably to the Sunni Arab sectors in 1985.

It was within this framework that Hafiz al-As'ad opted for a more pragmatic strategy with respect to the Kurds in Syria, and, as we will see in the following chapter, outside of the country, first in Iraq and later in Turkey. The overtures of the regime to certain segments of the Kurdish group do not, however, indicate the build up of a pro-Kurdish policy. Above all, it was a matter of seeking a balance between "redistribution and coercion" to manage the Kurdish problem and thus avoid losing control of the entire Kurdish group, a possibility which could lead to a revolutionary situation.

The coercion applied to the Syrian Kurds by the regime was not continual, but the "state of emergency," in place since 1963, with its arsenal of legal devices, was used to put into practice waves of repression or more intense repression to remind the Kurds of their boundaries. The intensity of the coercion was determined in part by factors such as the power of the Kurdish movement in the

The Ba'athist system and the Kurds 63

country. Thus, while in Turkey and Iraq, and to a lesser measure in Iran, the states felt forced to mobilize their armies against the Kurdish movement, weak capacity of the Syrian Kurdish parties to mobilize did not require Damascus to initiate harsh repressive methods.

All the same, Hafiz al-As'ad did not hesitate to take strong measures in his dealings with the Kurds. In the summer of 1973, security forces arrested twelve Kurds, including KDPS chairman, Daham Miro, and other party leaders shortly after they had addressed a memorandum to President al-As'ad protesting the living conditions of Kurds deprived of citizenship (HRW 1991: 98). Additionally, incidents with the police broke out in Damascus on the occasion of the Newroz Festival (Kurdish New Year) on March 21, 1986. On this occasion, hundreds of Damascus Kurds had anticipated celebrating Newroz at Rukn al-Din, in the heart of the Kurdish quarter of the capital, but the authorities forbade the buses from bringing the participants into the area. The people then decided to head for the presidential palace to protest. A young Kurd from Qamishli was killed. When the young man's body was returned to his birth village, there was an uprising.[22] The same night, security forces killed three other Kurds in Afrin (Vanly 1992: 164). In March 1990, a protest of Kurds who had been stripped of their nationality in 1962 was violently repressed by the police when the strikers wanted to submit a list of their demands to the president of the republic.

The time of Hafiz al-As'ad did not bring respite for the Kurdish language either. The teaching of this language remained prohibited, while Armenians and Assyrians had private schools, clubs, and cultural associations where their respective languages could be taught. During the 1970s, the public school became, for the Kurds, not only a place of Ba'athist indoctrination, as it was for other Syrians, but also a place of Arabization. With the increase in literate children in the Kurdish regions, a tight surveillance system was established there, following the example of the Turks, by means of "spies," to stop the children from speaking Kurdish among themselves. Children discovered in flagrant "defiance" could be physically punished.[23]

Though the ban on Kurdish publications had already begun with Adib al-Shiskakli's presidency (1951–54), under the Ba'athist regime measures of legal coercion were reinforced, obliging Kurdish authors and editors to have their publications printed in Lebanon, and afterwards they could be illegally brought back to Syria. Two decrees from the 1980s forbade the use of Kurdish in the workplace, as well as during marriage ceremonies and festivities.[24] Faced with the difficulty of enforcing this decree, a new circular targeting the work place was issued in 1996 (McDowall 1998: 147).

In May 2000, a little before the death of Hafiz al-As'ad, Resolution 768 ordained the closing of all stores selling cassettes, videos, and disks in the Kurdish language and re-emphasized the prohibition of using this language during meetings and festivities.[25] In the province of Hasaka, in 1992, officers of the civil state began to more strictly apply the restriction against registering children with Kurdish names, in accordance with decree no. 122. While Kurdish names continued to be registered, following the inevitable payment of a bribe to the functionaries,[26] the power of these decrees did not reside so much in their application, as in their existence, "in the fact that they could, at any moment, be applied." In this sense, it was theoretical coercion "whose legal existence mattered more for the state than its application" (Bozarslan 1997: 164).

*Incorporating the "other"*

Discursive strategies are the most influential and effective for imagining an ethnically homogenous geography and history. These are developed in central state agencies and disseminated at the local level to win the consent of members of the dominant *ethnie* to nationalist domination through cultural institutions.

The military defeats of the Arab countries by Israel and the distancing of the Hafiz al-As'ad regime from pan-Arab purist doctrine led the Ba'ath Party to emphasize the necessity of avoiding all references to any particularist tendencies. Thus, the Syrian Ba'ath Party decided in 1975 to recommend "the rewriting of Arab history." As a result of this initiative, the preparatory committee proclaimed that the guiding principle in rewriting Arab history should be to emphasize unity at all times. Therefore, the historian should give particular attention to politically and culturally unifying trends, "whereas, any kind of racism, fanaticism, and confessionalism had to be avoided" (Freitag 1994: 33).

Some of the Kurdish "heros," such as Salah al-Din Ayyubi, had been elevated to the level of a national symbol, without ever making any specific claims as to his ethnic origins. But from the point of view of "Arabness," an essential element of the imaginary construction of the new history, the symbolic integration of the Kurdish community into Syrian identity proved delicate. This obstacle had been partly overcome in light of the obvious Muslim identity, also common to the Arabs, of the majority of the Kurds. The recuperation of the history of certain ancient peoples – Canaanites, Arameens, Nabateens – to demonstrate the specificity of Syrians (Arabs), neglecting the evidence found in northern Syria of other nonsemitic people such as the Hurites,[27] also served to affirm the territorial unity of Syria. The integration of "the other" could also happen via the reinterpretation or appropriation of their symbols which were problematic for the official ideology. The most spectacular illustration of appropriation of Kurdish symbols was the case of Newroz or New Year's Day, March 21 to the Kurds. While Newroz was nearly unknown in Ottoman territories, Kurdish intellectuals reunited in Istanbul raised it to the status of a national Kurdish holiday at the end of the 1910s. As we have seen, the exile of these intellectuals to Syria and Lebanon had important repercussions in the politicalization of the Kurdish identity in these territories. Thus, Jaladat Badirkhan expanded upon the founding myth of Newroz[28] among the Syrian Kurds using the *Hawar* revue (Badirkhan 1942: 976–8).

If in the beginning Newroz had been an affair of a minority of intellectuals and nationalist militants, after the 1960s, this festival became a sort of ritual of Kurdish nationalism, most notably through songs and dances. This was also the time, under the presidency of Hafiz al-As'ad, of the most important affirming moments on the public position of Kurdishness, in the north of Syria and also in the Kurdish quarters of Aleppo and Damascus. After the events of Newroz that occurred in Damascus and Afrin in 1986, the regime imposed an official ban on this festival and attempted to eclipse it by making it coincide with a holiday honoring mothers.[29] Despite this decision, tension surrounding Newroz did not completely disappear and on more than one occasion (1995 and 1997) the Kurdish festivities ended with massive arrests.

Toponymical strategies to rearrange the historicity of places are a logical consequence of the strategy of the incorporation of "the other" (Kurd) into the hegemonic historiography. Therefore, the decree of Arabization of toponyms issued in 1977 was a clear manifestation of the regime's desire to erase all non-Arabic cultural and historic presence in Syria. For instance, in Jazira, the localities or towns of Tirbe Spî, Tel Kochak, Amuda, and Darbasiya were, respectively, renamed Qahtaniyya, Ya'Rubiyya, Adnaniyya, and Ghasaniyya, while Derik was made al-Malikiyya. In the Kurd Dagh, the place names of all Kurdish villages were changed from Kurdish to Arabic (HRW 1996: 44–6).

The incorporation of time (history, temporality) was accompanied by a strategy of incorporation of space, notably through the "Arab belt" policy, which aimed to put into practice ethnic cleansing and the dispossession of "non-national" landowner classes (Kurds) and the transfer of land to "national" elements (Arabs).

Once this had been done, the grievances of the Kurdish population towards the state and its local representatives began to grow and take an economic turn. In effect, the Ba'athist regime was not only incapable of allocating economic resources to the Kurds, urban and rural alike, but, moreover, they found that belonging to the Syrian state actually incurred costs (Wimmer 1997: 643–5). Thousands of Kurds had lost their lands and their citizenship following the publication of the results of the census taken in 1962, while the Arabs were clearly favored by the regime. The Kurds' accumulated cultural and economic grievances since the rise to power of the Ba'ath could, under the right circumstances, give wings to a Kurdish movement in Syria.

## *The co-opting of some kurds*

The exclusion of the Kurds from the top circles of power, lack of recognition of their cultural rights, the policy of the "Arab Belt," and the denial of citizenship for thousands of Kurds had been "compensated" by a series of selective measures during the years. Indeed, between 1970 and 1990, the Kurds participated in the Ba'ath system through the engagement of certain of their elites from the religious brotherhoods and official shaykhs such as Ahmad Kuftaru, *mufti* of the republic (1964–2004).

On the death of his father, Ahmad Kuftaru (1921–2004) took over the direction of the Kuftariyya, a branch of the *tariqa* (brotherhood) Naqshbandiyya in the Kurdish quarter of Damascus. From the 1950s, Shaykh Kuftaru began a prestigious career in Damascus. In 1964, he was named grand mufti of the Syrian Republic, but his career at the center of his movement did not begin until Hafiz al-As'ad rose to power in 1970.

Under the protection of the regime, Ahmad Kuftaru could develop his Kuftariyya brotherhood and establish himself as a very popular spiritual leader among the Kurds and Sunni Arabs at the same time. In exchange, Kuftaru, who had become a functionary of the republic, defended the separation between religion and state, thereby rejecting the idea of political Islam. He presented a simple and modern interpretation of Islam, distancing himself from the readings of conservative Islamic circles, enemies of the Alawite-dominated regime.[30] Furthermore, the brotherhood became a sort of liaison between the regime and the Kurdish community in Damascus, as well as in the northern region of Syria because, although Arabs are active in the *tariqa*, the Kurdish ethnic origin of the nucleus of the brotherhood remained the rule (Böttcher 1998: 125–38).

The case of Ahmad Kuftaru is not unique. Another Kurdish "newcomer" in the religious field, the Shaykh Muhammad Sa'id Ramadan al-Buti also became a protégé of the regime. Born in Jazira bin 'Umar in 1929, his family left Turkey, fleeing the secularist measures of Mustafa Kemal, to settle in Syria in 1934. Even though he was suspected of maintaining contact with the Muslim Brotherhood, al-Buti did not stop his contact with the regime and eventually became an official and mediating shaykh, all the while, holding on to his Islamic discourse. Without denying his ethnic origins,[31] Buti encouraged the Kurdish–Arab brotherhood to advance in a peaceful and progressive manner towards the creation of an Islamic state (Christmann 1998: 57–81). Following his intellectual advisor, Sa'id Nursi, also of Kurdish origin, and founder of the powerful movement, *nurca*, in Turkey, al-Buti was an advocate of the current political regime and did not hesitate to openly criticize the Muslim Brotherhood for attempting to lead Syria into civil war.

The choice of these two religious men as official representatives of Islam in Syria seems to have been, in effect, a political strategy. It was difficult to represent the Kurdish community in terms of their "Arabness" in an official discourse. The Sunni affiliation of the majority of Kurds was a considerable trump because, in creating the impression through this group of courting Islam, the regime succeeded in toning down the Sunni opposition's challenge to its legitimacy. The co-optation of individuals or groups of Kurdish origin was not limited to the religious field. After the takeover of Hafiz al-As'ad in 1970, membership of the party was opened to all Syrians, including non-Arabs such as (Arabized) Kurds, Circassians, and Armenians (Van Dam 1996: 18). Indeed, a few Kurds held positions of local authority. Some, like former Prime Minister Mahmud Ayyubi, Hikmat Shihaki, chief of Military Intelligence (1970–74) and chief of staff (1974–98), and General Mahmud al-Kurdi, former director general of the Military Construction Enterprise and later, Minister of Agriculture, have even been able to reach high-ranking positions. This has been, however, on the condition of not showing any particular Kurdish consciousness.

In 1976, as the opposition movement grew among Syrian Arabs, As'ad sought to placate the Kurds, announcing an end to forced transfers from Jazira. The next move was the reintegration of Kurds into the communal system by giving them military positions, not into the ordinary ranks of the Syrian army, but into the elite divisions, notably into the Special Units attached to the Ministry of Defense and

The Ba'athist system and the Kurds 67

the Defense Brigades, which were directly dependent on the presidency and were commanded by the president's younger brother, Rifat al-As'ad. Interestingly enough, the fragmentation of the regime's power elite between different military corps exacerbated the fragmentation of the Kurdish soldiers who were divided into different militias and, therefore, had different loyalties.

In 1980, the Alawite, Kurdish, and other "minority's" Defense Brigades and Special Units were used to repress the troubles in Aleppo and again, commanded by Alawite officers, to suppress the Muslim Brotherhood's revolt of Hama in February 1982. As a result of this action, in the course of which a large portion of the city was destroyed with a significant loss of civilian life, the Arab Sunni majority regarded the Kurds as the partners of the regime in repression, and occasionally, graffiti appeared "threatening the Kurds with direct vengeance" (Vanly 1992: 159).

In May 1990, while the government was feeling fairly stable, the proportion of seats reserved for independents in parliamentary elections passed from 18 percent to 40 percent, the remainder going to the National Progressive Front, dominated by the Ba'ath. At this conjuncture, the Kurdish voters could elect around fifteen candidates of Kurdish origin. Three among them were even presented on a common list supported by Kurdish organizations in Jazira: Kemal Ahmad, president of the Kurdish Democratic Party of Syria; Fuad Aliko, representative of the Kurdish Populist Party; 'Abd al-Hamid Hajj Darwish of the Kurdish Democratic Progressive Party in Syria (Chaliand 1992: 172). At this time in the Kurd Dagh, six Kurds, who presented themselves overtly as supporters of the PKK (Kurdistan Workers Party), were elected to the Assembly.[32] However, in August 1994, the government resumed control of the "independent" vote, and, from that point onwards, any Kurds were elected with the consent of the regime.

Elsewhere, the efforts at co-optation of certain segments of the Kurdish minority had led the Syrian state to cede some of its power. As an example of this, one can cite the complicity of local security services with certain families of active Kurdish smugglers in Jazira on the Syrian–Turkey and the Syrian–Iraqi borders. The Kurdish regions of Syria were underdeveloped, largely as a direct result of political decision making, and the redistribution of economic resources took on a great importance. The chronic financial difficulties of the Syrian state did not allow it to support all of the Kurdish populations. In light of this fact a certain permissiveness towards illegal economic activities, such as smuggling, helped to mitigate the negative economic consequences for Kurdish regions of having been abandoned by the government.

Certainly, smuggling was not an activity that originated with the arrival of the Ba'ath Party. To the contrary, it was already the "economic motor" of Qamishli during the time of the French Mandate. Tolerated and even encouraged by French officers and reinforced by the very elevated Turkish customs charges, smuggling allowed an avoidance of traditional commercial routes of Turkish villages such as Nusaybin, towards the new border towns of Syrian Jazira. This phenomenon took on such great proportions that the Turkish government decided to implement large-scale measures to reinforce their control of the borders. During the 1950s, the Turko-Syrian border, most notably in Upper Jazira, was mined to stop smuggling. In addition, the Turkish border guards undertook forays into Syrian territories to arrest smugglers, not without provoking a number of diplomatic "crises" between the two involved countries.[33]

Over the years, the goods which passed illegally through the Turkish and Iraqi borders changed. To the traditional trafficking in sheep were added cigarettes and arms, the former having been encouraged by the Kurdish revolts in Turkey and Iraq since 1984. Since the 1990s, "smuggling lords"[34] appeared in northern Syria with the complicity of the local authorities, thanks mostly to the growth of this lucrative venture. If Qamishli remained an important smuggling center for a diverse range of goods, other villages and border posts seemed to be more specialized. Thus, heroin traffic was especially important in Jarablus, while the arms trade was centered in Derik and cigarettes and archeological artifacts alike have been smuggled out of Iraq since 2003 by way of 'Ayn Diwar.[35]

The smuggling lords, faithful to the regime, have been able to build imposing villas in the upscale quarters of the border towns and put into place networks of patronage among the populations which suffered the most from a lack of financial resources. The case which received the most media attention was that of Majid Birkî who was "unmasked" by the German weekly, *Der Spiegel* and the Kurdish website, *amude.com*. The economic empire of Majid Birkî began in 1998 as a result of a small-scale human trafficking operation, for the most part of Kurdish candidates for asylum in Europe. Good relations with diverse branches of the *mukhabarat* permitted him to rapidly extend his mafia network into Lebanon, from where hundreds of Kurds, including stateless Kurds, were drawn towards Europe. Between 2001 and 2002, these refugees would have paid $3,000–4,000 per adult and between $1,700 and $2,000 per child, to Majid Birkî, who would also have accepted payment in kind for the amount demanded. In this way Majid Birkî accumulated no less than 2,000 houses in Qamishli and Hasaka. After being arrested in Lebanon in 2003, Birkî was freed after only 6 months according to German information services, thanks to intervention by Damascus.

# 4 The Kurdish issue and its transnational dimension

"Kurdistan" or the "Land of the Kurds" was integrated into the Turko-Iranian world through the expansion of the Seljuq dynasty (1040–1118) toward modern-day western Iran, Anatolia, Iraq, and Syria. This integration served to reinforce the composite character of Turko-Iranian society and culture (Canfield 1991: 6–13). Similar to other regions in this vast expanse of territory, Kurdistan became both a place of welcome for diverse religious groups steeped in pre-Islamic beliefs (Yazidis, ahl-i Haqq, Alevis, Shabak) and a centre of Sunni orthodoxy.

The growing political tension between the Ottoman and Safavid Empires encouraged Kurdish elders to develop strategic alliances with one or the other, in exchange for diverse goods and a certain degree of autonomy. In effect, relations between Kurdish tribes and imperial administrations recalled the feudal system, in that they were based on the exchange between sovereigns and tribal chiefs of land for armed contingents. These relationships developed largely as a result of the strategic location of Kurdistan at the border between the two empires. The "multifaceted" Kurdish area (Badie 1995: 94) was more than a border region; it was a buffer zone between the two competing empires.

In 1514, the Ottoman state managed to annex a large piece of the Kurdish regions by creating a political and military alliance with Kurdish amirs who were discontented with certain policies of the Safavid Empire, namely their tendencies toward administrative centralization and the "Shi'ification" of the Kurds, the majority of whom were Sunni. The two empires tried to exploit those Kurdish tribes situated close to the border within enemy territory. The problem of the exploitation of the Kurds by both dynasties, however, could not be resolved without a clearer definition of the borders between the two empires. With this aim in mind, the Ottomans and Safavids made attempts to end their disputes and come to terms with their differences through various international treaties (Kashani-Sabet 1999: 24–5). However, despite these treaties, the borders between the two empires remained open to dispute and continued to be disregarded by Kurdish populations in the border region.

If throughout the centuries the Kurds had adapted well to a certain "border culture," the creation of new state borders changed the status quo completely. The new states of Turkey, Syria, and Iraq demonstrated acute possessiveness with regard to their territories. Furthermore, the governments wanted control over not only their territory but the territory's populations as well. New citizens were expected to be loyal to the state, its institutions, its national language, and its national economy. As was the case for other Middle-Eastern populations, the political border meant for the Kurds the division of tribes, religious brotherhoods, villages, and even families, threatening to sever existing group bonds. In this way, these new political borders were in direct contrast to the group's actual borders as experienced by each entity as a delimitation of their immediate environment. But ethnic or, in this case, "macroethnic groups" like the Kurds can defy the state through the maintenance of networks of cross-border solidarity, such as brotherhoods and tribal confederations. On a cultural level, in Kurdistan the government's desire for cultural homogenization conflicted with the Kurdish wish to safeguard its relations with similar linguistic groups situated beyond the state border. Similarly, certain segments of these "macroethnic groups" regarded smuggling as a natural and even legitimate activity, because the continuation of commercial trade between the members of their community helped them to avoid a "betrayal" of their prestate social group.

Kurdish nationalism as a doctrine that lays claim to the existence of a Kurdish nation unjustly divided between four states is not conducive to the acceptance of restrictive border legislation. As Hamit Bozarslan asserts, Kurdish nationalism must oppose the creation of political borders in order to grow and even to survive (Bozarslan 1997: 293). In light of this, the feeling of being threatened that was shared by the various sectors of Kurdish society (tribes, brotherhoods, intellectuals) helps explain the emergence of armed, rebellious movements in the states in which the Kurds found themselves divided.

The League of Nations' decision in 1925 to divide the old "Ottoman Kurdistan" – east of Anatolia and the *vilayat* of Mosul – between Turkey and Iraq served only to entrench these positions. Everywhere Kurdish tribes, sometimes under the direction of the leaders of nationalist associations, rose up against the centralist policies of the new states between 1920 and 1945. Certain comities including *Azadî* ("Liberty") and Khoybun ("Be Yourself") soon discovered some of the advantages of border conflict by implicating themselves in a system of alliances with the competing states. By the same token, the Kurdish factor played a particular role during the diplomatic negotiations between France and Turkey in establishing the Turko-Syrian border. The dispute over borders thus became both a permanent source of armed struggle at the regional level and a determining factor in the transborder nature of the Kurdish question.

The peaceful years in Kurdistan (1946–61) constituted a period of consolidation for the new states born of the collapse of the Ottoman Empire. After World War II, most Middle-Eastern states turned their attention toward nation building and, with the exception of the Israeli–Palestinian conflict, the general attitude was one of acceptance of the regional *status quo*. In contrast, the revival of Kurdish nationalism at the beginning of the 1960s coincided with the first challenges to the status quo on the part of some state actors. The regional nature of the Kurdish question led some states to play the "Kurdish card," to various degrees, either against another competing state – as in the cases of Syria and Iraq, Syria and

Turkey, and Turkey and Iran – or in open conflict, as in the conflict between Iran and Iraq.

Syria became a master in the use of the Kurds for political gain in this new regional game. Despite weak financial resources, Syria managed to impose itself as a major force in the region, to such a degree as to play a determining role in the evolution of Lebanese and Kurdish situations. Being a relatively weak state, particularly between 1946 and 1970, Syria was the target of influence of other nations (Egypt, Iraq, etc.) of which the most marked chapter was its integration into the United Arab Republic dominated by Nasser's Egypt in 1958. When the Ba'ath Party came to power in 1963, the regime sought legitimacy by way of a militant political rhetoric against Israel, but in reality, Syria's foreign policy became one more weapon in the internal conflict between its diverse political factions.

During the 1970s, the Syrian state gained in strength as a result of various factors. These included the increased stability of the regime compared to preceding periods, the time elapsed since independence, the oil boom and Syria's relations with Saudi Arabia,[1] and Hafiz al-As'ad's leadership. As'ad's pragmatism led him to invest in the regional sphere by playing on the weaknesses of neighboring states, in an attempt to promote Syria as a "regional middle power."[2] Hafiz al-As'ad used different approaches in his foreign policy in order to increase his sphere of influence. In Lebanon, he was able to wage a war by proxy, guided by *realpolitik*, as illustrated by his support of Christian militias against the "progressive" militias. At the same time, his rhetoric regarding Arab solidarity helped him to legitimize Syrian intervention in the country. In the case of his ideological involvement in Iraq, an essentially geopolitical struggle for regional influence after the defection of Sadat in Egypt took on an ideological character.

With regard to the Kurdish issue, Hafiz al-As'ad put into place a policy of co-optation of certain segments of the Kurdish group, both within Syria's borders and abroad. In Syria, this policy was accompanied by an equally effective and selective policy of repression. Abroad, this policy of co-optation served both to facilitate the achievement of his regional ambitions and to disperse the Kurdish "danger" from the capital. Hafiz al-As'ad's regime succeeded in displacing "its" Kurdish problem toward Iraq and Turkey between 1970 and 1990, thus encouraging the polarization of the Syrian Kurds between partisans of the Kurdish movements in Iraq and Turkey.

## The emergence of Hafiz al-As'ad's game

The establishment of a Ba'athist regime in Baghdad in 1968, along with a shared Ba'athist ideology and common economic interests (notably the Kirkuk/Mediterranean oil pipeline and the use of the Euphrates' waters), far from encouraging Syro-Iraqi cooperation, long remained sources of controversy between the two countries. From 1968, tension between Syria and Iraq manifested itself primarily in the struggle for Ba'athist ideological legitimacy. The Iraqi leaders made no attempt to hide their ties with the Syrian Ba'athists exiled in Lebanon since 1966. Following As'ad's coup and the establishment of the Corrective Movement

72  *The Kurdish issue and its transnational dimension*

after 1970, the struggle over Ba'athist legitimacy remained unresolved. Having taken refuge in Baghdad, the Syrian Ba'athist leaders and founding members of the party, including Michel Aflaq, condemned the architects of the Corrective Movement for having denounced the right-wing tendencies of the "Takrit clique," referring to the clan of Saddam Husayn.

As Eberhard Kienle recalls, the period between 1972 and 1975 was a time of relative calm between two storms (Kienle 1990: 61). In spite of this apparent calm, new forces were coming into play at a regional level. The war of October 1973 clearly marked a turning point in Syrian foreign policy by accelerating the process of open diplomacy toward Arab partners and the western world. Thanks to the support of certain oil-producing states, Syria was empowered to challenge the regional *status quo*, whereas Iraq found itself weakened in the face of an armed Kurdish movement, led by Mustafa Barzani and supported by Iran. The experience of two crises related to exportation of Iraqi oil[3] via Syria and another connected to the sharing of the Euphrates' water resources[4] aggravated diplomatic relations between the two Ba'athist regimes and further encouraged the calculated containment and exploitation of the Iraqi Kurds, to the benefit of these parties.

The first sign of As'ad's "Kurdish policy" came to light during the Ba'ath Party's eleventh national congress in 1971 during which part of the discussion was dedicated to the Kurdish question and the congress finally agreed on a resolution proposing autonomy for the Iraqi Kurds. Four years later, the Ba'ath Party's twelfth national congress confirmed its position while denouncing the "fascist approach" of the "right-wing" Iraqi regime with regard to the Kurdish question.

Damascus showed unabashed support for those in political opposition to the Baghdad regime. But the Kurdish political scene in Iraq was also experiencing significant upheavals with the collapse of the KDP after the Alger Agreement[5] which provoked the collapse of the party. The former dissidents of this organization, like Jalal Talabani,[6] and other small parties of Marxist or Maoist orientation, like the Komala, created a new movement which would be dominated by Talabani's Patriotic Union of Kurdistan (PUK), in 1975. Talabani was able to open a permanent office around the same time in Damascus where he had been since 1972. In addition to the PUK, the Syrian regime also supported the Democratic Union of Kurdistan, a small organization founded in 1976 by Ali Sinjaghi. However, the importance of these gestures from Damascus should not be exaggerated, given that the main military force in Iraq remained, in spite of its defeat in 1975, the KDP. The active conflict between the PUK and the KDP rendered it impossible for Syria to make any serious attempt to play the Kurdish card against Iraq.

The attempted reconciliation between Syria and Iraq between 1977 and 1979, following Egyptian President Sadat's unilateral engagement in negotiations with Israel, was aborted in July 1979 after the discovery of a plot against the new Iraqi president, Saddam Husayn, who denounced Syrian complicity. Saddam Husayn initiated a new foreign policy which undermined the Syrian–Iraqi coalition formed earlier in violation of the Camp David Agreements. In 1979, Idris, son of the Kurdish leader Mustafa Barzani, came to Damascus and formalized relations

The Kurdish issue and its transnational dimension 73

between Syria and the KDP. This prevented the Syrian regime from maintaining and developing its relations with the PUK during the following years.[7] Nevertheless, the results of the material aid to the PUK were generally limited, as its political stronghold was in Sulaymaniyya, a Sorani-speaking region, far from the Iraqi–Syrian border.

Relations between Syria and Iraq worsened significantly during the 1980s, when Damascus sided with Iran during the Iran–Iraq War (1980–88), condemning the invasion of Iran by Iraq due to its weakening effect on the struggle of the Arab states against Israel. In exchange for this support, Iran allied itself with Syria at the time of the Israeli invasion of Lebanon in 1982. As the Iran–Iraq conflict dragged on, Damascus sought to weaken Baghdad by working for the reconciliation of the PUK and the KDP, which was accomplished in 1987 and reinforced by the creation of a United Front.

The Syrian regime turned a blind eye to the recruitment of hundreds of Syrian Kurds to the ranks of the *peshmergas* (combatants), mainly in Barzani's KDP. While the political myth surrounding Barzani and his family certainly played a role in this transborder engagement, other factors, namely cross-border social, economic, and familial ties, seemed to have played a more important role. From the time of the delimitation of the Syrian–Iraqi border during the 1920s, tribes such as the Hasenan and Miran (also known as the Kochar) were separated by the borders dividing Syrian Upper Jazira and Bahdinan in Iraq, a region dominated by Barzani's KDP. The members of divided tribes defied the borders until the 1970s,[8] through the survival of family, brotherhood, and economic ties. The case of the Bawalia clan (Hasenan), which maintains close ties with the Barzanis even today, is a perfect example of this. It goes without saying that the movement of goods and people went hand in hand with the movement of ideas and, just as important, of information and rumors regarding events in Iraqi Kurdistan.

The deep-rooted solidarity between the Kurds on both sides of the border in itself, however, does not sufficiently explain the engagement of young Kurds in the ranks of the *peshmergas*. When the Syrian government announced in the mid-1970s the results of the census of 1962 in the Hasaka province, it established that the inhabitants of the region situated between Derik and Karachok, where the clans related to the Hasenan and the Miran were located, were particularly badly affected by the withdrawal of their Syrian citizenship. Similarly, this region was also affected by the organized settlement of the "Arab Belt." If the departure of the young Kurds to Iraq could be seen as a victory for Damascus, in the context of its political externalization of the Kurdish question, the radicalization of these tribes was a strong indication of a growing threat to the regime. In light of these facts, Hafiz al-As'ad felt obliged to create stable channels of communication with the tribal leaders in order to assure that they continued to have the "right attitude."[9]

During the Second Gulf War (1991), Syria did not oppose allied intervention against the Saddam Husayn's Iraq. Furthermore, Syria became a member of the multinational force which eventually forced the Iraqi army to pull out of Kuwait. The main reason for this was that the Iraqi regime supported General Aoun's anti-Syrian militias in Lebanon and with Iraq's annexation of Kuwait came the added risk of Baghdad gaining a central position in the Arab–Israeli conflict, to the detriment of Syria's position (Ehteshami and Hinnebusch 1997: 80). Finally, Damascus' decision allowed Syria to break out of a certain international isolation brought on by its engagements, most notably, with Iran.

It was therefore in the context of renewed regional competition between Syria and Iraq during the 1990s that the Kurdish parties, which dominated parts of northern Iraq, strengthened their ties with Damascus. In effect, in the face of the human drama of thousands of Kurdish refugees gathering on the Turkish–Iranian and Iraqi–Iranian borders following the failure of the popular Kurdish uprising in the spring of 1991 against Saddam Husayn's regime, the western powers, relying on UN Security Council Resolution 699 on humanitarian interference, decided to create a "safe haven" to facilitate the return of refugees to their homes. From this moment, international protection came into effect over an area of about 40,000 square kilometers (approximately the size of Switzerland), with a population of 3.5 million Kurds. The remaining Kurdish territories (Kirkuk, Sinjar, Khanaqin) remained under the control of Saddam Husayn who pursued his policy of forced Arabization of these regions. The initial objective of the western powers was, above all, to relieve their Turkish ally of the destabilizing influx of Kurdish refugees toward the provinces of Turkish Kurdistan.

But this resolution opened the door to the establishment of a *de facto* Kurdish region, independent of Baghdad. The Iraqi government proceeded to withdraw its civil administration from the three political seats in the protected zone – Dohuk, Irbil, Sulaymaniyya – and ceased to pay the salaries and pensions of the functionaries who decided to stay. Under pressure from Turkey, the United States accepted the responsibility of protecting this territory, while, on the other hand, the Kurds found themselves faced with the challenge of managing a devastated region, without economic resources and with almost 80 percent unemployment rate among the working-age population. If the international community had imposed an economic embargo on Saddam Husayn's regime, Baghdad had responded in kind to the detriment of the autonomous Kurdish region.

Despite these early difficulties, the members of the United Front of Kurdistan assumed power locally and prepared elections for the establishment of a regional parliament. This took place on May 18, 1992, with the KDP and the PUK winning fifty-one and forty-nine seats, respectively, whereas the Christian minority made do with five. The rest of the Kurdish political groups (communists, Islamists, socialists, etc.) not having attained the minimum 5 percent of votes had no elected representatives, but finally became associated with the unified national government formed in July 1992. The "government" of Kurdistan was not, however, recognized internationally. The economic stranglehold of a double embargo, and the political isolation of the Iraqi Kurds, made contacts with Damascus all the more important.[10]

The KDP and the PUK were able to keep offices in the Syrian capital and in Qamishli up until 2003, allowing them to secure outside contacts and to maintain a second port of entry into Kurdistan in the extreme northeast of Upper Jazira, through which numerous journalists and political representatives could pass with relative ease.[11] The condition *sine qua non* of this support from Damascus was, of course, the abstention of the Kurdish parties of Iraq from any attempt at mobilizing Syrian Kurds against Hafiz al-As'ad's regime.

## The Damascus–PKK axis

In the 1980s, external pressure compelled Hafiz al-As'ad to take an interest in the Kurdish nationalist movement in Turkey. The conflict between Turkey and Syria was rooted in the transfer of sovereignty from the Sanjak of Alexandretta in 1939 during the French Mandate to the benefit of Turkey. Besides this territorial dispute, the Turkish dams on the Euphrates threatened Syria's water supply and the announcement of plans to build a dam at Keban in Turkey only served to exacerbate existing tensions between the two states, leading to border skirmishes.

A connection between these two issues emerged when Turkey proposed an agreement with Syria over the sharing of the Euphrates' waters in exchange for recognition of its borders. Syria, however, refused to integrate the border question into the negotiations, preferring to exert pressure on Turkey by allowing the Kurdistan Workers Party (PKK) to establish bases on its territory, from which Kurdish fighters launched military operations against the Turkish army.

Syria's open support of the PKK may be best understood in light of the Turkish government's announcement in 1977 of the launching of the Southeast Anatolia project (GAP – *Guneydogu Anadolu Projesi*), a vast program aimed at exploiting the water resources of the Euphrates and Tigris basins. Covering nine provinces with a total area of 74,000 square kilometers, the US $32 billion project became the largest development project ever undertaken in Turkey and one of the largest of its kind in the world. When completed, a total of 22 dams and 19 power plants would have been built on the two river basins. The newly irrigated land would increase the area under irrigation in Turkey by 40 percent. Officially, the GAP project aimed to develop the land and water resources of the region with a view to accelerating economic and social development in Southeastern Anatolia, an area inhabited by a large Kurdish majority.

However, Syria and Iraq claimed that the GAP project could cost Syria 40 percent and Iraq 90 percent of the Euphrates flow. In addition, although the Turkish government assured them that much of the water would find its way back into the river, Damascus and Baghdad feared that after irrigating Turkish fields the water would have a much higher salt content by the time it reached the Syrian and Iraqi farms downstream. The main concern for both countries was that the dams that Turkey intended to build would enable Turkey to exercise control over its downstream neighbors.

Hafiz al-As'ad responded by inviting dozens of different guerilla factions, liberation movements, and dissidents to set up their headquarters in Damascus. Among those who accepted this invitation to Damascus were young members of *Dev Genç* and *Dev Sol*, of the Turkish People's Liberation Army and other small factions of the revolutionary left. Many of them returned to Turkey once they had completed their first courses in guerilla warfare and played their part in gradually converting Turkish cities into urban battlegrounds (Bullock and Darwish 1993: 60). In 1977, a group of young students at the University of Ankara, including a young man named Abdullah Öcalan, founded the PKK (*Partiya Karkerên Kurdistan*), a Marxist–Leninist organization which sought to create an independent and united Kurdistan.

As Turkey prepared itself for a third *coup d'état* in 1980, Abdullah Öcalan fled to Damascus. Other members of the PKK followed him and organized a training camp for their group north of Damascus. Hafiz al-As'ad then decided to up the stakes using the Kurdish card by encouraging the PKK to step up its recruiting campaign. New instructors would be provided, bank accounts were opened, and more weapons and better premises would be found for their use. The PKK was moved from the camp they shared with others north of Damascus to the Masum Korkmaz training base in the Biqa valley in Lebanon, part of the area under the control of the Syrian army. Improved relations with Palestinian groups, especially Nayif Hawatmeh's Democratic Front, gradually helped secure the PKK training facilities (Bruinessen 1988: 44). In addition, the Syrian and Lebanese Kurds were engaging both individually and communally in the Lebanese War. During the Lebanese conflict the PKK took up arms for the first time in the name of solidarity with the Palestinian cause, thus creating the nucleus of a professional army. In August 1984 the PKK officially launched its armed struggle against the Turkish state.

Thanks to the cooperation of the As'ad regime, northern Syria became a breeding ground for PKK militants during the 1980s and 1990s. While no figures exist as to the exact number of youths who were active members of the PKK, certain sources estimate that between 7,000 and 10,000 Syrian Kurds died or "disappeared" during clashes with the Turkish army (Montgomery 2005: 134). According to certain critics of the PKK, families of the disappeared never received call-up papers for these young men, with the clear implication that the Syrian government either quietly accepted enrollment in the PKK "in lieu of compulsory military service, or alternatively, that it was informed by the PKK of Syrian Kurdish casualties" (McDowall 1998: 65).[12]

In keeping with the cross-border dynamics which explain the militant engagement of local tribes in the ranks of the PKK's *peshmergas* in Iraq, certain clans of the Hasenan tribe – split between Turkey, Syria, and Iraq – and the Miran sent dozens of their members to the PLAK (People's Liberation Army of Kurdistan), the armed branch of the PKK. Certain clans of the Miran tribe abandoned Barzani's KDP and turned instead to the PKK, while others supplied fighters to both organizations. While these tribes were traditionally orientated toward Turkey and Iraq, the war in Turkish Kurdistan offered them the chance to continue to defy international frontiers by strengthening interstate networks of solidarity.[13]

Other rumors reported incursions by bands connected to the PKK against members of other Kurdish political parties in Syria, notably the KDPS, during the years of high tension.[14] This aggressive strategy was typical of the PKK and exactly in line with their approach in Turkey when trying to monopolize the Kurdish political arena. In 1987, Turkey and Syria came to an agreement which included an implicit agreement to end Damascene support for the PKK in

The Kurdish issue and its transnational dimension 77

exchange for guaranteed access to Euphrates' water. However, despite some posturing, As'ad refused to extradite the Kurdish leader Abdullah Öcalan and allowed the continued development of the PKK in Kurdish enclaves in Syria. According to David McDowall, by 1987, the PKK had offices in Damascus and in the following northern cities: Qamishli, Darbasiya, Derik, Ras al-'Ayn, Afrin, Aleppo, and Hasaka (McDowall 1998: 65).

Furthermore, six candidates from Kurd Dagh, overtly declaring themselves as representatives of the PKK, ran for office in the Syrian elections in May 1990. As asserted by Ismet Sharif Vanly, relations between the PKK and the Syrian government were mutually beneficial, the former having a base in Syria for its military activities against the Turkish state while the Syrian Kurds provided Hafiz al-As'ad with a shield against its internal and external opponents (Vanly 1992: 169).

In response to the Syrian regime's nonchalance with respect to the actions of the PKK, from mid-January to mid-February 1990, Turkey stopped the flow of the Euphrates, in order to hasten the refilling of the Atatürk dam. In an attempt to appease Turkey, Syria labeled the PKK as a terrorist organization and declared that it was willing to cooperate with Turkey in arresting members of Öcalan's party. However, Syria did not want to lose the leverage afforded to them by the PKK's presence in Syria in their negotiations with Turkey over the water supply. In addition, the military reconciliation between Israel and Turkey initiated at the beginning of the 1990s under the aegis of the United States and sanctioned by two security agreements in 1996 reinforced the Syrian regime's position with respect to the location of the PKK. Their interest in maintaining this strategic relationship with the PKK was such that As'ad eventually asked the Kurdish leaders to simply relocate all the organization's military cells, some of which were active in the old Sanjak of Alexandretta between 1993 and 1994, initially to Lebanon and afterward to Syria's ally Iran.

Between May and June 1996, the escalation of tension reached a climax, as the number of troops concentrated on both sides of the border increased proportionally to the growing animosity between the two sides. At the same time, there were a number of bombings in Syrian cities, most notably in Damascus. Turkish agents were apparently behind these bombings, which were designed to signal to Syria that its support for the PKK would only continue at great cost (Zisser 2001: 93).

*Limits to the PKK's structural dependence vis-à-vis Syria*

Resorting to "parallel diplomacy" led to increased pressure and caused collateral damage for all the parties involved. Thus, all the while using the Kurdish movement against Iraq and Turkey, Hafiz al-As'ad's regime had to accept the strengthening of cross-border relations between the Syrian Kurds and Kurds in neighboring countries, despite having strived since 1946 to strengthen Syria's borders and to spread an ideal of unity between its various ethnic and religious factions.

By the same token, Syria relinquished part of its sovereignty, particularly in its relations with the PKK. Therefore, the PKK's militants took *de facto* control over a few small portions of Syrian territory, notably in Kurd Dagh, and managed to replace the state in the minds of some young Kurds in, for example, an ideological (military) framework and to control illegal traffic through a few border posts. Additionally, portraits of Abdullah Öcalan and Mustafa Barzani replaced those of Hafiz al-As'ad in public spaces such as shops and workplaces. Finally, state support for the Kurdish movement could be construed as the betrayal of official Syrian ideology, of Arab nationalism and pan-Arab solidarity, especially regarding its conflict with Iraq.

This diplomacy also incurred a high cost for the Kurdish movement in that it was obliged to collaborate with an "enemy," in this case the Syrian state, possibly against its "brothers" across the border. This involvement in "parallel diplomacy" constituted, for the Kurdish movement, a betrayal of pan-Kurdist doctrine. Moreover, Damascus' strategic alliances with the PKK, the KDP, and the PUK served to create tensions between these three competing parties and their local bases, PKK, KDPS, and 'Abd al-Hamid Hajj Darwish's KDPPS (Kurdish Democratic Progressive Party in Syria), respectively. This resulted in the polarization of the Syrian Kurds, especially between the PKK and the KDPS and dealt a serious blow to the ideal of Kurdish national unity.

As previously illustrated, with the complicity of the Kurdish "clients" – KDP, PUK, and PKK – Syria steered its Kurdish nationalists toward the "true Kurdistans," which is to say, the Kurdish regions of Turkey and Iraq. Therefore, as David McDowall asserts, the Kurdish leaders Jalal Talabani (PUK), Abdullah Öcalan (PKK), and probably Masud Barzani (KDP) either denied the legitimacy of a Syrian Kurdish movement or dismissed it as a small-scale movement that distracted from the "real struggle" for Kurdistan (McDowall 1998: 69–70).

An additional step in this direction was made by Öcalan, when in 1996, he publicly adopted the line that Syria had no Kurds of its own and that those living there were refugees from Turkey. Furthermore, Öcalan implicitly downplayed the problems faced by Syrian Kurds and invited them to join the ranks of the PKK in Turkey, in what the regime considered their place of origin. Although this type of argument can be easily understood in light of pressure from the Syrian "boss," it nevertheless created a certain discomfort in Syria that resulted in the alienation of some PKK sympathizers after Öcalan's declarations.

In addition to carrying the high price of credibility in the eyes of other minority groups, relations between "minority clients" and "patron states" also turned out to be extremely risky for the minority group concerned. While a geostrategic rationale could lead states to form alliances with Kurdish parties, it could also lead to the sudden rupture of these alliances by the state with dramatic consequences for the minority group. Threatened by the Turkish–Israeli alliance of 1996, isolated internationally and dependant on water from the Euphrates, Syria finally succumbed to Turkish pressure to withdraw all support for the PKK and hand over its leader to the Turkish authorities. Following Egyptian and Iranian mediation, Damascus expelled Abdullah Öcalan on October 9, 1998. The Kurdish leader fled to the former Soviet Union before arriving in Italy on November 12, 1998. He was immediately placed under house arrest, but no European power was willing to take the responsibility of trying Turkey's public enemy number one. In January 1999, Öcalan began the long journey that took him to Kenya where he was arrested and transferred to Turkey.[15] The Kurdish leader appeared before the television cameras blindfolded and wrapped in two Turkish flags. The valiant symbol of Kurdish resistance had been reduced to the status of mere mortal, a man like any other, at the mercy of the enemy.

Even though at first thousands of Kurds (sympathizers or otherwise of the PKK) in Turkey, Iraq, Iran, Syria, and Europe demonstrated their anger at the humiliating treatment of the PKK leader, eventually his party found itself alone to face the enormous challenge of maintaining the direction of an organization which had up until then centered on the persona of Abdullah Öcalan. His later declarations only added to the confusion in the Kurdish nationalist camp in Turkey. Clearly drugged, Öcalan proclaimed his love for Turkey and the Turkish people and later declared that the PKK's struggle had been a big mistake. On August 2, 1999 he called for a cease-fire, accepted by the PKK three days later. Demands for the creation of a Kurdish state were replaced by those for the democratization of Turkey and the right to speak the Kurdish language.

Confronted by the rapid evolution of events, the organization had to respond to two outwardly incompatible demands: first, to democratize its structures with a view to gain credibility abroad – mainly in Europe and the United States – and second, to limit dissident rhetoric in order to conserve internal cohesion (Grojean and Küçük 2006: 70).

The repercussions of the PKK's crisis were also felt in Syria. Since 1998, various PKK leaders have been handed over to Turkey by the Syrian authorities and former PKK fighters returning to Syria were given prison sentences ranging from 1 to 10 years.[16] PKK militants attempted to create new parties with the double objective of escaping state repression while maintaining support from its thousands of members and sympathizers. In doing so, the PYD (Democratic Union Party), founded in 2003, strengthened its position as successor to the PKK, with only the SKDCP (Syrian Kurdish Democratic Concord Party) or *Wifaq*, created in 2004 following a split in the PYD, as a possible challenger.[17] Despite attempts at reconciliation and although still considered the only true Kurdish popular party in Syria, the PKK–PYD has been unable to maintain its influence in the Kurdish political arena in Syria.

## The fall of Saddam Husayn and the collapse of Syrian strategy

The impact on the Middle East of the American intervention in Iraq, on March 20, 2003, remains difficult to measure. Accused by the United States of supporting Iraqi insurgents and Shi'ite militias in Lebanon, Damascus had to bow to pressure from Washington to accept UN Resolution 1559. The rapid, unilateral retreat of Syrian troops from Lebanon in April 2005, following the assassination of Lebanon's former prime minister Rafiq Hariri, constitutes an example of the changing power relations at the regional level.

Moreover, as previously discussed, by delivering Öcalan to the Turkish authorities, Syria lost an important advantage in the game of the exploitation of the

80  *The Kurdish issue and its transnational dimension*

Kurdish card in the regional sphere. Syria's relations with the Kurdish parties in Iraq also suffered a major blow after the fall of Saddam Husayn. The Iraqi Kurds were among America's closest allies during the last Gulf War in 2003, allowing them to besiege Kirkuk, the oil-rich historic capital of Iraqi Kurdistan.[18] The "territorialization" of Kurdish nationalism – an important step in the process of nation building – initiated in 1991 and strengthened in 2003 raised serious concerns among neighboring states regarding the birth of a Kurdish state that could pull in other Kurdish regions in the Middle East (Olson 2005: 233–4).

When diverse Kurdish leaders arrived in Damascus in order to reassure the Syrian authorities, the Kurdish party's offices in Damascus and Qamishli were temporarily closed. Despite their reopening in Damascus, such "diplomatic" representations lost their importance in a climate of high tension confirmed by the closure of the border, on both sides, between Syria and Iraqi Kurdistan (Montgomery 2005: 143). The "Qamishli revolt" of March 2004, which is discussed later, and the police repression of Kurdish demonstrators in Syria became a new source of tension between Damascus and the Kurdish parties of Iraq, particularly after Masud Barzani, first president of Iraqi Kurdistan, had openly urged Bashar al-As'ad to soften coercive measures against the Kurds and to undertake reforms.[19]

During the elections of January 30, 2005, the unified Kurdish list (Kurdistan Alliance) won 92 percent of the votes in the three northern provinces placed under Kurdish control since 1991. At the same time, an unofficial referendum, which was implicitly encouraged by the two principal Kurdish parties, suggested that 90 percent of Kurds were in favor of independence. The acceptance in the constitution in 2005 of federalism as the new Iraqi state's system of organization only served to strengthen the centrality of the Iraqi Kurds, both in Iraq and in the Kurdish arena in the Middle East (Bozarslan 2005: 26–7). Almost immediately, demands for administrative autonomy following the Iraqi model were made with varying degrees of intensity in Turkey, Iran, and even Syria, confirming the cross-border character of the Kurdish issue.

Incidentally, the Iraqi Kurds succeeded in expanding their maneuvering room through an alliance with the United States, but without resorting to forming counterintuitive alliances with "enemy" states. As a result of this relationship, Turkey, Syria, and Iran saw their sphere of influence in Iraqi Kurdistan diminish following America's second intervention in Iraq, particularly between 2003 and 2005.

*Toward a new balance of regional power*

However, if the American invasion of Iraq in 2003 triggered the expansion of the Kurdish sphere, the difficulties encountered by American troops and the Baghdad government in imposing their authority over the whole Iraqi territory helped Syria and Iran, allies against the American giant, to gain back any lost ground in the balance of military power on the regional scale. The White House is well aware that in order to stabilize the situation in Iraq, it will need the collaboration not only of Teheran and its local Shi'i intermediaries in the south of the country, but also of the Iraqi capital. In addition, the United States' difficulties in Iraq have convinced certain sectors of the American administration as well as the Democrat opposition of the need for "critical dialogue" with Syria in order to move toward a resolution of the Arab–Israeli conflict and, to a lesser degree, to avoid the spread of "jihadism" toward Iraq.

Incidentally, the improvement in economic and political relations not only between Damascus and Ankara since 1999, but also between Ankara and Teheran and Damascus and Teheran allows the three countries to keep a keen eye on the Kurdish parties of Iraq, who live in uncertainty with regard to the future of their autonomous government. In addition to the constant threats of military intervention by Turkey in Iraqi Kurdistan should Turkish interests in the Kirkuk area be considered in "danger" (in other words if Kirkuk and its oil comes under Kurdistan regional government or KRG control), Ankara seeks to bypass the Kurdish autonomous region in order to establish direct economic relations with Baghdad. In early 2007, following the refusal to sign a protocol to export oil products through the Kurdistan region into Iraq, Baghdad and Ankara decided to extend their deal in accordance with the previous agreement signed by both sides. Even more importantly, Turkey announced intentions to close the Ibrahim Khalil gate, the only official border point between Iraq and Turkey, which was controlled by the KRG and through which all trade passes, and that Ankara had started negotiations with the Syrian authorities to renovate the way of Nusaybin to be the trade route between Iraq and Turkey.[20]

The withdrawal of American troops from Iraq would only serve to reinforce the fragility felt by the fledgling power in Iraqi Kurdistan. However paradoxical as it may seem, the Kurdish parties in Iraq convert this uncertainty into symbolic and political resources which permit them to strengthen the peoples' sense of "national unity" and to legitimize the construction of power already under way. In other words, just like the other state actors of the Middle East, the KDP and the PUK use their capacity to anchor themselves for the duration, as a political resource. Reactive or deliberate, the strategies that they have put in place have adhered to two complimentary temporalities: in the short term, aiming to manage daily affairs (institutions, development of territory, relations with neighboring countries, etc.), the other long term, aiming at the continuity of Kurdish nationalism, likely to lead, in time, to independence (Bozarslan 2005: 34–5).

For the moment the KRG is duty bound to compromise with its Syrian, Turkish, and Iranian neighbors, thus, once more normalizing the KRG's relations with Damascus. The official visit to Damascus in January 2007 of the Iraqi President Jalal Talabani, hoping to bring the two countries closer together, gave him the opportunity to meet the leaders of the Kurdish parties of Syria close to the KDP and the PUK with Bashar al-As'ad's blessing. It is easy to imagine that there would be a price to pay for this collusion with Damascus via the compromise made by the KDP and the PUK not to interfere in Syria's internal affairs. In other words, a commitment could have been made by the Kurdish parties of Iraq not to encourage the Kurdish nationalist movement in Syria in exchange for Syria's "constructive" attitude toward Iraqi Kurdistan, constituting a scenario not unlike that prior to 2003.

# 5 The Kurdish response and its margins

## "Dissimulation" of a hidden conflict

Even though it can be said that the Kurds had been subject to a certain "linguistic Arabization" and that, as Syrian citizens, they had been imbibed with Arabo-Syrian cultural and political references – through education, television, and, for men, the army – the diverse expressions of Kurdish culture have maintained their vivacity.[1]

Kurdish ethnic identities in Syria are articulated in various forms of group affiliation, such as tribe, locality, or class, depending on the social context in which they are produced and expressed. The geographical fragmentation of the Kurdish pockets stresses this variety of articulations. Nevertheless, there is a shared sense of belonging to a Kurdish community defined as a cultural community with a common history, which articulates the various social and cultural realities of the Kurds in Syria. This community is delimited by the objectification of cultural diacritical features, which are used to signal the cultural distinctiveness of the Kurds in relation to other ethnic groups in Syria. The collective emphasis on the maintenance and public expression of certain cultural features, such as the use of the Kurdish language or folklore festivals, aims to mark the ethnic boundary that defines the translocal Kurdish identities (Pinto 2007: 259).

Although ethnic awareness is an important feature among Kurds in Syria, the translocal identities have not traditionally been conducive to a nationalist mobilization. There are a number of approaches taken in an attempt to explain this paradox. The demographic arguments that explain this fact in light of the relatively small number of Kurds seems insufficient given that the Alawites managed to take control of the state from the 1960s despite their similarly small numbers. Nor does the geographic distribution of the Kurds in several enclaves explain, in itself, the political absence of the Kurds in Syria until 2004. Like the Alawites and the Druzes, the Kurds took part in the massive rural exodus toward Syrian towns and cities and now populate both rural and urban locales.[2]

A dialectic approach based on the evolution of the Syrian state and that of Kurdish communities can, however, provide some explanation for the Kurdish predicament. As previously illustrated, during the years of the French Mandate, there was no well-defined Kurdish group to speak of, as a result of their diverse origins, local histories and the fact that each Kurdish group experienced a different process of integration into their Arab environment. Furthermore, for Kurds coming to Jazira from Turkey and Iraq since the 1920s, except for a minority of intellectuals, the first concern once established in Syria was economical survival. The Syrian state being almost nonexistent in the Jazira, Kurdish peasants and tribesmen were framed by tribal and religious leaders, in spite of the Khoybun's efforts to mobilize them around a Kurdish nationalist project. On the other hand, at that time, Kurds were able to live normal lives with their ethnic identity. Kurdish was the language of communication among Kurdish communities and even between Kurds and Christians in Jazira.

Despite the end of the mandate, the Syrian state and the elites who succeeded one another until 1963 possessed neither a unanimist ideology nor a sufficiently coercive powerbase to pose a serious threat to Kurdish identity. State authority was more of an illusion than reality, especially in the countryside where real sovereignty lay in the hands of rival notables and landowners "who did little to encourage any feelings of national identity" (Perthes 2002: 91–2). In this context and according to reports of the French Legation in Damascus:

> The old Kurdish colonists, the majority of whom can be found in Jazira, live in harmony with the Syrians. They continue to speak their national language and wear typical Kurdish clothing, but as long as the government does not force the issue of taxes, and closes its eyes to the lucrative smuggling of illegal goods, an activity in which Kurds in border areas engage with such pride, there is no Kurdish problem to speak of in Syria, where numerous functionaries and high-level officers belong to this community.[3]

If the rise to power of the Ba'ath led to the imposition of a unanimist ideology on the Syrian population, the new regime suffered from internal divisions which prevented it from ever establishing viable official institutions or even a myth of national integration which would have given it some legitimacy. It was not until Hafiz al-As'ad came to power in 1970 that a coherent and dominant power structure was finally established. Paradoxically, the progressive betrayal of the most ideological aspects of the Ba'ath under Hafiz al-As'ad went hand in hand with the consolidation of an authoritarian regime, which was for the first time capable of shaping the whole of Syrian society, and of monopolizing means of organized violence in the name of the party's principles. The absence of liberty in this situation was the price for the promise of economic development, progress, and the liberation of traditional allegiances and the emergence of a "new man." Finally, it was time for Syrian society to "emerge unified and cleansed of its ethnic, denominational, social, and clannish blemishes" (Chiffoleau 2006: 10).

In reality, behind the official unanimism, significant fissures, exacerbated by the foundation of the regime's political culture, continued to exist at the margins of the Syrian legal political system. For example, Arab nationalism excluded Kurds and other non-Arab groups by denying the legitimacy of these groups' differences and their symbolic resources. While the government in Damascus cultivated the loyalty of their Kurdish "clients," the majority of Kurds opted for a policy of "dissimulation." This sociological concept, which is related to the religious term *taqiyya*,[4] means that under certain adverse sociopolitical conditions actors disguise their differences or distinguishing traits in order to challenge the official unanimist ideology at its deepest roots. But when conditions permitted, the formerly hidden group ceases to play this game of conformity and insists on being visible and exposing their differences.

The existence, albeit precarious, of certain groups, movements, or organizations (secular and religious) which had become "abeyance structures" during the period of "crossing of the desert" is extremely important for an eventual re-emergence when the context is more favorable (Taylor 1989: 761). Together, militancy, maintenance of activist networks, and the promotion of a collective identity constitute an important reservoir for such groups, available for remobilization at the opportune time.

In light of this, "dissimulation" should not be considered synonymous with accommodation. Dissimulation exists as a middle ground between the basic dichotomy of passive acceptance and revolution, and therein lie the attitudes, practices, and discourses which betray a persistent defiance and refusal to submit to the powers that be. The different forms that "daily resistance" to authority can take in a nondemocratic setting are, in fact, extremely diverse. Such resistance can take the form of, for example, discursive practices (flattery of elites, coded language, and jokes), unwillingness to complete tasks (uncooperative and unproductive at the workplace), exhibiting behaviors that are disapproved of by the elites (consumption of jute, wearing of the veil by women), illegal dealing in material goods (smuggling), sabotage of the means of production, or electoral absenteeism (Fillieule and Bennani-Chraibi 2003: 46–57).[5]

In Syria, it is the Ba'athist regime itself which favored the dissimulation of the various divisions that existed throughout Syrian society. An ambiguous relationship was established between the Ba'athist power and the Syrian people during Hafiz al-As'ad's presidency. The various official institutions (schools, military, administration, public television, etc.) encouraged the personality cult surrounding As'ad and his Ba'athist principles, while simultaneously highlighting the boundaries that should never be crossed and, by consequence, highlighting the possible means of escape from the regime. In this sense, citizens have not been required to believe the cult's fictitious statement, but they have been required to act as if they did[6] (Wedeen 1998: 506).

The Kurds, along with other components of Syrian society, were invited to either adhere to the principles of the regime or to maintain a passive obedience while participating in the unanimist myth created by the Ba'ath. Like all Syrian citizens, the Kurds were subjected to the state of emergency, in effect since 1963, with its norms and restrictions of expression and association. Certain essential principles of the regime, notably that of Arab nationalism, and certain laws, including restrictions on Kurdish language and folklore, were direct attacks on the core of Kurdish identity which threatened the survival of Kurdish groups. Given the specific nature of these attacks on the Kurdish people, their methods of resistance also maintained a certain particularity.

The focus of this chapter is on the daily resistance methods employed by the Kurds with respect to the "abeyance structures" belonging to the political, cultural, and religious fields.[7] In doing so, the aim is to explain, on one hand, the dynamics which resulted from the dissimulation strategy and, on the other hand, the dynamics that have encouraged the Syrian Kurds to move away from the dissimulation of their conflict with the regime toward the evolving "Kurdish problem" at the dawn of the new century.

## The Kurdish parties at the margins of the legal system

The Kurds are dispersed between four different states and therefore fall under the authority of four distinct political, economic, and military jurisdictions. The nature of these authorities decides to a large extent which mode of action will be taken by the Kurdish nationalist movements in each country. It was inevitable then that the Kurdish political movements would follow distinctive trajectories in Iran, Iraq, Turkey, and Syria. According to Hamit Bozarslan, there are three common features that connect the Kurdish opposition political movement in each of these countries. First, they are identifiable by their use of a limited number of modes of action: political engagement, armed conflict, or negotiation. Second, the Kurdish movement has borrowed universalist doctrines, such as westernism, Marxism, and Islamism, aiming to connect the Kurdish world with other opposition groups and establish control over Kurdish society and transform it. Finally, the political divergences observed in the involved states have rarely sufficed to completely eliminate one of these modes of action, though they may play a role in determining their success or failure (Bozarslan 1997: 191–2).

An analysis of the history of the Kurdish movement in Syria confirms, to a large degree, that the Kurdish parties of Syria constitute an "exception" in the framework of oppositional Kurdish nationalist movements. With respect to the question of political choices, Syrian Kurdish parties had never taken up arms against the government of Damascus, although inversely armed struggle has represented the primary mode of opposition for the Kurdish movement elsewhere. As a result, Syrian Kurdish parties were unable to impose themselves as legitimate actors and open negotiations with the central government, a step which normally only takes place after a period of armed conflict.

Political participation has been limited over the years, to such an extent that more often than not the Kurdish parties remained outsiders, marginal actors in the political arena. This fact was more the result of the exclusivity of the political system, rather than the nature of the Kurdish movement, which had traditionally contented itself with cultural and civic demands (for example, the lifting of the ban on the Kurdish language and the return of citizenship to those "stateless" Kurds affected by the census of 1962).

The Kurdish movement in Syria followed, up until 1980, the same ideological evolution as in other Kurdish regions in the Middle East, which is to say that it borrowed from westernist (1919–50) and Marxist doctrine (1950–80). However, its singularity was evident in the fact that not one Kurdish party in Syria embraced an Islamist doctrine as was the case in both Turkey and Iraq.[8] Finally, and as already highlighted in the previous chapter, the Kurdish movement was encouraged to focus its attention on Turkey and Iraq, which spared Damascus the potential threat of destabilization of the country from the inside.

A brief return to the origins of the Kurdish movement in Syria may help us to explain the distinctive evolution of the Kurdish political movement in the country. The first Kurdish nationalist committee in Syria, the Khoybun (1927–44), followed two trajectories. First, Turkey was the target for its diplomatic and violent activities, as it was the country of origin of the majority of its members. Conscious of the Khoybun leaders' freedom of action in the Levant thanks to the French Mandate, the Kurdish nationalists focused their attentions on France and Syrian nationalists. This trajectory was sustained by the Kurdish League (1945–46), the Khoybun's successor, and through Kurdish actors connected directly or otherwise to these committees. Additionally, neither Kamuran Badirkhan, acting as a free agent and "representative" of the Kurds, nor the Kurdish League would include Syrian Kurds in their demands put forth to world powers after World War II in order to avoid antagonizing the authorities in Damascus.[9] In fact, it was felt that Kurdish enclaves in northern Syria could be sacrificed in exchange for an autonomous Kurdish body in Turkey.

Secondly, the Khoybun's leaders favored a strategy of political participation for the Kurdish representatives since the beginning of the mandate. Thus, the notorious members of the nationalist committee eventually became deputies in the Syrian parliament and some, including the sons of both Ibrahim Pasha and Hasan Hajo, kept their seats throughout the 1950s. However, never once did the Kurdish members of parliament present themselves under the banner of an openly nationalist party. They were considered "independents," known for their origins and for their notability, but who did not seek to create a true political apparatus around these aspects. Therefore, for the better part of the 1950s, the militancy of the politicized Kurds would be associated with the Syrian Communist Party (SCP).

It was not until the creation of the Kurdistan Democratic Party in Syria in 1957, which soon became the Kurdish Democratic Party in Syria, that a popular Kurdish national party finally appeared on the Syrian political scene. Even at this point, the party kept a "Syrianized" agenda in that the objectives of the party did not include the liberation of Syrian Kurdistan, though it did include the improvement of living conditions for Syrian Kurds. The KDPS managed to reunite former members and sympathizers of the Khoybun, such as Nur al-Din Zaza and 'Uthman Sabri, and former SCP militants such as Rashid Hamo. The KDPS was able to utilize the militant know-how of these two groups, rapidly establishing itself in every small town in Jazira, Jarablus, and Kurd Dagh. Despite the clandestine continuation of its activities – specifically awareness-raising activities such as publication and printing of tracts and bulletins on Kurdish issues in Syria – after the accession of UAR in 1958, the party managed to create a network of some 30,000 members and thousands more sympathizers.[10]

The arrest in September 1962 of 32 eminent members of the party represented the first serious blow to the KDPS. However, the KDPS's popularity was effectively measured for the first time during the legislative elections in December 1961. Nur al-Din Zaza and Shaykh Muhammad Isa Mahmud, both founding party members were elected as independent candidates in Jazira. Despite these positive results, the KDPS was unable to develop as a legal political body afterward. Zaza's election was nullified and on March 28, 1962 there was an antisecessionist *coup d'état*. The return to civil rule did not bring any significant changes for the KDPS and, in March 1963, the military reclaimed power and declared a state of emergency. When the charismatic party leaders, such as 'Uthman Sabri and Nur al-Din Zaza, were thrown into prison several times between 1960 and 1965, the KDPS leadership fell into the hands of 'Abd al-Hamid Hajj Darwish, a young law student.

The fragility of this new formation was also due in part to internal dynamics. Since its inception, the KDPS was subject to various divisions due to generational and ideological differences. Though the party had succeeded in bringing together the ex-members of the Khoybun and the SCP, this union was not sufficient to neutralize the tensions between its left (ex-SPC members, young students, teachers, and manual laborers) and its right wings (notables, religious leaders, and landowners). These differences were added to by the division which separated the partisans of the "progressive" approach of the KDP in Iraq, centered on Jalal Talabani, and the "conservative" approach led by Mustafa Barzani. This division at work within the KDP also had repercussions for the KDPS. This party was divided into three camps: one pro-Barzani and two contesting parties split between the left ('Uthman Sabri and Muhammad Nayo) and the right ('Abd al-Hamid Hajj Darwish). However, 'Abd al-Hamid Hajj Darwish eventually joined the Marxist camp of his schoolmate Jalal Talabani in 1965, even though he was not a leftist.

In 1970 Mustafa Barzani attempted to reunify the KDPS by inviting all of the factions to Iraqi Kurdistan. Despite this effort, he was unsuccessful in reuniting the contesting factions under his party's banner and a new party was created by Daham Miro, a notable. Though this new formation succeeded in uniting the conservative party members, the "young wolves," led by Mullah Muhammad Nayo and 'Abd al-Hamid Hajj Darwish, were not reintegrated into the KDPS, known henceforth as "The Party."

The left wing came to be led by Salah Badr al-Din in the Kurdish Leftist Democratic Party. In 1975, the year of the Kurdish movement's defeat in Iraq and the breakup of the Mustafa Barzani's KDP, Jalal Talabani made his own attempt to unite the Syrian Kurds. He made contact with the "left" and the leaders of the KDPS, attempting to position himself as the leader of the Kurdish movement in Syria. A congress was held, but those loyal to Barzani refused to participate. Furthermore, the Kurdish Leftist Democratic Party broke into two parts, though it kept the same name until 1980.[11] In reality, the differences in the agendas of the various Kurdish parties in Syria were minimal. The majority of Kurdish parties professed Marxist and anti-imperialist ideologies, following the example of political parties of non-Kurdish regions, and demanded a degree of autonomy and legal rights vis-à-vis the Arab majority.[12] In the face of pointless ideological disputes, many of which were driven by the personal differences between members, many Kurds left the parties and were consequently condemned to live in a state of political lethargy (More 1984: 205).

As of 2007, thirteen Kurdish parties existed for a population of around 1.5 million, organized into three "Blocs": the Kurdish Democratic Front in Syria

88  *The Kurdish response and its margins*

(*Eniya* or *al-Jabha*, or the Front), the Kurdish Democratic Alliance in Syria (*Hevbendiya* or *Al-Takhaluf*, or the Alliance) and an alliance comprising three independent parties (see Appendix). Finally, the Democratic Union Party remains alone though it often collaborates with the latter.

*The Kurdish political parties: a theoretical framework*

Rather than recount a detailed history of the successive schisms in the Kurdish movement since the 1960s, it is more important to focus on the reasons behind the Kurdish parties' unwillingness or inability to escape this pattern which resulted in the chronic splintering of the Kurdish political movement in Syria. The period between 1970 and 2000 offers an interesting observational framework because these three decades have witnessed the stabilization of both the regime and its policy toward the Kurds, and the Syrian opposition (Arab and Kurd).

The present analysis approaches the subject from three different vantage points by studying the Kurdish movement first as a social movement taking place in a sociopolitical context with various constraints and opportunities (opportunity structures), second, as a social movement that was well resourced and which had recourse to a certain repertoire of actions[13] (resource mobilization), and third, as a movement within a certain cultural framework, playing the role of mediator between opportunity and action (Lichbach and Zuckerman 1997: 142–73). Finally, a synthesis of this theoretical framework is proposed here in light of some of the recent works on social movements (Lichbach and Zuckerman 1997; McAdam *et al.* 1996; Bennani-Chraïbi and Fillieulle 2003) and on the Kurdish movement in particular (Romano 2006).

The Kurdish movement, like all social movements, must maintain collective action in time and space. Structures of political opportunity, defined as a series of coherent dimensions of the political environment which can both encourage and discourage people from taking political action (Tarrow 1994: 17), take on great importance in this context. Generally speaking, at moments when the elites and their political groups become vulnerable to the opposition, social movements are more likely to be initiated and to inspire collective action. At the same time, such political opportunities can be missed due to the lack of an organized social movement.

In addition, the types of opportunities which present themselves come to bear on the types of collective action employed by social movements. Thus, political systems that enable minority groups to participate and administer their own communal affairs encourage constructive center/periphery relationships, allowing for the development of legal nationalist political organizations, internal cohesion, and compromise. By contrast, restrictive spaces stifle opportunities for political growth and negotiation between nationalist and state elite. Finally, ambiguous spaces encourage both compromise and hostility between the center and periphery (Natali 2005: xxviii–xxix).

The Syrian political arena falls into this last category of ambiguous space. This helps to explain why, for example, Kurdish parties can be outsiders in the system, outlawed and persecuted, and at the same time can be openly tolerated and even party to the regime through members of their civil and religious elite. However, as in Morocco, the crux of the matter is that it is the Syrian regime that has created a moving dividing line between inclusion and exclusion (Roussillon and Ferrié 2006: 170).

Rather than incorporate[14] the Kurdish parties into the Ba'athist system, thereby allowing them a certain degree of legitimacy, the Syrian regime opted instead to engage in a series of "collusive transactions," that is to say, the spreading and "publicity" of certain interactions between the regime and different sectors of Syrian society with a double objective. By way of these tactics, the Syrian state, like the majority of Arab regimes, sought and achieved stability on the one hand, and, on the other, the Syrian state managed to prevent Kurds – and all other ethnic and religious groups – from coming together, interacting, forming a group ethnic consciousness and organizing into movements that would facilitate the spread of this process and eventually challenge the regime to pursue their own objectives. The eventual neutralization of the Kurdish movement was a consequence of this effort on the part of the Syrian regime. Furthermore, the "deregulation" of the partisan market only added confusion to the political supply and to social demands.

The Syrian regime's policy of alliance with the Kurdish nationalists starting in the 1970s introduced a new divisive element to the movement. Each party leader sought to establish himself as a "representative" of the Kurdish people of Syria and as a legitimate interlocutor of the government in Damascus. As a result, the Party quickly developed a bad reputation amongst certain Kurdish nationalist groups. Its leaders, especially Daham Miro, were accused of having accepted anyone as a member, allowing members of the Intelligence Services to infiltrate the party. He was also accused of having collaborated with Damascus. The parties which stemmed from the KDPS did not escape similar accusations of having collaborated with Syrian Intelligence Services, with the cases of 'Abd al-Hamid Hajj Darwish[15] and Salah Badr al-Din[16] attracting the most attention. Hafiz al-As'ad collaborated since the 1980s with Iraqi Kurdish parties and Kurdish parties in Turkey, and also with various Kurdish groups in Syria, with a view to containing the Islamist threat in Syria. These collaborative relationships served to reinforce the friendly ties between the regime and its security forces and Kurdish groups.[17] By way of these collaborations, he was even successful in improving the regime's ties with Arab opposition parties and minority groups such as Armenians in Aleppo (Migliorino 2006: 108–9) and Syriacs in Jazira.[18]

This explains how Muhammad al-Mansura, head of security in the Hasaka province between 1980 and 2002 and later promoted to the head of *Firh Filistin* branch of the Secret Police in Damascus, came to control the Kurdish movement in Jazira. He resided in Qamishli where he established patron/client relationships with Kurdish party leaders and tasked himself with establishing certain limits for the movement which should not be breached. His deep understanding of the Kurdish movement also helps explain his role as mediator between the Syrian regime and Kurdish parties following the Qamishli uprising in March 2004.[19]

However, the Syrian regime's relations with the Kurdish parties were of a particular nature. First, disregarding religious personalities, not a single Kurd has ever attained an important position in Syria's government system. In addition, the limited role of Kurdish representatives in Parliament remained one of a consultative, rather than legislative nature. More often than not, they have remained in the margins of the legal system. The principal reason for this is that the demands of the antiestablishment minority are not analogous with those of most other social movements or political Islam in that it asks for an additional ethnic group to be recognized by the state. In order to meet these demands, the state would be required to accept that the "national establishment" was also a type of resource which could be shared. The acceptance of this idea could result in the weakening of the state monopoly on group representation and its symbolic capital and would imply a move toward sharing of administrative and political power (Bozarslan 1997: 150).

The intervention of the state does not provide sufficient explanation for the fragmentation of the Kurdish political arena or for the neglect of the Kurdish problem for almost three decades. Resource mobilization theories provide some answers to these questions. Mobilization refers here to the processes by which a discontented group "assembles and invests resources for the pursuit of group goals" (Obershall 1973: 28). Resource mobilization can refer to both material and nonmaterial resources, such as people, money, weapons, and means of communication, or legitimacy and commitment. Resource mobilization theories view groups as rational strategic actors. Thus, this approach takes different key variables into consideration, such as resources that are both internal and external to the movement, the costs and benefits of participation in the movement, the availability of social networks for reaching and mobilizing support, and the state's capacities and weaknesses.

It is difficult to imagine what resources the Kurdish movement could possibly have at its disposal for their use in confronting the Syrian government. Since 1963, the state has strived to maintain an unfair advantage over other political organizations by obstructing the institutionalization of a liberal political system which could potentially create political advantages for partisan organizations. The Syrian political scene has thus become a political arena lacking in the typical power play of such settings. Candidates must be approved by Syrian authorities and therefore must adhere to the Ba'ath Party political agenda, accept the decisions of Ba'ath Party congresses, or at least abstain from promoting any other political agenda. The immediate consequence is that the Kurdish parties cannot offer their people goals that matter to them, to the point that it could even be considered an example of the "depolitisization of political activity" (Roussillon and Ferrié 2006: 168).

By the same token, Kurdish parties cannot present a credible image, vision of the future, or any successful action, which would allow them to gain the trust of the people. The Kurdish parties, who were typically very moderate with respect to any proclamation of identity, identified themselves as secularist parties that were also aligned with national liberation movements characterized by a tendency toward Marxist and socialist discourse, which prevented them from clearly distinguishing themselves from Arab parties. Having evolved in a common environment, the Kurdish parties shared, up to a point, the same ideological framework which was influenced by the region's political currents and the Cold War ambiance that lasted until the 1980s.

The Kurdish parties which came into being after the KDPS were small clandestine groups which were generally organized around a central personality and in connection with one of the Kurdish entities in Iraq or Turkey. In the first case, these "heads" of certain parties, which sometimes comprised as few as ten to twenty-five members,[20] often contented themselves with mobilizing weak segments without any continuity in time, which allowed them to engage in "reticular actions."[21] The dependence of these parties on their leaders and their personal networks offers some explanation as to why these parties have been unable to establish a system by which the organization may change leadership. 'Abd al-Hamid Hajj Darwish is one such example, having led the Kurdish Democratic Progressive Party since the 1970s.[22]

In the case of Kurdish organizations connected to parties in Iraq and Turkey, it is interesting to note that these are the organizations that contain the higher number of militants, greater financial means, a larger capacity to create and disseminate propaganda, and greater legitimacy. Consider, for example, the aura surrounding the great hero of the Kurdish movement in Iraq, Mustafa Barzani; the strength of his reputation helps to explain why the Syrian counterpart of his party, the KDPS, managed to hold its ground as one of the foremost Syrian parties, despite the numerous schisms which divided the party and its progressive inaction as a political organization.[23] One can find portraits of Barzani in the homes of KDP supporters and Kurdish nationalists of varying degrees. Visits to Jazira made by Masud Barzani, Mustafa's son and current president of the Kurdish Regional Government (KRG), has served to maintain and increase the number of young Kurds belonging to the party and who remain committed not only to the party and its agenda, but also to the Barzani family.[24]

Despite these advantages, all Kurdish parties survive in an uncertain and precarious political environment. They suffer from a lack of internal opportunities for advancement, leaving them with few attractive characteristics for members (McAdam *et al.* 1996: 3). Kurdish parties, and especially the smaller ones, are unable to offer economic incentives for joining the party or possibilities for advancement either within the party or in the state government. The words of Sa'id 'Abd al-Majid, representative of the Kurdish Democratic Progressive Party of Syria in Berlin, eloquently speak to this problem:

> The people are very frustrated with the Kurdish parties. They expect them to solve their problems, but this is unrealistic. It is dangerous to be a member of a Kurdish party as you risk prison and we have no money. When people learn this, they leave the party for another. For me, my commitment stems from a certain family tradition, given that my father was also involved in politics.[25]

The Kurdish parties have been unable to launch significant political activities and propaganda. As in the case of Syrian opposition parties, the parties with the most resources can publish magazines and pamphlets, while parties or individuals in exile can maintain Internet sites.[26] However, the economic vulnerability of the parties leads them to avoid confrontation with the state, as any such confrontations would threaten their very existence. When a party member is imprisoned, for example, the party must assume economic responsibility for his family for the duration of his imprisonment. Therefore, the mass arrests of party militants can lead to a veritable crisis in the party.[27] This economic vulnerability also explains why some parties are eventually persuaded to create ties with the state or Intelligence Services.

If Kurdish parties in Syria are unable to offer either political success or large-scale political action, then what purpose do these parties actually serve? With the exception of members of certain political parties, the majority of Kurds interviewed on the subject were extremely severe in their judgments of the Kurdish parties. Accusations of having done nothing for the "Kurdish cause" or for the people and a general distrust of the Kurdish parties are very much present in their testimonies. However, longer interviews often revealed more complex and contrasting sentiments with respect to the Kurdish parties.

If the regime had established the rules of the game regarding the unanimist fiction of the Kurdish problem, the stabilization of Kurdish communities nevertheless came about through a process in which Kurdish actors, either political, tribal, or religious actors or intellectuals were in constant contact. In this way, the Kurdish parties took responsibility for guiding different groups' actions so that they remained within certain limits. However, the interpretation of these limits required by such a guiding role is not without risk. Practices such as the covert sale of books in the Kurdish language or the holding of a public conference can be tolerated at one time and can be suppressed at another. The Kurdish political parties acted, unknowingly, as guinea pigs for testing the limits imposed by the regime with regard to the Kurdish problem.

Moreover, the parties' entrenchment in rural areas, employing the functional familial and clan structures, has allowed them to replace local authorities in resolving certain social problems. In this functionality, Kurdish parties often act as mediators in, for example, land disputes or in certain public awareness campaigns against social practices such as "honor crimes."[28] Their substitution for local state and religious authorities was further aided by the fact that these actors were not inclined to involve themselves in disputes of this nature.

The most important function of the political parties is the "cultural framing" of the community. "Framing" can be defined as "conscious strategic efforts by groups of people to fashion shared understandings of the world and of themselves that legitimate and motivate collective action" (Snow et al. 1986: 464). Since 1957 the KDPS assumed the function of cultural framing, following the strategic approach of the Badirkhan brothers and of the Khoybun. The KDPS continued to promote the teaching of the Kurdish language in Latin characters and to cultivate the nationalist doctrine of the Syrian Kurds, using the Kurdish myths (Kawa and "Greater Kurdistan"), the martyrs and heroes (Shaykh Sa'id, Mustafa Barzani), and literary and intellectual figures (Ahmad Khani, the Badirkhan brothers, 'Uthman Sabri, Cigerxwîn).

Though this cultural framing of Kurdish communities was achieved despite the considerable obstacles during the 1960s and 1970s, after 1980 the improvement in relations between the parties and the Syrian government allowed cultural activities to blossom. This took place largely through the mobilization of affluent Kurdish students in Damascus and Aleppo by way of institutions, such as schools, theater and folk groups, athletic organizations or publishing houses based in Lebanon, charged with organizing social events, the foremost of which was the Newroz festival (Gauthier 2006: 222).

*Toward a theoretical synthesis*

The history of the Kurdish movement reveals a certain continuity during the period beginning with the French Mandate and lasting until the presidency of Hafiz al-As'ad. These continuous aspects included its moderate political platform, the pursuit of a participatory role in Syrian political arena, and the general direction of the movement toward other Kurdish areas. Without assuming a determinist stance, it could be said that these elements have come to comprise a "cultural tool kit" or, in other words, "ideational themes" and prevalent attitudes within the Kurdish movement in Syria (Romano 2006: 21).

Even though the ambiguity of the Syrian arena did not offer any real political opportunities, it did serve as a venue in which the Kurdish organizations were able to survive. While the dissimulation of the Kurdish conflict in Syria promoted by the Kurds was a reaction to the constraints imposed by the Syrian regime, it was also the result of certain constraints within the movement. Divided by personal and ideological quarrels, lacking in human, material, and symbolic resources, and tortured by its ambiguous (at best) relationship with the government, the Kurdish parties in Syria lacked a clear political project with the strength to attract Kurds and inspire them to publicly proclaim their Kurdish identity and attachment to a nationalist ideal. This idea can be further examined by drawing a comparison with the evolution of the PKK in Syria during As'ad's presidency, based on the three levels of analysis discussed previously in this chapter: opportunity structures, resource mobilization, and cultural framing.

During the 1980s and 1990s, the PKK was the only organization capable of becoming a veritable popular party in Syria, and the only organization given the authority to do so by the regime. Unlike other Kurdish parties, the PKK had the advantage of certain opportunity structures which facilitated its development in Syria. The PKK's success can be explained to a large degree by the complicity of Damascus in their recruitment and propaganda activities. There are, of course, additional reasons behind the engagement of thousands of Kurds in this guerrilla movement.

First of all, the slogan of a united and independent Kurdistan aroused great sympathy across all social classes in the Syrian Kurdish community in the 1980s.[29] As in Turkey, many Syrian Kurds, whether allied with or opposed to the PKK, recognized that the PKK's discourse of the "new man," which implied renouncing his former personality in order to become a "real Kurd," helped to restore, and even reinvent, Kurdish identity and place him on equal footing with Arabs.

94  *The Kurdish response and its margins*

The armed struggle led by the PKK also aroused sympathy because it brought the possibility of real political achievements, in contrast to the clandestine activities of other Syrian Kurdish parties, which rarely bore fruit.[30] The repressive practices of the Turkish army in Turkish Kurdistan also gave rise to sympathy for the PKK's cause. The appeal of the guerrilla warfare employed by the PKK was not in itself surprising. Even though other Kurdish parties have declined to take up arms as a means of action in Syria, it is important to bear in mind that the Kurdish revolt led by Shaykh Sa'id in 1925, the Ararat revolt (1927–31) in Turkey, and the armed movement led by Mustafa Barzani in Iraq constitute important aspects of the Kurdish nationalist myth in Syria. Notably, Syrian Kurds had joined forces with Kurdish guerrillas in Iraq since the 1960s.

Secondly, the role played by Abdullah Öcalan, the charismatic leader of the PKK, should not be underestimated (White 2000: 162–74). To engage with the guerrilla movement of the PKK increasingly translated into engagement in Öcalan's army, as he imposed himself as the embodiment of a certain political myth. At once loved and feared by his supporters, following internal purges and the establishment of a rigid hierarchy, Öcalan came to be perceived as an incarnation of Kurdishness (Bozarslan 2003: 111).

Thirdly, in certain regions, such as Kurd Dagh and Jarablus, the PKK filled a vacuum left by other Kurdish organizations mainly based in Jazira.[31] Well organized and supported by the Syrian government, the PKK's officials created a highly effective network which allowed them to recruit men for their armed contingent and also managed to accumulate significant financial resources from Kurdish-owned businesses.

Finally, certain young men from poor areas in border towns such as Darbasiya and Kobane ('Ayn al-Arab) may have seen military engagement in the PKK as a potential means of economic and social advancement. On one hand, the complicity of the Syrian authorities with the PKK allowed organized gangs, trained by the PKK, to control the illegal traffic in drugs and weapons across the border. On the other hand, their access to weapons and the very fact of belonging to such a gang allowed some young Kurds to emerge as powerful local players, set apart from the older generations of their families and communities.[32] In other words, military engagement offered Kurdish youth an opportunity to challenge the Kurdish social order and to renegotiate their own place in it.[33]

The reality of the Kurdish parties in Syria was very different during the 1980s and 1990s. That is, Hafiz al-As'ad was no longer in complete control of his own game. Having evolved under his leadership, the Kurdish movement in Syria could hardly have been unaffected by the cultural and political disruption caused by the PKK's activities and doctrine. This party started promoting gender equality[34] among the Kurdish population in Syria and searched to undermine the basis of the tribal and religious allegiances that formed the basis of the traditional Kurdish political elite.

Furthermore, the relative freedom of action related to propaganda and training that was available to PKK representatives, and to a lesser extent to members of the KDP and the PUK, in Iraq and Turkey, led to a certain revival of Kurdish identity and to the strengthening of the pan-Kurdist ideal in Syria by "proxy."

Additionally, the Kurdish movements in Iraq and Turkey facilitated the effervescence of the Kurdish nationalist sentiments in Syria, in spite of the Syrian Kurdish parties' inability both to establish themselves as parties with widespread appeal and to mount any significant political opposition to speak of.

The most obvious political consequence of this dynamic was the adoption by certain Kurdish parties of the expression "Syrian Kurdistan" referring to northern Syria, as opposed to the traditionally used phrase "Kurdish regions of Syria." Thus, at the end of the 1990s, the foundations for the dissimulation of the Kurdish conflict in Syria had collapsed.

## Kurdish identity at the margins of official Islam

The rise of political Islam was observed during the 1970s in the Middle East, including Syria. However, this modern rise in religious zeal is "a religious phenomenon with complex contours, whose boundaries are blurred and whose turns and detours, we try to follow" (Ghazzal, Dupret, and Courbage 2007: 33).

Even though there have been no Kurdish Islamist oppositionist initiatives in Syria, the various Kurdish communities have participated in this religious development in the Syrian public arena. Whether in the Kurdish districts of Aleppo and Damascus or in towns such as Amuda or Qamishli, individual displays of piety – such as the wearing of the veil for women or of beards by men, and frequent visits to the Mosque – can be observed. The "Islamification" of the Kurdish arena is easily explained as the Kurdish movement did not follow an autarchic or self-sufficient evolution and also by the mixing of Arabs and Kurds in various religious brotherhoods (e.g. Kuftariyya).

The Kurdish case, however, retains a certain singularity. The growing evidence of this religious phenomenon among Kurdish communities went hand in hand with the revival of Kurdish identity. At first sight paradoxical, the Islam and Kurdish identity equation proves to be a complex one. This raises the question of whether Islam contributes to the strengthening of community identity or, conversely, functions as an obstacle to the rise of a national consciousness. Would it serve to bind Kurdish communities or further divide them by generating additional ambiguity? Rather than attempting to provide a generic response to these vast questions, we propose a historical and anthropological analysis[35] of one of the most influential forms of Islam amongst Kurds, that of Sufism.[36]

As Martin van Bruinessen points out, "Sufi orders have been prominent in Kurdistan, and the Sufi shaykh is more representative of Kurdish Islam than the official religious representative" (Bruinessen 1998: 26). Furthermore, most of the best-known '*ulama* in Kurdish history were Sufis. Various Sufi orders were present in Kurdistan, but for the past few centuries the scene has been dominated by the Qadiriyya and the Naqshbandiyya. These two orders have at certain moments played important social and political roles in Kurdistan, because they represented a pattern of social organization independent of the tribes as well as the state.

With regard to Kurdish identity, Sufism has played an important role in the processes that led to the emergence and affirmation of ethnic and national identities among the Kurds. *Madrasas* (Koranic schools) and Sufi *zawiyas* (lodges) were the intellectual centers where the Kurdish dialects emerged as written language. In particular, the Naqshbandiyya contributed to the systematization of the Kurdish literature culture and to its diffusion across their network of *zawiyas* and *murids* (disciples). Thus, for instance, Mullah Ahmad Jaziri (Meleyê Ehmedê Cezirî), 1570–1660, is the author of a famous diwan of Kurdish metaphysical poetry, while Ahmad Khani (Ehmedê Xanî), 1651–1706, adapted a popular romance, *Mem û Zîn*, into his long poem of the same name.[37] By the same token, the fact that the Sufi communities often used vernacular languages made the Sufi *zawiyas* privileged spaces for the adaptation of the religious tradition of Islam to the local cultural and social contexts of the Kurdish communities.

The process of centralized administration set in motion by the Ottoman authorities toward the end of the nineteenth century unleashed a decentralizing force in the tribes and religious brotherhoods in Kurdistan, an area peripheral to the empire, in the form of a wave of uprisings. The effect was that tribal and religious chiefs, sometimes in league with one another, filled the local power vacuum left behind after the destruction of the Kurdish emirates. The radicalization of the shaykhs was confirmed after the founding of the modern states, when the hostility of shaykhs and tribes toward the centralized power escalated into armed protest.

However, from the 1950s, the strong Marxist influence felt throughout the Middle East, including the Kurdish nationalist parties, created a gulf between Islam and Kurdist nationalists, the Islamists being seen by the Kurdists as an obstacle to national liberation because of its preaching of Muslim community (*umma*) above any other identity. According to the Kurdish nationalists, Sufism, being nothing more than a folkloric vestige of the past, should disappear in the modernism of the twentieth century. The reality turned out to be more complex.

## *The reformation of the Kurdish Sufi brotherhoods in Syria*

In 1925 the Turkish state abolished mystic orders, forcing Kurdish and Sufi brotherhoods into hiding. Many Kurdish shaykhs took refuge in northern Syria[38] and Iraqi Kurdistan, creating a "very high density of shaykhs per unit of population" (Bruinessen 1992: 30). Such was the situation for two popular Kurdish Shaykhs, Muhammad Sa'id Ramadan al-Buti and Ahmad al-Khaznawi.

Since 1927, the leaders of the Khoybun League tried to spread the Kurdish nationalist ideal through all sectors of Kurdish society in Syria, including the shaykhs and the mullahs, who were responsible for the Koranic schools. The attitudes of the shaykhs and mullahs differed in regard to their attempts at nationalizing Kurdish ethnic identity. Certain religious leaders emphasized Kurdish identity in their teachings, while others promoted a more apolitical approach in their activities, which were centered rather on Sufism.

Among the former was Shaykh 'Abd al-Rahman Garisi, an active member of the Khoybun, and the mullahs, Anwar, Bashir al-Hasani, and Ubeydallah Jangir. The latter two were responsible for a *madrasa* in Amuda and engaged in the military training of Kurdish fighters who would later (end of the 1920s) join rebels active in the Ararat region of Turkey (Ehmed Namî 2000: 193).

The Kurdish response and its margins 97

Certain Koranic schools in northern Syria effectively became "Kurdish schools" where Kurdish classics (epic poems and mystical works) found a place. According to Pierre Rondot, in 1932 the Kurdish language served as the primary language of communication, in a dozen religious schools in Jazira.[39] The teaching materials, much reduced during this period, comprised a few Kurdish volumes in Arabic characters. The reviews and notebooks edited by the Badirkhan brothers during the 1930s, completed the collection of study materials in Latin characters.[40]

The latinization of the Kurdish alphabet, however, had a divisive effect among the Kurdish shaykhs. While the religious circles close to the Khoybun considered this reform a progressive step forward and a move toward the full development of the Kurdish language (Badirkhan 1932: 224), the conservative sectors considered the substituting of Latin characters for the Arabic characters an attack on the Koran, the Muslim religion, and the unity of the Muslim community.

With the departure of the French from the Levant and the stifling of the Kurdish nationalist movement in Syria, most Kurdish shaykhs used the Arab–Kurdish brotherhood "card," based on their common affiliation with Islam. The postmandate era was marked by the growth of certain Kurdish brotherhoods and, even, by the integration of Arab followers into brotherhoods of Kurdish origin, such as the Kuftariyya led by Ahmad Kuftaru and the *zawiya*, directed by al-Khaznawi. Despite state attempts to gain control over the Sunni religious establishment since 1949, *'ulamas* and shaykhs had at their disposal much room for maneuvering up until 1961, when the government created the Ministry of *Waqf*.[41] From this date, all mosques and most *madrasa* and other religious institutions came under its control. Furthermore, the Ministry of *Waqf* became responsible for the organization and surveillance of religious men, particularly the production of the theological and juridical opinions of both provincial muftis and the Mufti of Syria, the highest position in the official hierarchy.

This centralized structure, which was, in part, a legacy of the Ottoman Empire, attracted the attention of the Ba'athist regime which saw it as the ideal instrument to have its political and social projects approved by the Sunni religious establishment. Thus, the regime played an important role in the election of Shaykh Kuftaru to the post of *Mufti* of the Republic. In 1964, Shaykh Kuftaru became a key figure in the teaching and spreading of interpretations of Islam which were in accordance with the religious policy of the Syrian state. He exploited his privileged relations with the regime to transform his Sufi network into a veritable transnational brotherhood. And yet, despite the common interests shared by the Kuftariyya and the Ba'athist regime, the former had always "expressed some degree of autonomy from the state in its religious activities as a Sufi order, which increased after the death of Shaykh Kuftaru" (Stenberg 2005) in 2004.

Efforts by the Ba'athist regime to impose direct control over the religious establishment failed to attain the full legitimacy of unanimous approval from the Sunni Muslim population. A large number of the religious leaders refused to cooperate and went so far as to condemn the secular character of Ba'athist policies. The Islamic opposition represented, in particular, by the Muslim Brotherhood and the Sufi shaykhs with salafist tendencies was able, during the 1970s, to capitalize both

98  *The Kurdish response and its margins*

on the discontent of the brotherhoods, which remained outside of "official Islam,"[42] and of the sectors (traditional, commercial, industrial and agrarian) affected by the Ba'athist regime's economic reforms. The over-representation of Alawites in key positions in the party and the regime only served to confirm the apparent conflict between Sunni Muslims and Alawites (Batatu 1988: 112–19; Perthes 1995: 103–4). Subsequently, Sufi shaykhs had played a fundamental role in recruiting members for the "Islamic Front," which was created in 1980, with a goal of mounting an armed opposition movement. This development was not ignored by the regime, which targeted prominent Sufi shaykhs and sometimes disbanded their communities, particularly after the revolt prompted by the Muslim Brotherhood in the city of Hama in 1982 (Seurat 1989: 72–83).

Although precise data are not available, it is important to recall that the largest Kurdish brotherhoods in Syria remained outside of the process of radicalization of Islamic policy. The Kurdish militias were used in the repression of the Islamist movement at Hama and Aleppo between 1980 and 1982. Furthermore, the Arab–Muslim synthesis of Muslim Brotherhood ideology apparently prevented a large number of Kurds from participating in the armed combat against the Ba'athist regime, which, since 1975, had adopted a more conciliatory policy with regard to ethnic and religious minorities in Syria. Nevertheless, it is possible that the Kurdish shaykhs or the followers of certain mixed brotherhoods (Arab–Kurd), particularly in Aleppo, had joined the Islamist opposition.

The Hama revolt of 1982 was crushed by military intervention and resulted in the destruction of most of the city and a massacre of many of its inhabitants (Van Dam 1996: 111). Subsequently, both the regime and the Islamic opposition changed their strategies. On the one hand, despite having consolidated his rule over Syria, As'ad adopted a more accommodating position toward the public expression of Islam, which was paralleled by a gradual liberalization of the regime and the integration of Sufi shaykhs into the clientelistic state apparatus. On the other hand, there was a shift among the Sunni population from an articulated social and political goal, centered on the conquest of the state, "toward the intensification of public displays of expressions of piety and religiosity as an individual practice" (Pinto 2003: 6). This new social movement had strong connections to Sufi shaykhs such as the shadhili shaykh from Aleppo, 'Abd al-Qadir Isa, who highlighted the social relevance of the Sufi notions of personal morality as a way to bring a solution to the state of corruption and materialism into which the Islamic community had fallen.

*When Sufism is synonymous with Kurdism*

The Sufi brotherhoods, deeply impregnated with popular culture, could not remain immune to the process of re-ethnicization of the Kurdish communities from 1980, which took place particularly as a result of the alliance between Hafiz al-As'ad and Kurdish parties in Iraq and Turkey. The effects of this process on the Kurdish brotherhoods were felt to varying degrees and at different times, within the various Kurdish communities in Syria.

Local Sufi communities in Syria can be classified into three institutional categories: centralized Sufi orders, decentralized Sufi networks, and autonomous *zawiyas* (Pinto 2006: 161–2). Brotherhoods such as the Kuftariyya, a Sufi order to which we have already referred to several times, are in the first group. In the Kuftariyya *tariqa*, the Kurdish language is not spoken; its usage is limited to a few chants and expressions. Yet Shaykh Ahmad Kuftaru made no attempt to hide his Kurdish heredity, often referring to it in his courses (Böttcher 1998: 128). However, he cultivated an ambiguous relationship with Kurdishness, his objective being to establish himself as an intermediary between the state and the Syrian Kurds.[43]

The expansion of Sufism[44] among Kurds in the last decade can be seen in the new *zawiyas* in the neighborhoods of Aleppo which are located on the northern part of the city. These new *zawiyas* tend to be part of larger decentralized Sufi networks, based on hierarchical (initiation) and/or horizontal (marriage, kinship, or friendship) personal ties that connect their shaykhs over large geographical areas.

Finally, the Sufi networks can also integrate and connect rural and urban *zawiyas* following ethnic boundaries, as is the case with Kurdish Sufi networks that link *zawiyas* in the villages of Kurd Dagh, and of Jazira with the Sufi communities of Aleppo (Pinto 2005: 212). These local *zawiyas* have a high degree of autonomy, and they remain the main locus of production of Sufi identity. It is in these local *zawiyas* that the phenomenon of re-ethnicization had been most profound.

The *zawiyas* in the Kurdish regions, particularly those connected to the Rifa'iyya, habitually use Kurmanji as the liturgical language and introduced Kurdish cultural elements (songs, music, and dance) into their religious rituals. The cult of the saints is also a very important practice among the Kurdish Sufis because it allows the introduction of the sacred history of Islam into the framework of Kurdish history. Thus, important sacred places, such as the lavishly built Roman tomb of Nabi Hur in Kurd Dagh, have become places of pilgrimage which connect the dispersed communities and create emotional attachment to its territory in the form of sacred sites.

In Kurd Dagh, where the tribes had disappeared and the power of the aghas had been decimated since the application of Ba'athist agrarian reforms, the Sufi shaykhs enjoyed religious authority and a certain social prestige. The almost total absence of Kurdish parties in this region, until the arrival in force of the PKK during the 1980s, only reinforced the local authority of the Sufi shaykhs. When the PKK established itself in Kurd Dagh, with the complicity of the Ba'ath regime, shaykhs and PKK officials became competitors in the struggle for the material (recruitment and finance) and symbolic (religious and national legitimacy) resources of the region. After an initial phase of conflict, reminiscent of the struggle between the PKK and the Kurdish shaykhs in Turkey, the two groups came to an unwritten, mutually accommodating agreement. Thus, while the PKK proclaimed itself a "revolutionary" party, with the aim of putting an end to the domination of the people by aghas and shaykhs, the PKK officials felt obliged to re-examine their position with regard to the religious situation and to admit that religious reference was in fact of great importance to the Kurds.[45]

The mutual accommodation of the political and religious fields allowed many Kurds from Kurd Dagh, Aleppo, and to a lesser degree Jazira to belong to both a brotherhood and the PKK, triggering, at the same time, a Sufism of Kurdish character and a Kurdish nationalism with a Sunni character, leaving the other ethnoconfessional groups such as the Kurdish Yazidis, present in Kurd Dagh and Jazira, somewhat alienated. Shaykhs and PKK officials devoted themselves to a "division of labor"; while the PKK's recruitment and propaganda activities were concentrated on Turkey, Kurdish "religious nationalism"[46] allowed the Kurdish shaykhs to intervene as cultural and political agents and to act as mediators in relations between their followers and Syrian society, including the Ba'athist regime (Pinto 2007a: 264). In this way, the shaykhs could be perceived by the local population as defenders of Kurdish culture and social autonomy and, by consequence, leaders in a non-Kurdish state.

The fact that Sufism with a Kurdish following assumed a Kurdish quality is corroborated the fieldwork conducted by Paulo G. Pinto in Kurd Dagh. Acording to this author, for example, the Sufi identities that were produced at Shaykh Mahmud Husayn's *zawiya* in the Afrin area were marked by a strong ethnic framework, which defines Sufism as a form of "Kurdish Islam." According to this shaykh, who died in May 2000, Kurds had the "true Sufism," while Sufism did not "exist among the Arabs." Pinto concludes that the self-image of this Sufi community demonstrates how claims to religious distinction, in this case the purity of their mystical tradition, allowed the definition of Kurdish ethnic boundaries as opposed to the religious practices and identities of the Muslim Arabs (Pinto 2008). However, recent field studies did not reveal a desire by all the shaykhs to create an imagined Kurdish community bound by equal relations. On the contrary, many of them, like Shaykh Mahmud Husayn, saw Kurdish society as structured by a hierarchical order created by the unequal distribution of social and religious power. In fact, the articulation of religious and ethnic discourse is coupled with the establishment of hierarchical social relations between the religious community and the rest of the local society, whether they are Kurds or not. Therefore, while Shaykh Mahmud defended Kurdish religious and cultural distinction, he aimed to establish positive relations with the web of political and bureaucratic clientele which structured the channeling of the Ba'athist regime into the local areas of power.

Other shaykhs favored less hierarchical relationships at the heart of their *zawiya*. Such was the case of Shaykh Yasin in the Kurdish quarter of Ashrafiyya in Aleppo. All the members of his *zawiya* were Kurds, but even more significantly, the language, music,[47] and Kurdish dances were integrated into private and even public rituals. The incorporation of elements from Kurdish cultural traditions into the ritual of the *dhikr* (the mystical evocation of God) created a complete identification between being Sufi and being Kurd. Moreover, the mixture of different local musical and dancing traditions showed the construction of a larger "national" Kurdish tradition through the articulation of elements taken from various local cultural traditions (Pinto 2008). In more concrete terms, the disciples of Shaykh Yasin encouraged, at the urging of the political parties, Kurdish literacy in Kurmanji whether it was supported in the *zawiya* or not. An important consequence of this identification between Sufism and an objectified Kurdish ethnic identity is the downplaying of local or social differences, allowing the construction of a version of Kurdish "religious nationalism" that has a more inclusive and egalitarian character.[48]

However, if local, autonomous *zawiya* expansion went hand in hand with the penetration of PKK cells in northern Syria, naturally resulting in a certain degree of "Kurdish Sufism," the definitions of the "imagined community" of Kurdish "religious nationalism" are influenced and limited by the forms of religious codification and, consequently, by the styles of religiosity present in each Sufi community. So much so, in fact, that Kurdish Sufism was accompanied, in certain cases, by a greater fragmentation of Kurdish communities. Hence, if for Kurdish nationalism, in Kurmanji dialect, the capital of Kurdistan is Diyarbakir (Turkey), for the followers of the Kurdish Sufi *tariqas*, there are different capitals, Afrin, Amuda, or even Qamishli.

Political risk was a completely different matter for the regime faced with the transnational *tariqa* because, as shown by the Kurdish insurrections of the 1920s in Turkey and Iraq, the brotherhoods can effectively become the "torch bearers" of political protest. In Syria the largest Kurdish transnational brotherhood is without a doubt that managed first by Ahmad al-Khaznawi and later by his sons and grandsons. Originally from the village of Khazna in Upper Jazira, Ahmad al-Khaznawi (1886–1950) based his brotherhood, of the Naqshbandiyya branch, at the beginning of the twentieth century, in the Kurdish province of southeast Anatolia. Fleeing Kemalist repression, he settled in Tell Maruf in northeast Syria. Despite his living in Syria, Ahmad al-Khaznawi continued to have considerable influence over the Kurdish populations living on both sides of the border, thus defying state logic because "the clientele of charismatic leaders is not tied to one particular state, but willingly crosses the border for pilgrimages or to ask assistance from a shaykh" (Zarcone 1992: 101).

Among the grandsons of Ahmad al-Kaznawi, Muhammad Mashuk al-Khaznawi was very popular, thanks to his natural charisma and the religious authority that he inherited from his father, Izz al-Din al-Khaznawi. Moreover, Mashuk could count on the support of the government which sanctioned his liberal and modernist reading of the Koran, influenced by Salafism. This support from the regime was apparent by the space for maneuvering that was offered to him. Thus, Mashuk al-Khaznawi was one of the rare shaykhs in Syria to have at his disposal an electronic website launched in 2002. At the time of the "Qamishli revolt" and the repression that followed it in March 2004 (two events which will be studied in the next chapter) Shaykh al-Khaznawi called on his political establishment contacts to position himself as mediator between the Kurdish protesters and the government.

However, relations between the shaykh and the government deteriorated rapidly. The religious dignitary, then 46 years old and vice-president of the center for Islamic Studies in Damascus, came to demand the granting of cultural and political rights for the Kurds. In addition, while traveling in Europe, he met other Kurdish leaders and Ali Sadr al-Din al-Bayanouni, head of the Muslim Brotherhood of Syria, in Brussels. Interviewed by the daily newspaper, *The Canadian Globe*, he showed himself to be extremely critical of the Syrian regime, which, according to him, should "change or be terminated." Finally, he confessed that he could speak out like this because the Americans were in the process of trying to put an end to dictatorships and help the oppressed.[49]

Under circumstances that remain unclear, Shaykh al-Khaznawi was kidnapped on May 10, 2005. His body was discovered three weeks later, buried in the Dayr al-Zur province. Al-Khaznawi's website was frozen in June 2005, when his sons started to use the Internet to broadcast their critical ideas and to accuse the regime of being behind these acts. (Christmann 2007: 4–26). The Syrian authorities denied involvement in al-Khaznawi's killing, but Kurdish parties and western diplomats noted that the shaykh's death coincided with a crackdown by the regime against internal political dissent.

Regardless of who killed al-Khaznawi, it is clear that the mediation between the state authority and the local communities that is performed by the Sufi shaykhs can secure them a central role as producers of order in the Kurdish community. Thus they may become major political and social players after an eventual liberalization or even disintegration of the Ba'athist regime in Syria. Mashuk al-Khaznawi had indeed become a potential threat for the regime after the events of March 2004. As a Kurdish representative, he played two roles, one related to his identity as a Sufi shaykh, and the other was his role as cultural and social mediator for the Kurdish (Sunni) communities.

Furthermore, his aura as Kurdish leader had grown to transnational dimensions. Thus, two months before his assassination, Shaykh al-Khaznawi was welcomed by thousands of Kurds, whether they were faithful or not to his brotherhood, as a national hero in Diyarbakir during the Newroz festivities of 2005. His role as Kurdish leader, even in the eyes of secular nationalists, was consecrated by the interview granted, by the Kurdish television channel, close to the PKK, Roj TV. Mashuk al-Khaznawi's evolution immediately brings to mind those of other actors from the Kurdish religious scene, such as Shaykh Sa'id in Turkey, Shaykh Mahmud Barzanji and Mullah Mustafa Barzani in Iraq, who all used their religious charisma, combined with nationalism and tribal solidarity.[50]

However, the reasons for the rupture between al-Khaznawi and the regime remain unknown. For certain Kurdish nationalists, al-Khaznawi had simply broken the silence over the Kurdish question after having observed the regime's repressive reaction to the events in Qamishli in March 2004. Some go as far as to claim that the shaykh had always been a "Kurdish patriot."[51] For others, Mashuk al-Khaznawi's "discovery" of the Kurdish identity as a means of mobilization can be explained by the fratricidal struggle for the control of resources, both material (land and money) and symbolic, in the brotherhood after the death of Izz al-Din. Whatever the truth, al-Khaznawi's story is an illustration of how collaboration between Sufi communities and state authorities can easily turn into open opposition, if the sociopolitical and even internal conditions (as with the *tariqa*) demand it.

## The defense of Kurdish culture

The Kurdish language is the principal distinctive cultural trait of the various Kurdish ethnic identities, although the significance changes depend on the region inhabited by Kurds in Syria. Thus in Kurd Dagh, the Kurdish language is spoken "naturally" in a very homogenous Kurdophone environment.[52] In Jazira, where the population has a more heterogeneous character, particularly in urban areas like Qamishli or Hasaka, public use of the Kurdish language marks the boundaries which define the Kurds from other ethnic groups. In Damascus, on the other hand, the Kurds use, to a large degree, the Arab language, in public as in private life. In this case Kurdish identity is defined, not in terms of common language, but by Kurdish patrilineal ascendance and the observation of cultural practices, such as the Newroz festival (Pinto 2007: 261). In Aleppo, the Kurdish language is far more present because the geographic proximity of Kurd Dagh allows a "come and go" continuity for the Kurds between the village and the countryside, and consequently, a continuity in cultural *habitus*. The situation is slightly different for Kurds who have settled permanently in Aleppo, for one or two generations, tending toward a more marked cultural Arabization.[53]

In fact, the Syrian Kurds possess diverse cultural traits: from language to folklore via ethnoreligious affiliation, as in the case of the Yazidis, who, by tradition and in response to legal constraints imposed by the various political regimes, are codified in both written and spoken language. Thus, Kurdish culture is passed on through folklore and various structures that originated during the mandatory period, such as political parties and intellectual groups which are formed around reviews or cultural associations.

These collectives have proved to be surprisingly consistent in their conservation strategy, the passing on of the Kurdish identity, and in knowing the importance of the individual effort in spreading of the language and in the "protection" of Kurdish identity in a predominantly Arab cultural environment. The Badirkhan brothers realized, when first confronted by a lack of sensitivity from the French authorities and the National Bloc in regard to gaining official recognition of the Kurdish language, that individual action would be required to overcome these obstacles. Each literate Kurd (agha, shaykh, intellectual) had to act as an instructor for others.[54] There should also be a family effort, with women ("the mothers of the nation") in particular (Tejel 2007a: 213) taking responsibility for the reproduction of Kurdish culture.[55]

The result, direct or otherwise, of these appeals launched by the Badirkhans since the 1930s, is that the "Kurdish mothers" and the individual engagement of intellectuals had assured the transfer of the Kurdish culture by informal channels, creating a certain "privatization"[56] of cultural practices.[57] The family has, in fact, played an important role in this informal transmission, being the basic unit of social organization and protector of alternative norms in linguistic and cultural matters. It may have been through the use of the Kurdish language in private[58] that Kurdish toponyms replaced official names (Öktem 2004: 559–78). Kurdish names were selected for children in an attempt also to conserve a "memory" (family origins, tribal affiliation). One is faced with a kind of "family ethos," in which individuals felt authorized to express values, opinions, and objectives which differed from those promoted by the state. The extended family was also an area of transgression where one listened to radio broadcasts in Kurdish, by Radio Yerevan and Radio Baghdad. Finally, since the Newroz celebrations were forbidden up until the 1980s, religious festivals, particularly *qurban* (the sacrifice festival), and marriages became areas where the expression of Kurdish identity could be expressed through musical interpretation and traditional dance.[59]

With regard to literature, between 1960 and 1980, only three books in the Kurdish language were published. This was accomplished in Beirut after which they were secretly distributed in Syria (Malmîsanij 2007: 127). In the domain of cultural reviews, *Gulistan* (1968), edited by the poet Cigerxwîn, and *Gelawêj* (1979) operated under extremely difficult circumstances. In the words of Michel Seurat, "In such a repressive climate, one sees that little remains of the cultural movement that, in the 1930s, had stirred the Kurdish community in Syria and Lebanon" (Seurat 1980: 105).

Legal constraints explain, to a large degree, the continuation of the strategy of privacy, related here to the "dissimulation," of the Kurdish culture until the 1980s, because whenever it seemed possible, Kurdish activists presented demands of cultural order to the Damascus government, during the mandatory period (1928, 1932, 1940, 1945) as well as during the postmandatory era. The end of Adib al-Shishakli's presidency (1951–54) was capitalized on by Kurdish intellectuals, such as 'Uthman Sabri and Rewshen Badirkhan, who had actively participated in the cultural movement of the 1930s. In 1955, they founded the society for Reviving Kurdish Culture in Damascus with its principle objective the teaching of the Latin alphabet to Kurds. In 1957, the KDPS launched the publication of the newspaper, *Dengê Kurd* (The Kurdish Voice) in Latin characters. At the time of the accession of the UAR in 1958, proposals made directly to Nasser by spokesmen for the Kurds in Syria, that the Kurdish language be taught in schools and that Kurdish language broadcasts be organized by Radio Damascus,[60] were refused.

*The politization of Kurdish culture*

As Harriet Montgomery says, the Syrian state was complicit in defining Kurdish cultural activity as political by treating expressions of Kurdish identity as such. This complicates the examination of Kurdish politics as a purely political phenomenon, and of Kurdish culture as a purely cultural issue (Montgomery 2005: 116). When the Syrian state and the PKK sealed a strategic alliance against the Turkish government in the 1980s, the intermingling of cultural and political fields created a great upset in the cultural realm. Following the example of other political parties, the PKK took over the cultural framing of the Syrian Kurds with an aim of achieving greater room for maneuvering.

In order to attract followers, the PKK started sponsoring literacy programs and very quickly succeeded in steering Kurdish culture away from the private sphere toward the public arena, using means such as openly celebrating the Newroz festival. For example, after the PKK's establishment in Kobane where the Newroz festival was unknown before the 1960s and celebrated secretly between 1960 and 1970, thousands of people began gathering to celebrate the Kurdish New Year.[61] However, a distinction had to be drawn between events and activities organized by Syrian Kurds and those organized by the PKK. Kurds claim that many Newroz festivals suffered from restrictions while the "PKK Newroz" celebrations were never obstructed (McDowall 1998: 51).

The PKK did not stop at ensuring a greater visibility of Kurdish culture, but also played a role in the process of its reinvention. Folklore groups close to the PKK used the colors of the Kurdish flag: green, white, yellow and red, to decorate the "traditional" dress of dance groups. The music, dances, "national" history, and even the place reserved for Yazidism in Kurdish identity[62] were revitalized with a new sense of political unity under the party.

Additionally, the PKK pulled the other parties and collectives into this process of re-invention and inspired in them the desire to publicly display their Kurdish culture.[63] Political parties and intellectuals took advantage of the opening created by the PKK to develop their activities. The fruit of this cultural awakening was seen mainly during the 1990s with the growing number of literary journals and various publications in the Kurdish language. Whereas only three books had been published in the Kurdish language up until the 1970s, 111 appeared in the 1990s, mostly in Lebanon (Malmîsanij 2007: 127).[64]

Kurdish writers organized clandestine language courses where books in Kurdish were read and circulated. Kurdish intellectuals[65] managed to publish some journals, such as *Gurzek Gul* (1989–92), *Zanîn* (1991–97), *Aso* (1992), *Pirs* (1993), *Hêvî* (1993), *Delav* (1995), and *Xwendevan* (1995). In addition, since 1980, political parties launched various newspapers: *Stêr* (1983–95), *Xunav* (1986–95), *Roj* (1991), *Deng* (1995), and *Newroz* (1995). Finally, Kurdish students were very active in sponsoring clandestine literacy courses, particularly at the University of Aleppo.

However, the politization of Kurdish culture has had, however, negative repercussions on the culture itself. The fragmented Kurdish political scene is then reflected in a fragmented cultural arena with multiple initiatives spearheaded by a small nucleus of intellectuals.[66] While competition between publications could usually be interpreted as a sign of a robust "cultural market," in the Kurdish case, competition, often the result of personal quarrels, only serves to weaken the viability of each initiative due to a lack of capital, the shortage of readers,[67] problems of distribution and sales, and legal constraints. Furthermore, the market for cultural journals is divided by the same ideological lines which divide the Kurdish political arena.[68]

In addition, though all the cultural journals have been declared independent, their economic fragility and their problems with distribution have created conditions favorable to dependency on political parties. Thus, for example, the review *Pirs* is printed by the Yekîtî (Demokrat) party, while *Gelawêj* is traditionally tied to the KDPS (el Partî) and *Hevind* to Yekîtî (Kurd). The political organizations assure the distribution of cultural reviews and, in certain cases, decide even the linguistic criteria and style.

Finally, the divisive struggle on the cultural terrain is manifested at the time of the Newroz festival, an important date in the affirmation of the Kurdish identity. On this occasion the parties with more financial resources come forward as sponsors of the festival. In this way, the political power and the social prestige of each party is measured by the quality of the artists and the number of spectators. Additionally, the artistic performances are perceived by the public as variations on the "envisioned Kurdistan," modern and traditional, transcending party lines with music and dance styles (Pinto 2007: 262–3).

## Militants in the Kurdish cultural field

Contrary to appearances, the cultural activities of the Kurds in Syria between 1980 and 2000 were not launched without difficulties, in spite of the connections of Hafiz al-As'ad to the PKK, KDP, and PUK and other established parties. Kurdish cultural activists, at the urging of political activists, continued to operate in an ambiguous space marked by indistinct boundaries between the cultural and political spheres. One of the rare movie producers of Kurdish origins, Mano Khalil (Qamishli, 1964) paid the penalty for this ambiguity. In 1992, he secretly filmed the documentary, *The Place Where God Is Sleeping*, in the Kurdish language, on the politically sensitive subject of the Turko-Syrian border. In the film, Khalil denounced the miserable living conditions in the Kurdish villages on the border and showed the popular support there for the PKK. Even though the alliance between the PKK and the government was known by all, this fact was not considered an appropriate topic for presentation inside of Syria. Discovered by Secret Service agents during the filming, Khalil was forced to send his negatives out of Syria to Europe. The film was finished there and won a prize in Germany in 1993. Three years later, Mano Khalil left Syria.[69]

The militant career of Muhammad Hamo (Afrin, 1961) closely resembled that of a number of Kurdish cultural activists. Poet, journalist, and co-proprietor of the Khani Book Store[70] in Aleppo, Muhammad Hamo went to prison several times because of his involvement in the cultural field. A member of a family of "nonexploitive land proprietors," Hamo received a formal education.[71] After earning his Baccalaureate, he became interested in the Kurdish language and began to frequent the circles of intellectuals and political activists in Kurd Dagh, and later in Aleppo.

Encouraged by what seemed to be a favorable context for the Kurds in Syria, Muhammad Hamo founded an art group in 1988, the Khani's Club (Koma Xanî), which was a reference to the classical Kurdish author, Ahmad Khani, in Aleppo. This club founded, on the anniversary of poet Cigerxwîn's death (October 22, 1993), the Festival of Kurdish Poetry. Later, this date was called the Day of Kurdish Poetry in Syria. The following year, this festival took place secretly in Afrin, Qamishli, Aleppo, and Derik (Malmîsanij 2007: 109 and 112). During the 1990s, other cultural groups, which were part of the same network, organized short story contests and several commemorative meetings to celebrate Kurdish writers who had passed away such as Jaladat and Rewshen Badirkhan and 'Uthman Sabri.

However, the success of the initiatives of Muhammad Hamo and other cultural activists caused a certain alarm in Damascus. In 1995, Hamo was arrested for possession of Kurdish books and tortured in a military prison in the Syrian capital. He was forced to agree to a "pact": freedom and a salary in exchange for working as an informer for the information services of the Kurdish political parties. His refusal resulted in more torture. Released in 1996, he reopened his book store but was arrested several times for short periods, until 1999, when he was incarcerated in Aleppo for six months, accused of printing books without governmental permission.[72] In 2000, he was again arrested for three days after the publication of one of his works in French, then, again, in 2001 for "distribution of Zionist propaganda" in his book store.

Despite the regular arrests, Muhammad Hamo did not change the direction of his militant career. After each release, he reopened his book store where forbidden books written in Kurdish were sold. His critical opinions in regard to the Kurdish political parties were apparent in these actions. In effect, Hamo considered that the Kurdish parties in Syria "did nothing for the culture" and that from that time on, it was up to the intellectuals to give direction to the resistance. It was clear that Muhammad Hamo, as other cultural activists, had been influenced by the resurgence of identity demands in the 1980s, a process to which the PKK and the political events of Iraqi Kurdistan were no strangers. Despite the end of the strategic alliance between the PKK and the government in Damascus, in 1999 the dynamics created by this alliance, particularly the challenging of the strategy of "dissimulation," escaped the control of both parties.

In 1994, the Kurdish parties asked the people to not celebrate Newroz as a sign of respect for the As'ad family, after the death of Basil al-As'ad in an automobile accident in January of the same year. Nonetheless, thousands of people went out into the streets of the Kurdish villages of northern Syria to celebrate the New Year and to publicly affirm their attachment to Kurdish "national" identity.[73]

Hamo was not ready to return to the period before the Kurdish cultural "spring" at the beginning of the 1990s. The death of Hafiz al-As'ad in 2000 and the optimistic ambiance generated by the "Damascus Spring" allowed thoughts to turn to progressive reductions in prohibitions in the cultural sphere. However, the security forces decided otherwise. In 2001, he was invited to Dohuk by the Writer's Union of Iraqi Kurdistan to participate in a literary festival. While Muhammad Hamo was away he was informed that the police had invaded his home searching for compromising materials. What is more, his book store had been broken into, and all of his books had been confiscated. At that point he made the decision to stay in Iraqi Kurdistan where he works to this day for a television channel and a library in Sulaymaniyya.

# 6 The Qamishli revolt, 2004

## The marker of a new era for the Kurds in Syria

Violent surprisings that erupted in the northern Syrian Kurdish enclaves and the Kurdish areas in Aleppo and Damascus marked the emergence of Kurdish anti-establishment protests on the Syrian political scene in March 2004. The Syrian government was previously unaware of the Kurdish capacity for action and was surprised by the scale of these protests. The visibility of the "Kurdish problem" in Syria was heightened by worldwide media coverage causing these events and the protests that followed (and which continued until 2005) to resound, giving even greater importance to the Kurdish factor.[1]

In several ways, the Qamishli revolt (*serhildan*) signified the beginning of a new era for the Kurdish populations of Syria. First, all players on the Kurdish cultural and political scene immediately abandoned any attempt to conceal the conflict. Whether it was in northern Syria or in the two largest towns in the country, Damascus[2] and Aleppo, thousands of Kurds continued to openly defy the Ba'athist regime by means of mobilizations, the so-called "identity mobilizations"[3] and various types of collective[4] actions, such as marches, commemorations, cultural festivals, and demonstrations. For the first time in the history of contemporary Syria, the protest movement had touched all of the Kurdish territories, thus reinforcing the symbolic unity of the Syrian Kurdish arena – "Syrian Kurdistan." Henceforth, victims of the revolt or *intifada* of March 2004 in the town of Qamishli would be added to the pantheon of martyrs of the Kurdish nationalist movement in Syria and other Kurdish areas.[5]

Secondly, since 2004 the Kurdish parties were courted by other Syrian opposition groups. Abroad, the National Salvation Front (NSF), established in early 2006,[6] and the Reform party of Syria, led by Farid Ghadri and based in the United States,[7] were said to be on the verge of offering a "democratic" solution to the Kurdish problem in Syria. Inside the country, intellectuals, human rights activists, and the secular opposition had also established stable connections with Kurdish organizations. The Syrian regime had also carried out certain well-intentioned declarations with respect to the Kurds. Finally, for the first time in history, political parties and populations from other Kurdish regions had showed their solidarity with the Syrian Kurds by means of public declarations[8] and demonstrations in Diyarbakir (Turkey), Irbil, and Sulaymaniyya (Iraq). What were the factors which brought about this spectacular response to the "Kurdish problem" at that time?

Upon the death of President Hafiz al-As'ad, on July 10, 2000, Bashar al-As'ad, his son, succeeded to the "throne." He quickly acceded to the highest positions which had been held by his father; however, the succession was not limited to the transfer of power from the "king" to the "crown prince." At the time of the Ba'ath Congress, held from June 17 to 20, 2000, Bashar al-As'ad made new appointments to the regime's key positions, and the Ba'ath underwent a profound change in its position of authority. As a result, a new generation progressively took its place.[9]

It was during the new president's speech of investiture that a second round of changes was announced. The accent was on internal questions, calling particularly on the ethical responsibility of everyone to work toward common objectives and the defense of general well being. In other words, it was a shift of "control" in the political domain, particularly in the area of economics. Soon, a new atmosphere emerged. Freedom of speech was granted, first to political officials, and subsequently to intellectuals (*al-muthaqqaf*) and "civil society,"[10] understood to be a mixture of associations, clubs, guilds, syndicates, federations, unions, parties, and groups that provided a buffer between the state and the citizen (Norton 1995: 7). Marginalized by the Ba'athist revolution of 1963, Syrian associations, with a rich history going back to the Ottoman Empire, had been confined to charitable organizations and limited, for the most part, to a specific geographic area and a denominational group (Le Saux 2006: 194). Since 2001 a change in the associative world in Syria[11] had occurred. The political debate went through some surprising evolutions with regard to the long reign of Hafiz al-As'ad, which began in November 1970[12] (Droz-Vincent 2001: 19).

In September 2000 intellectuals held a "national dialogue" in a suburb of Damascus, where the participants could listen to two unedited conferences about Syrian political organizations. Starting with this dialogue, debates, forums, and assemblies began to be organized all over the country. Documents were publicly distributed or published by the Arab press, which had never been subject to censure since its introduction in Syria. The "Statement of 99," a short text signed by ninety-nine intellectuals specifically asking for the lifting of the state of emergency and martial law, was publicly released on September 26, 2000 in the *al-Hayat* newspaper. It was followed by the "Statement of 1,000" or the "Fundamental Document," distributed on January 11, 2001, the "General National Accords," and the "Communiqué of 185 Expatriated Syrians."

"The Statement of 1,000," the longest and most analytical of the documents released by the media, encouraged a national dialogue and the initiation of certain measures: (1) lifting the state of emergency and martial law; (2) recognizing freedom of politics, opinions, and thoughts; (3) revising the law that controlled publications; (4) promulgating a democratic, electoral law. The following week, the "independent" deputy, Riad Seif, announced the formation of a party for the Movement for Social Peace. From outside the country, in May 2001, the Muslim Brotherhood launched the "Charter for the Construction of a Modern State in Syria." Also, certain parties inside the PNF, like the Communist Party (the Wisal Farha-Bakdash or the Yusif Faysal branch), or those which stayed outside, like the Syrian Socialist Nationalist Party, demonstrated their desire to launch legal and autonomous political activities (Droz-Vincent 2004: 228). At this stage, the regime's hard-liners initiated a crackdown on the "Damascus Spring" (George 2003: 30–46).

The Kurdish parties and cultural activists also participated in the "Spring." In Qamishli, a group of Kurdish intellectuals founded the "Badirkhan" forum and, in a more general manner, began to contemplate establishing relations with the representatives of the "Syrian opposition"[13] such as political parties, and "independents," but also human rights activists.[14] In August 2002, aware of these developments, Bashar al-As'ad made the first visit by a Syrian president to Upper Jazira in over forty years. Despite this, no concessions were forthcoming after 2002, leading Kurdish activists to engage in a new strategy to gain visibility based on ethnic and national claims.

## The events preceding the Kurdish upheaval

The years 2002 and 2003 bore witness to a paradox in Syrian political life. Between 2000 and 2001, at the end of the "Damascus Spring," when Arab collectives and political parties were playing a major role in articulating political opposition to the regime, the opposition's center of gravity was displaced toward the "periphery" of the Syrian political field, toward the clandestine Kurdish parties. This transition was all the more paradoxical because it occurred within the closed context of Syrian public space.

In 2001 discussion forums organized across the entire country, including Qamishli, were closed, and the most visible figures in the movement were arrested. In September 2001 the Syrian government replaced the General Law on Printed Matter. The substitute Decree No. 50, which applied to publishers, printers, journalists, editors, authors, distributors, and book shop owners, consisted of more than "fifty articles which restricted printed media and expanded state control over it" (Montgomery 2005: 101). Kurdish language publications were subject to this decree, because they could be misconstrued as seeking to change the constitution or threatening the unity of the state by association with Kurdish demands for recognition and rights. In fact, in 2002, a number of Kurds, including the authors Ibrahim Nasan and Habib Ibrahim, were arrested and condemned to up to five years in prison for possession and distribution of Kurdish language publications and for teaching in secret Kurdish schools. Individuals organizing festivals and practicing Kurdish music, long tolerated by Hafiz al-As'ad, also risked arrest (Amnesty 2005: 2–4).

It was at that time that a previously marginal party, the Yekîtî (Kurd), and not Kurdish "civil society" organizations, decided to bring various public actions denouncing the injustices to the Kurds to the Syrian capital. One constant thing in contemporary Syrian history and in other Kurdish regions of the Middle East has been the dominating role of the political parties in their relationship with "civil society" in the Kurdish enclaves. The nationalist movement has been the sole motivating force for social, cultural, and even charitable initiatives, including *The Society of Beneficence for the Poor of Jazira* founded in 1932, which were tied to the political parties, and as a result, to the hazards of political developments. The nonexistence, from the very beginning, of a "civil society" in the Kurdish enclaves of northern Syria until 2005[15] could perhaps be explained by the underdevelopment of these regions, the pre-eminence of strong tribal connections in the population, the ethnicization by the regime of every demand that came from the Kurdish community, and the explicit prohibition against the forming of any association in the Hasaka province.

According to Abbas Vali, there was another factor which resulted in the weakness of civil society among Kurdish populations. In his opinion, Kurdish political parties have been neither willing nor able to create such a culture, "on the contrary, they have thrived on the persistent weakness of 'civil society' in Kurdistan" (Vali 1998: 83). Also, the semiorganic relationship between the rare initiatives launched by the Kurds in Syria and the political parties appears to have been modeled on a certain perception of nationalist leadership. That is to say that the relationship between political parties and so-called "civil society" activities resemble the relationship between nationalist actors and the society which they aspire to rule, in the sense that these nationalist actors develop policies which reflect their perceptions of their own society and how it must be organized: "In fact, they (the nationalists) argue that these initiatives are determined by their assumptions, that they are the spokesmen for the nation" (Breuilly 1993: 63).

*The Yekîtî party*

The Partiya Yekîtî ya Kurdî li Suriyê or Yekîtî (Kurd) was created by reshuffling several Kurdish partisan groups of diverse origins which could be simply separated into two main camps: the first was leftist and included Marxist allies and proponents of national liberation, the other consisted exclusively of Kurdish nationalists. Members of the leftist group included important party figures like Marwan 'Uthman (Amuda, 1959), an activist, poet, and journalist who defined himself as a "Marxist according to the Trotsky model" (Den Hond 2004). Like lots of politicized students, 'Uthman embraced Marxism in the 1970s at university. In 1983, with other Kurds, he founded a small Trotskyite party, affiliated with the IV International. After some public success, particularly the Newroz celebration in 1986, repression crashed down upon the small group. As a result, 'Uthman and his comrades sought to create ties with other left leaning Kurdish groups. The Kurdish Peasant Party accepted the Trotskyite trend and the two organizations, together with three other small parties, created the Yekîtî Party in 1992. Yekîtî was headed by individuals who went on to make their mark on party life, Fuad Aliko and Hasan Salih, but also other groups such as Isma'il Amo and Muhi al-Din Shaykh Ali of the Yekîtî (Demokrat).

In the beginning, situated at the left end of the political spectrum, the Yekîtî did not offer a very different profile from the other "progressive" and "secular" parties, but certain sociological differences were discernable when compared to other groups. First, although the leaders of Yekîtî included in their ranks representatives of all social strata, students, intellectuals, and liberal professionals (e.g. doctors, lawyers) dominated their ranks. Also, the party was situated mainly in urban centers, particularly in Qamishli, Hasaka, Damascus, Aleppo, and Latakia.[16]

Finally, perhaps as a natural occurrence after this sequence of events, members of Yekîtî were making attempts at reorganizing their resources and militant knowhow. In contact with various groups of "civil society" and the Syrian opposition either at the universities,[17] in the newspapers, or human rights associations,[18] the leaders of Yekîtî tried to expand the boundaries of the "Kurdish problem" beyond the narrow limits of an "identity movement" to encompass the broader role of a "civil society" movement and respect for all human rights, a context to which the various groups could relate. This restructuring had also been promoted by the "Damascus Spring" and the rapid increase of activities that followed was very much in this same spirit.

Nevertheless, unlike the forces driving the Syrian opposition, Yekîtî knew how to draw the youth into their ranks. Thus, the "old guard" of Yekîtî was joined by new arrivals in the political field. This was a young generation, born in the era of Hafiz al-As'ad which had been far more affected by key events in "ethnic" memory, such as the exodus of thousands of Iraqi Kurds to Turkey in 1991, and later, by the creation of Kurdish autonomy in northern Iraq, than by the ideological debates of the Cold War.[19] Similarly, Yekîtî used more direct language and demonstrated its ambition to change the Kurdish movement's modes of action by giving more visibility to its demands (this was also an important strategy of the PKK movement) and arming itself with a "Syrianized" program, around the slogan "the Kurdish problem is being settled in Damascus."

Thus, the founding act of the party was also the source of its first rupture. To commemorate the thirty years since the special census of 1962 in the province of Hasaka, a small group of militants hung posters denouncing the policy of the government with regards to the "undocumented" Kurds on the walls and public buildings of several large cities in the country. As Julie Gauthier put it, the novelty was not so much in "the content of the poster as in the new visibility of the demands" (Gauthier 2005: 99).

The new "repertoire of actions" demonstrated by the party, as well as its more radical program, particularly the reference to the "Syrian Kurdistan," revived tensions in the party which resulted in a first schism in 1995.[20] The more aggressive and demanding partisans led the way for the party. In November of 1999, at the time of the third party congress, the party's two pillars: more "visibility" (publications, campaigning, protesting, demonstrations, assembling, striking) and territorial demands (Syrian Kurdistan), were incorporated into the Yekîtî program.

The party's leftist position remained intact, for although the party "derived its power from the enormous force of the Kurdish people in Syria," it relied heavily on the engagement of the "working class."[21] With regards to finding a solution to the Kurdish issue, the party stressed the need to review the Syrian constitution so that a new article acknowledging the existence of the Kurdish nation could be added. Besides the traditional cultural demands, such as making the Kurdish language the official language in Kurdish regions and allowing the establishment of local radio and television broadcasting channels in the Kurdish regions, the Yekîtî party called for the acknowledgment of the Newroz festival as a national holiday not only for the Kurds but for the whole country. On a political level, the party demanded that "all the local authorities, assemblies, directorates, and establishments in the Kurdish regions" should be "established, organized, and run by Kurds."[22]

### New action: new reaction

Various events which occurred between 2000 and 2002 had a powerful effect on the political perspective of the leaders of Yekîtî. First, the end of the strategic alliance between the PKK and the regime had plunged the former into a crisis involving its reorganization and its platform, and the Yekîtî aspired to fill the void left after the decline of the PKK in Syria. Also, the first overtures of Bashar al-As'ad in 2000, including retiring some of the *mukhabarat* agents and some north Syrian police posts, as well as the encounter of August 2001 between the upper management officials of the Ba'ath and representatives of the Kurdish parties involved in the Front and Alliance, led the leaders of Yekîtî to think that the time to move from talk to action had arrived.

On December 10, 2002, International Human Rights Day, between 150 and 200 members of Yekîtî demonstrated in front of the Syrian parliament shouting slogans such as "Citizenship for the Kurds," "Down with the Prohibition of Kurdish Language and Culture," and "Respect Human Rights in Syria" (Montgomery 2005: 119). The demonstration was the first of its kind since 1984. The unanimist ideology of the Ba'ath was torn apart in the street, a space previously limited to use for public acts affirming adhesion to the regime. During the demonstration, a communiqué protesting discrimination against the Kurds in Syria was published, mentioning the injustices to which they had been subjected, such as "the refusal to accord them citizenship, Kurdish towns and villages renamed with Arab names, economic discrimination, rejection of the Kurdish language and culture, and the failure on the part of the constitution to recognize Kurdish nationality."[23]

Marwan 'Uthman and Hasan Salih were among those who presented a memorandum to the president of the National Assembly, 'Abd al-Qadir Qadurah, demanding greater protection for the rights of Syrian Kurds. The memorandum evoked the suffering of the Kurdish people in the face of this discrimination, the necessity of constitutional recognition of the presence of the Kurdish people in Syria as a second nationality, the recognition of their cultural and linguistic rights, the problems faced by Kurds who were denied citizenship, and the distribution of Kurdish lands to the Arabs in the provinces of other regions. Marwan 'Uthman and Hasan Salih were arrested five days later following an invitation to a meeting by the Interior Minister, Major General Ali Hammud.[24]

On June 25, 2003, Yekîtî organized a peaceful demonstration before the seat of UNICEF in Damascus, on the occasion of World Children's Day. Once again, Yekîtî had chosen a symbolic date in order to associate Kurdish demands with more universal issues. Close to 380 demonstrators, 200 of whom were children, assembled to ask the government to accord civic and political rights to the Kurdish population in Syria, including the right to teach in the Kurdish language.[25] This time, Yekîtî was not alone as it had succeeded in convincing other Kurdish parties to participate. In the face of increased visibility of Kurdish demands, the police and security forces violently dispersed the demonstrators and several participants were arrested and tortured.

Yekîtî agreed to participate in a silent demonstration with other Kurdish parties in front of Parliament on October 6, 2003, to commemorate the census of 1962. Even though, for Yekîtî, it seemed like a retreat from its strategy of visibility, this gesture of flexibility made it possible to gather the Kurdish parties and representatives of the Syrian opposition, particularly human rights associations, for the first time. This cooperation was confirmed again on December 10, 2003, International Human Rights Day, in the form of a unified demonstration involving around a thousand participants before the Syrian Parliament.

Bashar al-As'ad's regime did little to change the defiant attitude of the Yekîtî. In August 2002, Bashar al-As'ad delivered a message targeting the Kurds of Jazira. This message in summary indirectly stated, "Yes, we will look into your problem, but don't use this as a card to press for more."[26] Only four months later, Yekîtî overstepped the redline established by the regime by organizing a demonstration in the Syrian capital on International Human Rights Day. The security force's repression did not come down on the Kurdish leaders alone. With each action, the number of people taken into custody increased.

On March 8, 2004, when a demonstration organized by the Kurds and Arabs occurred in Damascus, hundreds of Kurds united in Qamishli to celebrate the recognition of Federalism in Iraq. World Women's Day was the "politically correct" pretext for yet another assembly. In reality, it was used as an excuse to affirm Kurdish identity in a public place, with performances by folkloric groups and the organization of poetry festivals in the Kurdish language. Even so, the security forces clashed violently with the participants, and eight activists of Yekîtî were arrested. Four days later, the Qamishli Revolt erupted.

## The Qamishli revolt

A study of mobilizations, some of which lead to violent riots, suggests that the participants are prone to diverse and mixed motivations (anger, feelings of deprivation, hope, despair), which leads to diversified and complex group configurations. Rather than favor one single perspective over another, in order to analyze the violence that broke out in Qamishli in 2004, it is necessary to make a detour from these "facts," to later be able to critique the explanatory approaches to violence by taking into account all of the long-term factors (under-developed economy, symbolic violence) and the immediate environment (international context, subjectivity of the actors). Having done this, it is still not possible to arrive at definitive truths on this unprecedented chapter in the history of the Kurds in Syria, but nevertheless it facilitates a better understanding of the complexity of this violent episode.

## The "facts"

The writing of history as it occurs is a problematic task. On the one hand, the memory of recent events is extremely volatile and fragile. It is deceiving because it is saturated with emotion and passion, exposed to the effects of disinformation or misinformation. On the other hand, security obstacles in conducting ample field work inquiries with the participants of the actions make all attempts at exhaustive analysis difficult. Nevertheless, by combining the information relayed by the media and the information gathered from witnesses and participants, a relatively realistic version of the facts can potentially be established.

Most media sources reported that on March 12, 2004, during a football match in the town of Qamishli between the local team and Dayr al-Zur, the insults between the fans of the two sides escalated into a riot which spilled out into the streets.[27] Other sources reported that the riot originated in the provocative attitudes of the Dayr al-Zur fans, a town traditionally associated with the Sunni Arab tribes who sympathized with the Iraqi regime.[28] Riding around the town in a bus, the fans of that team chanted slogans insulting the Iraqi Kurdish leaders, Barzani and Talabani, while displaying portraits of Saddam Husayn. When fans of the local team responded with chants praising President George Bush ("We will sacrifice our lives for Bush"),[29] the battle between the "Dayri," armed with knives, stones, and sticks (Danish Refugee Council 2007: 6), and the Kurdish supporters erupted inside the stadium, which turned out to be to the disadvantage of the latter.

The governor of Hasaka, Salim Kabul, gave the order for the security forces to open fire, resulting in six dead, all Kurds, three of whom were children. This sparked rioting throughout Qamishli where residents burned grain warehouses and destroyed scores of public buses and private vehicles (Gambill 2004: 4). The same evening, Kurdish students from the University of Damascus attempted to approach the UN building as a sign of protest against the inaction of the United Nations in the defense of the Kurds (Gauthier 2006: 227). Later that night, some Kurdish parties including Yekîtî decided to assemble a group, by means of placards and communication by portable phones,[30] to protest against the actions of the security forces, capitalizing on the funerals planned for the victims.[31]

The next day, the Kurdish political parties' expectations for a turnout were greatly surpassed. Thousands of people joined the procession accompanying the coffins to the cemetery of Qudur Beg, in the traditional Kurdish quarter of town. That day, Christians, and Arabs of Qamishli, although less numerous, were part of the integrated group.[32] Security forces, supported by armed militias from Arab tribes, countered this demonstration by again firing into the crowd, triggering violence (attacks against public buildings and the railroad station) culminating in the destruction of statues of Hafiz al-As'ad.[33] Rumors of a real massacre quickly circulated and thousands of people demonstrated in other Kurdish towns, and even in Arab cities with a strong concentration of Kurds, like Hama, Raqqa, Aleppo, and Damascus.[34] In Derik and Amuda, rioters destroyed statues of Hafiz al-As'ad, and also several official buildings, such as the Ba'ath Center, the Arab Farmers' Club, and the customs station. In Ras al-'Ayn, stores were closed and young people threw stones at the commissariat. In Kobane, rioters set fire to a government civil registry office and attempted to free prisoners from the local jails (Gambill 2004: 4).

The anniversary of the massacre at Halabja on March 16 encouraged an increase in action and Arab solidarity with the victims of the Qamishli massacre on March 12 and 13, 2004. Eleven political and cultural movements and human rights defenders called for a solution that would put an end to the riots in Qamishli.[35] Despite this call to action, the demonstrations in Qamishli and elsewhere took a markedly political turn. The participants brandished Kurdish flags and chanted Kurdish slogans. Christians and local Arabs withdrew from the protest movement which became entirely Kurdish.

The reaction of the security forces between March 12 and 25 was surprising in its brutality.[36] In Derik, the Guardians of the Republic arrived by train and the militias were deployed along the Turkish–Iraqi border.[37] In the same town, when the demonstrators attacked the military intelligence and state security buildings, a 16-year-old youth and a 6-year-old child were killed by gunfire (United Nations 2005). In Ras al-'Ayn and Hasaka, street fighting broke out between the Kurdish demonstrators and the Ba'ath militias, including Arab tribes armed by the regime. In Ras al-'Ayn, the battle between the members of the Kurdish family descended from Ibrahim Pasha and the *Gamar*[38] militias resulted in the death of three Kurds. In Zorava, a Kurdish enclave of 5,000 inhabitants in a suburb of Damascus, just below the presidential palace, the suppression of the riots was very severe, resulting in one death and at least 700 arrests, including 25 children. At the end of March, the final count was 43 dead (7 were Arabs), hundreds wounded, around 2,500 arrested, and more than 40 Kurdish students thrown out of Syrian universities.[39]

Reports indicated that torture had been routinely used against Kurdish detainees, causing the deaths of five prisoners.[40] The brother of one of the victims told how thousands of military men were stationed in the town: "They demanded that my father turn over his sons, telling him that nothing would happen to them. My brother, Ferhad, surrendered to the commissariat. He was immediately imprisoned in Hasaka." After seven days of detention "my family received the body of my brother in a coffin covered with a shroud. My father looked at him. The evidence indicated that Ferhad had been tortured to death."[41] Kurds arrested in connection with the uprising faced charges such as "involvement in cells seeking to weaken nationalist consciousness and to stir up racial sectarian strife," "aggression aiming to incite civil war and sectarian fighting and incitement to kill," "affiliation with a secret association," and "attempting to sever part of the Syrian territory and annex it to a foreign state" (Amnesty International 2004: 7). The repression touched Kurdish children, too. Amnesty International collected the names of more than twenty children, between the ages of 14 and 17, who were reportedly subjected to various types of torture and ill treatment while detained for more than three months in the wake of the events of March 2004.

The violent dispersal of demonstrations was officially justified as a means of preserving Syrian national unity. At the same time the Syrian vice-president,

'Abd al-Halim Khaddam, accused foreign powers of exploiting the problems in the Kurdish regions for their own gain. By the same token, official media described the unrest as the work of bandits "controlled by foreign hands" and saboteurs "from neighboring countries" intent on undermining the country's stability.[42] Subsequently, Arab governments expressed solidarity with Syria and the Gulf Cooperation Council (GCC), made up of Saudi Arabia and five other oil rich Arab monarchies, condemning "Kurdish acts of sedition."[43]

Although Bashar al-As'ad made an unprecedented statement denying foreign influence on the demonstrators in Qamishli and dispatched a delegation headed by his brother, Maher, and Defense Minister Mustafa Tlas to meet with local Kurdish leaders in Jazira in order to quell the local mobilizations,[44] an anti-Kurdish opinion flourished across the country. As at the end of the Ottoman Empire and the end of the French Mandate, Kurds were considered again by public opinion and Arab nationalists as the "Trojan horse" of a foreign power. The result of this anti-Kurdish atmosphere was the death of six Kurds under suspicious circumstances during their military service in 2004.[45]

It remains unclear as to why the Syrian regime, which had traditionally sought to gain the cooperation of certain sectors and individuals in the Kurdish community, reacted in such a violent manner in March 2004, at the risk of starting a conflict which could have unforeseeable consequences. The Kurdish nationalists spread their view that this was part of a plot set up by certain powerful branches of the Syrian Government, aimed at provoking the Kurds in order to eliminate the leaders of their political parties, notably the Yekîtî and PYD, who were seen as especially distrustful of Damascus.[46] This deliberate provocation would explain why, since the signing of the Provisionary Constitution of the Federation of Iraq on March 8, 2004, Syrian Special Security forces and Secret Services had been discretely deployed in the Kurdish enclaves. Two days before the riots of March 12 in Qamishli, Syria had closed its borders with Iraq to avoid any suspicion as to their intentions. While this version may seem plausible, it is worth noting that only a small number of political leaders figured among the victims of the violence during the month of March 2004.

A second explanation, following the logic of deliberate provocation, was endorsed by some members of the Kurdish community. According to this view, the events of March 2004 could have been the result of an internal struggle between some of the powerful branches of Syrian government, the "fragmented tyranny" to which Charles Tilly refers (Tilly 2003: 42), in particular between certain sectors of the Intelligence Services and groups closely tied to Bashar al-As'ad. The growing marginalization of the Sunnis from the spheres of power since the arrival of Bashar al-As'ad in 2000, along with the reforms to the apparatus of the state interior promised by al-As'ad and the closing of several posts of *mukhabarat* since 2001 in Jazira, could all have served as the triggers of discontentment among some sectors of the Secret Services which had wanted to show in Qamishli the control they had over the country's stability. In this version, the Kurds were simply the unfortunate victims of this power struggle.[47]

In spite of the opportunity to use this event to gain the attention of the larger population, the Kurdish parties opted instead to calm the situation. Ironically,

Sirwan Hajji Husayn, who is responsible for the website *amude.com* which played an essential role in the dissemination of photos and videos of the uprising in Qamishli, recalled "it was the first time that the Kurdish parties of Syria were united on a point."[48] Thus, the parties, rallied around the Front, the Alliance, and the Kurdish notables of Jazira, reaffirmed their loyalty to President Bashar al-As'ad and decided to suspend the festivities of Newroz, in order to avoid a violent reprise.[49] In return, As'ad declared amnesty for 312 detainees between March 12 and 16. In doing so, the regime destroyed any possibility of unified action by the Kurdish movement by favoring relations with certain parties as official representatives (the Alliance) of the Kurds, to the detriment of other parties, most notably Yekîtî and the PYD.

*Making sense of violence*

The social sciences offer some analytical tools which help us discuss the phenomenon of violence. The classical paradigms explain violence either by rational choice or by the concept of "relative deprivation." In the first case, we find social scientists like Charles Tilly who has suggested that violence aims at the construction of new power relationships (Tilly 1991). In the second case, authors like Ted Gurr assert that individuals and social groups could perceive a given situation as preventing them from accessing the resources to which they believed they were entitled, and initiate violence in response (Gurr 1970). Traditional approaches, however, have typically neglected brands of violence that were gratuitous or irascible in nature.

More recently, sociologists like Michel Wieviorka have emphasized the fact that violence emerges when conflicts are criminalized or when the actors involved in these conflicts are unable to negotiate the legitimacy of their conflicts. Then, violence is not a consequence of conflict, but, on the contrary, the consequence of the denial of conflict (Wieviorka 1999). Finally, Hamit Bozarslan contests the idea that economic, religious, and cultural factors are to blame for all kinds of violence in the Middle East. To him, both sporadic and organized violence are linked to unequal power relationships manifested in material and symbolic domination. Symbolic domination in particular denies the dignity of social, political, ethnic, and sectarian groups by labeling them as groups of flawed citizens. Dominated groups regard this symbolic domination as even less tolerable than economic inequality, potentially leading them to violently defend and legitimize their symbols (national, sectarian, or political). When violent struggle does not succeed in removing the stigmatization imposed by the regime, violence, fueled by despair, degenerates in some situations into nihilistic,[50] sacrificial,[51] and/or messianic[52] forms of violence (Bozarslan 2004).

The emergence of a political, religious, or ethnic group from a "dissimulation" strategy does not necessarily occur through violence. However, when political avenues are blocked by an authoritarian regime, the probability of a group's entrance by violent means into a phase of "visibility" is much greater, which was confirmed by the case of the Kurds in Syria in 2004. The radicalism, or violence of opposition which emerges, is driven by the rejection of the unanimist system of representation imposed by the reigning power. We can observe various signs which confirm the passage of the Syrian Kurds from dissimulation to visibility, through an extreme politicization of primary membership, such as the incidence of ethnicity, revived as a basis for political action. The slogans, "Free Kurdistan" and "Kick Out the Arab Settlers," chanted by the demonstrators and symbols (the Kurdish flag, portraits of Abdullah Öcalan, references to the massacre in Halabja) clearly indicate that the Kurdish were moving in this direction.

Following the writings of Philippe Braud, it is clear that the violence which occurred in Qamishli had a certain "irrational, spontaneous, expressive" dimension (Braud 1993: 28), the expression of an anger that had been accumulating for too long.[53] Without under-rating the "identity" aspects of the mobilizations which occurred in March 2004 and the irrational dimension of the violence, other factors have been introduced, particularly socioeconomic, which may facilitate an improved understanding of the occurrences at Qamishli (Tejel 2006: 117–33, 2007b: 269–76).

The Kurdish mobilizations between 2004 and 2005 were not an exception in the Syrian political landscape. A few months after the arrival of President Bashar al-As'ad to power in 2000, trouble broke out in the southern province of Suwayda, where Bedouin clans and Druze farmers clashed over land rights. In 2003, Syria witnessed some Assyrian led riots and by mid-2005, two major outbreaks of violence between Alawite and Isma'ili (both Shi'i Muslim) communities erupted in Qadmus and Misyaf. All these occasions of sudden violence seemed to have one point in common. Despite the fact that socioeconomic grievances were at the heart of all these issues, "the rioting took place along sectarian and ethnic fault lines" (Abdulhamid 2005: 37).

The transition from economic demands to political and ethnic demands is a phenomenon which is well described by Donald L. Horowitz for whom "by far the largest number of secessionists can be characterized as backward groups in backward regions" (Horowitz 1985: 236). It is true that the Druzes, Isma'ili, and Kurds are found at the political, economic, and geographic periphery, with weak representation in government posts, especially noticeable in Upper Jazira. Peripheral groups or groups separated from economic development would be more likely to use ethnic or religious identity as a "political resource" (Breuilly 1993: 260). To put this another way, though the demands of the Kurdish minority are not limited to greater access to economic means, the inability to satisfy this demand would further radicalize their nationalist demands (Bozarslan 1997: 174–80).

Certain elements gave weight to this perspective. The rapid urbanization of towns like Qamishli and the migration of Kurdish peasants toward Arab cities like Damascus or Aleppo introduced a new dynamic: the marginalization of certain social classes of urban Kurds. In Qamishli, while the traditional Christian and Arab quarters had been improved and upgraded (paved roads, electricity, street lights, refuse collection) in the last few years, the Kurdish suburbs still resemble large third-world villages suffering from a lack of sewers, potable water, and electricity. In Aleppo, industry had drawn thousands of unskilled Kurdish immigrants from the countryside. These Kurdish immigrants were located mainly in the working class neighborhoods of Ashrafiyya, Shaykh Maqsud, and Sh'ar.[54] In Damascus, the Kurdish immigrants came from Jazira and Afrin. They were crowded together in the informal neighborhoods of the capital, called officially "informal and spontaneous residential zones"[55] just like the thousands of Syrians who migrated from all over. Zorava, one such informal neighborhood inhabited mainly by Kurds, is distinguishable because of its deplorable state. Unlike other working class areas, there is no school or public dispensary, nor are other numerous indispensable services available in this area (Abboud 2007: 175).

Although the fragility of the Syrian economy had affected the entire population of the country, Upper Jazira had, in addition, been affected by the policy of the "Arab Belt" (confiscation of land), the census of 1962 and its social consequences, a chronic lack of investment by the state, mechanization of agriculture, and between 1995 and 1999, a major drought which caused great difficulties for the thousands of families who relied on the cotton harvest. The Kurdish middle class of towns like Qamishli had also been penalized by the increase in the price of housing which resulted from the policy of harboring Iraqi refugees (Sunni Arabs primarily from Mosul and Baghdad) practiced by the Syrian government.[56] Dramatic population growth was added to these economic difficulties as this growth was far too rapid to be sustained by the available resources. The Kurdish population experienced the highest demographic growth in Syria.[57] With close to 1 and 1.5 million members by 2006, the population has increased sixfold in a half century and has come to represent the second largest ethnic group after the Alawites (Dupret-Schepens 2007: 190).

According to an analysis based on the concept of "relative frustration," for the Kurdish migrants, the compounded effects of various factors including the dissatisfaction of Kurdish migrants with the reality of their situation in contrast with their expectations and the demographic evolution of the Kurdish population during the last half century proved an explosive mix. Certain inhabitants of the working class neighborhoods have attributed the participation of young Kurds from Damascus in the violence of March 2004 to poverty, coupled with the repression to which the Kurds were subjected (Abboud 2007: 175). In fact, riots in these areas continued on September 15, 2005. On that day, a Kurdish woman was beaten to death during clashes between police and demonstrators attempting to stop the demolition of illegally built housing in west Damascus.[58]

The high level of participation of the popular districts at the time of the riots in Qamishli has been confirmed by several witnesses to acts of violence.[59] *Ajanib* Kurds were particularly active in the protests (Lowe 2006: 6). It was above all the youth from these areas who, free from the control of the small traditional Kurdish political parties which were more in favor of peaceful confrontation, attacked the symbols of the regime (statues of Hafiz al-As'ad, Ba'ath party buildings), public buildings (commissariats, etc.) and engaged in street battles with security forces.

But the analytical tool which constitutes the theory of "relative frustration" rests on assumptions of a certain degree of determinism, leaving little room for the study of social relations, related to the integration of participants into conflicts which have been institutionalized, and the manner in which they take action, or the lack of direction that may lead to a recourse to violence (Wieviorka 2004: 155). In the Middle East, as everywhere, there are examples that show that political participation through demonstrations, protests, and collective violence is not a regular feature of the behavior of the migrant poor. On the contrary, some studies indicate that the most violent demonstrations are those in which the middle classes form the core group (Kazemi 1980: 83–4).

Finally, why did this explosion of violence occur in 2004 and not before? This further raises the question of whether this occurrence constitutes a "popular, spontaneous" action, which arose independent of all political parties, or explicit direction.

*Violence as a "repertoire of action"*

Quite different from the hypothesis of "relative frustration," but not necessarily contradictory, is another paradigm which attempts to examine violence from a utilitarian perspective, where it is just one resource among many (the repertoire of collective actions), a tactic used in a rational manner by the participants who "calculate elaborate strategies, and use violence as a means to an end" (Wieviorka 2004: 162). The actor, according to this hypothesis, is not defined by his frustrations, but by his goals. If the anticipated gains are high and the anticipated losses relatively low, particularly in terms of repression, then the probability of recourse to violence increases when circumstances conducive to this violence arise.

The theory of "resource mobilization" (McCarthy and Zald 1977: 1212–41) has been expanded by other writers such as Charles Tilly, who considered violence a natural part of social and political life and far from an anomaly. It has a clear place in normal relations and furthermore should be thought of as "normal." According to this theory, violence is not necessarily the product of a will of rupture because it is a fundamental feature of functional society (Obershall 1973). From this point of view, the instigators of violence are not elite actors, distinguishable from the population they represent. On the contrary, they would be "typical" of that population, established in their community, integrated in their "reference group."

According to this reasoning is that violence is considered an expression of action, one of its forms and modalities, and cannot be analyzed outside of that specific action. Charles Tilly asserts that group violence springs from the ordinary, from collective actions which are not intrinsically violent (festivals, meetings, demonstrations, strikes, etc.), but without which collective violence would rarely occur (Tilly 1972: 74). In this sense, "resource mobilization" theory can help us to analyze the violence which arose in March 2004 in the Kurdish enclaves of north Syria because it corresponded to ongoing political conflicts. After the death of Hafiz al-As'ad, and the end of the "Damascus Spring," and despite the political context which was less than ideal, the Kurdish party, Yekîtî, decided to conduct various political actions aimed at increasing the visibility of the "Kurdish problem" in Syria. With few material or symbolic resources, this party revealed itself as an entity to be reckoned with in the Kurdish space and, more importantly, in the Syrian space between 2002 and 2004.

The Yekîtî's example proved that social and political movements could create their own opportunities. Opportunities are products of both objective conditions and subjective perceptions of the parties involved in a conflict. From this, one can infer that the parties are not necessarily in agreement or synchronized in their respective positions. To put this another way, far from being pre-existing reserves of action and structurally insensitive, opportunities are continually cropping up by virtue of the relationships of social movements to the contexts in which they occur (Fillieule 1997: 1461–632).

In their engagement in "peaceful confrontation," the Yekîtî leaders organized actions (sit-ins, demonstrations) that, according to Charles Tilly, were susceptible to degenerating into collective violence (Tilly 2003: 200–1). In fact, between 2002 and 2004, the regularity of organized actions by the Yekîtî, alone or in collaboration with other parties and associations, and the regularity of arrests and torture seemed to revive feelings of solidarity among the Kurds. Thus, when in February 2004 the two leaders of the Yekîtî, Marwan 'Uthman and Hasan Salih, were freed after nearly fifteen months in prison, something occurred which surpassed a strictly partisan framework. A procession accompanying the two Yekîtî leaders from the prison in Adra, near Damascus, to Qamishli, extended for two and a half miles along the road. Between 5,000 and 10,000 people accorded them a triumphant welcome.[60]

However, the Yekîtî's success attracted criticism even in the Kurdish camp. The repertoire of collective actions (demonstrations, slogans) and demands for autonomy were perceived by certain Kurdish parties, particularly the Kurdish Democratic Progressive Party (KDPP) of 'Abd al-Hamid Hajj Darwish, as a provocation to the regime.[61] Furthermore, the KDPP issued a statement condemning "acts of sabotage" and calling upon the Kurds to "extinguish the sedition" (Gambill 2004: 6) making the Yekîtî party appear responsible for the Qamishli riots. A few Arab sources asserted that certain Kurdish political parties had used the riots which ensued during the football match to garner more support for greater autonomy for Jazira. According to these Arab sources, the unrest was prearranged "by Kurdish parties of which Yekîtî and PYD (ex-PKK) were the most aggressive," and it was their members "who did all the burning" (Danish Refugee Council 2007: 6).

The accusations of the KDPP, although biased by their relationship to the regime, and of certain neighboring Arabs, seem to suggest that it would be difficult to explain the extent of the Kurdish actions without taking into account their organized character. The role of the Yekîtî in the revival of the Kurdish confrontation since 2002 has already been established. With respect to the PKK, we must remember that relations between the regime and the party (re-established in October 2003 under the name of Partiya Yekîtiya Demokrat, or PYD) had changed completely since 1999, following the arrests of dozens of its members. The involvement of PYD members in violent actions after March 12 was evident in the tone of strongly nationalist slogans, the banners with the face of Abdullah Öcalan displayed at the time of burials of "martyrs," and certain forms of violence like the self-sacrifice of a youth on a central plaza in Aleppo,[62] in honor of the victims of Qamishli. In addition, the actions of other Kurdish enclaves, Afrin and Kobane, where the Kurdish parties (except PYD) were weakly rooted appeared to confirm the central role of PKK cells in the riots.

The Yekîtî and PYD did not, however, take the steps which would have confirmed them as spokespersons for the opposition movement. During the first days, Yekîtî leaders attempted to channel the movement[63] and affirm their will to continue with peaceful actions, particularly in the Syrian capital, but, little by little, the Yekîtî and the PYD folded under pressure from the security forces,[64] and the other Kurdish parties[65] resigning themselves to a tactic of "wait-and-see."

However, the two parties succeeded in deepening the mechanism of "boundary activation" (Tilly 2003: 21). Through violence and victimization, the two parties had an opportunity to build the contours of the Kurdish "national community" or the "we-group" as opposed to "them," the Arabs, the "enemy" with whom conflicts cannot be resolved. At each burial, several thousand people attended the ceremony, singing songs of the renowned Kurdish singer Shivan Perwer, particularly his song about Halabja, the Kurdish village in Iraq which was the target of chemical attacks in 1988. The assemblies organized by these families, shouldered by the political parties, allowed the casting of the Syrian Kurds in the "tragic destiny" of their Iraqi brothers.

The brutality of the security forces made this projection easy enough. From March 13 to 25, the list of martyrs continued to grow, which served to define these conflicts in community terms and ruled out the possibility of other lateral protests. In effect, the martyr is seen as a deceased who is "one of ours," who is remembered by those belonging to the group or cause for which he/she gave their life. So, in the sense of identity affirmation, the martyr inspires a feeling of collective belonging or provides a kind of "education in solidarity." Also, to recognize that a martyr is "one of ours" accentuates the distance which separates the "we-group" from the executioner, whose descendants can still be identified as the enemy and antagonist (Albert 1998: 20). The commemoration of Newroz, invoked by the Yekîtî and the PYD, was a new opportunity to emphasize "ethnic boundaries" using these martyrs. There were little girls wearing the Kurdish folk costume in green, yellow, and red (the colors of the Kurdish flag), flying black banners bearing the slogans "Long live the Martyr" or "Newroz weeps for the Martyrs."[66] The Yekîtî and the PYD proclaimed March 12 the "Day of the Martyred Kurd."[67]

The memory of events gave way finally to new methods of collective action. There were visits to the graves of the martyrs, candlelight vigils, and commemorative assemblies which occurred in northern Syria or Damascus. The Syrian Kurds were already used to mourning ceremonies for the martyrs who fell in the ranks of the guerilla forces of the PKK in the 1980s. However, these gatherings around the martyrs of the PKK also served as opportunities to express fidelity to Abdullah Öcalan, though these were not used as opportunities to express political demands of the Syrian government or to use the martyrs as a reference for "Syrian Kurdistan."

To summarize, the repression of Kurds and the resentment it generated allowed the Yekîtî and the PYD to politicize the Kurdish ethnicity proclaiming: "look what the state does to us because of our ethnicity. They repress us as a group. We must band together and seek redress as a group" (Romano 2006: 111). The Yekîtî also sought to integrate the Qamishli revolt as a new "cultural tool kit" of Kurdish nationalism in Syria.

While the instrumentalist approach has allowed us to question the role of political parties in the events of March 2004, it is nevertheless not without certain limits. The idea that violence is just another resource, among many, implies that the actor compares it to other resources that could be used and contemplates its use in terms of its costs and benefits. It also implies that the "challengers" are in complete control of the action, from start to finish, in spite of permanent risks of losing control. Our inquiries as to the organization of Yekîtî and the participants in the demonstration of March 13, 2004, the largest and bloodiest ever, revealed that participants had not anticipated the harshness of the state repression.[68] Bearing this in mind, is it possible to infer that the riots in Qamishli took place as a result of a deliberate "cost–benefit" analysis? Are there other factors to explain the defiant attitude of the Kurds toward the authorities? Finally, considering that the Kurdish parties had traditionally possessed a low capacity for mobilizing the Kurdish community, how can the massive gatherings in Qamishli, the rest of the Kurdish enclaves, and the Kurdish neighborhoods in Arab cities be explained?

*The subjectivity of the actors*

The classic approaches to violence are less likely to focus on the creators of the violence, but rather to dedicate their attention to the conditions that are favorable to violence. There is little in these approaches that actually touches on the meaning of the action. To do this, it is necessary to place the *subject* at the heart of the analysis and, by consequence, to take into account the subjectivity of the participants.

According to this approach, moving toward a state of violence occurs in a state of mind that can be defined as a "regime of subjectivity." The first regime of subjectivity would be tied to "positive violence" where actors resort to violence because they are convinced that it is the only way to change the social or political order. This violence is invested in a regime of hope. The second regime, to the contrary, is not based on the hope of establishing another political or social order by violence. It is a "negative violence," and it often replaces the first wave of "positive" violence (Bozarslan 2005: 101–3). This perspective may allow us to grasp the subjectivity of the actors in the "revolt" in Qamishli.

In effect, the regional context marked by the fall of Saddam Husayn's regime in Iraq along with the deterioration of relations between Damascus and the Iraqi Kurdish parties,[69] the imminent punishment of Syria by the United States who accused them of supporting terrorism, the suspension of the agreements between Syria and the European Union, and the emergence of a Syrian opposition had placed the Syrian regime in a precarious situation between 2003 and 2004. The possibility of the fall of the regime of Bashar al-As'ad, following that of Saddam Husayn, seemed imminent. This interpretation of the events in Iraq was shared among many members of the Kurdish opposition, particularly among the Kurdish nationalists (Leenders 2007: 70–1).

Many of those interviewed for this book confirmed that the events occurring in Iraq had a great influence on the Syrian Kurds.[70] This view was expressed explicitly by Kurdish activists such as Mashal Tamo: "The Iraqi war liberated us from a culture of fear.... [P]eople saw a Kurd become the president of Iraq and began demanding their cultural and political rights in Syria" (Landis and Pace 2006–07: 53). In the same spirit, an eyewitness recounted how when certain demonstrators saw the large numbers participating in the demonstration of March 13 they began to chant slogans for independence and launched attacks against public buildings in Qamishli because "anything seemed possible."[71]

The influence of the Iraqi experience was reflected not only in political demands, but also in the types of demonstrations which occurred in Qamishli and in other localities during the March 2004 riots. In several Kurdish towns, statues of Hafiz al-As'ad were destroyed, the demonstrators probably wanting to remind the Syrian regime of the treatment to which the statue of Saddam Husayn in Baghdad had also been subjected. This act of destruction, which had been heavily represented in the media, came to symbolize the fall of the Iraqi regime. Other riots took place on the occasion of the anniversary of the bombing of the Iraqi Kurdish town of Halabja.

According to Muhammad Hamo, a Kurdish intellectual exiled in Iraqi Kurdistan, the hope for the imminent fall of the Syrian regime, inspired by foreign intervention, could also be heard in the tone of certain slogans, such as "Long live Sharon," which until then, had never before been heard in Syria.[72] These pro-Israeli slogans did not indicate any "alliance" of Kurdish activity with the "Zionist" enemy of Damascus. In fact, at this time there were many references to state actors (United States, Israel) and individuals or organizations (Barzani, Öcalan, the Palestinian Intifada[73]). The violent actions of the demonstrators were a response to objective changes in the situation (international threats, the fall of Saddam Husayn) and also to regimes of subjectivity (of hope, to be specific), tied to the Kurds' own temporality.[74]

Even if the influence of the Iraqi experience is clear from the local perspective, it does not increase our understanding of the direction in which the principal actors in the violence, the young people, wished to guide the movement. Certainly, the central role of youth in acts of violence can be explained by a tendency of the young to be more radical in their views and expectations (consumer goods, employment, etc.). However, subject to the results of more in-depth studies, certain clues help us to form a hypothesis according to which the central role of youth[75] at the forefront of the Kurdish political scene in March 2004 – confirmed by the results of the police repression on this sector of the Kurdish population (Amnesty International 2005)[76] – must be partly seen as an attempt by the young to confirm their separateness from the mainstream of (Kurdish) society.[77] By a logic comparable to that endorsed by a large number of young Kurds from the ranks of the PKK, the radical nature of youth protests responded to their desire to distinguish themselves from their elders (families, quarter leaders, political parties) and prove their independence. In this way they wished to establish a new place for themselves in this patriarchal society, ruled by its "wise elders."

126  *The Qamishli revolt, 2004*

Following this same logic, the objective of peace in the streets, advocated by the Kurdish parties, including the Yekîtî and the PYD, could be read to some extent as a decision taken by Kurdish elders to counter the aspirations of Kurdish youth, who seemed likely to escape their control. Thus, for example, the decline of protests led by Yekîtî and PYD at the end of March 2004 revived tensions between the partisans of a sustained mobilization against the regime and the defenders of a more moderate strategy for the Yekîtî[78] and between partisans of an open confrontation with the regime and the defenders of a negotiated reconciliation with Damascus for the PYD. In general, these divisions served to re-emphasize the generational line of separation, with the youth siding with the "radicals."

Despite the "victory" of the elders (local notables, religious dignitaries, and political party leaders) in this conflict, the young Kurds took recourse in acts of violence several times following the Newroz festivities in 2005 and 2006[79] and at the time of the mass gatherings protesting the kidnapping of Muhammad Mashuk al-Khaznawi. On June 5, 2005, several thousand Kurds demonstrated in Qamishli demanding to "know the truth" about the killing of Muhammad Mashuk al-Khaznawi. The Syrian government announced it had arrested two of a five-member "criminal gang" charged with kidnapping al-Khaznawi, but Kurdish officials and al-Khaznawi's family remained skeptical and called for a complete investigation. Later, al-Khaznawi's funeral in Qamishli attracted thousands of people. At a demonstration which followed the service, the police beat protesters and arrested around sixty participants.

## Toward a radicalization of ethnic divisions?

Between 2002 and 2004, members of the Syrian opposition, particularly human rights associations, initiated a collaboration with the Kurdish party, the Yekîtî. The events of March 2004 and the new Kurdish actions initiated in June 2005 created a consciousness among the opposition movements of the significance of the Kurdish opposition in the Syrian arena. In a first gesture of solidarity, human rights organizations joined in with the Kurdish parties' demands, calling for a commission of inquiry to establish responsibility for the disproportionate repression of March 2004.[80] Riad Darar, an Arab activist, was arrested in June 2005 after having spoken to the crowd at the time of the funeral of al-Khaznawi. He was charged with "inciting ethnic strife" and later sentenced to five years in jail. In March 2006, several leading Arab figures of the opposition attended demonstrations organized by Kurdish groups in Damascus and other cities to commemorate the Qamishli riots and were arrested, among them the former deputy Riad Saif.

The establishment of the "Kurdish problem" on the political agenda of the Syrian opposition came on October 16, 2005 with the introduction of an explicit reference to this problem in the Declaration of Damascus, a document which established a unified platform for democratic change. The signers committed themselves to

[f]ind a just democratic solution to the Kurdish issue in Syria, in a manner that guarantees the complete equality of Syrian Kurdish citizens with the other citizens, regarding nationality rights, culture, learning the national language, and the other constitutional, political, social and legal rights on the basis of the unity of the Syrian land and people. Nationality and citizenship rights must be restored to those who have been deprived of them, and the file must be completely settled.[81]

The eruption of the Kurdish issue in Syria at that moment was not conducive to the creation of a common strategy for the Kurdish movement. Therefore, when Kurdish parties organized around the Front and the Alliance signing the Declaration of Damascus, four parties – Yekîtî, Azadî, Kurdish Future Movement, and PYD – did not endorse the text. At the same time, an additional Kurdish constituency, represented by Salah Badr al-Din, integrated itself into the National Salvation Front (NSF), reuniting 'Ali Sadr al-Din Bayanouni (chief of the Muslim Brotherhood) and 'Abd al-Halim Khaddam, the former Syrian vice-president.

What alternative is offered by the Syrian opposition for dealing with the Kurdish problem? 'Ali Sadr al-Din al-Bayanouni, the chief of the primary organization in the Syrian opposition, the Muslim Brotherhood, rejected every autonomist plan for the Kurds and asserted that the solution to the Kurdish problem must be dealt with through the democratization of Syria in order to ensure equality for all citizens and respect for diversity.[82] The majority of Syrian parties and human rights associations engaged in the opposition[83] saw the Kurds as normal Syrian individuals who had been deprived of some of their rights. In other words, the Syrian opposition and even certain Kurdish parties confined the Kurdish problem to the single issue of the census in 1962, a point of view that was rejected by the Yekîtî and its allies (Azadî and the Kurdish Future Movement) and the PYD, who consider the Kurds a separate nation: "We are not guests in this country. We are living in our land."[84]

The basis of the problem is in the concept of the nation-state in Syria. While it is considered acceptable for Syrian Arabs to proclaim that "We are Syrian Arabs who are part of the Arab nation," it is not permitted for the Syrian Kurds to say "We are Syrian Kurds who are part of the Kurdish nation."[85] This issue has resulted in a significant fracture between the Kurdish parties which had provoked the political and social mobilization between 2002 and 2005 and the rest of the Syrian parties, who are less open to the possibility of administrative decentralization than their counterparts in Iraq.[86] As a Yekîtî's representative put it, "the Syrian (Arab) opposition isn't ready to listen to demands aimed at Federalism. First, they will have to accept the principle of administrative decentralization."[87]

In fact, the reticence of the Syrian opposition to look at the "Kurdish problem" from a new perspective fed a certain mistrust with regard to the "hidden objectives" of certain Kurdish parties, including the Yekîtî and its allies. Certain acts, like the destruction of statues and public buildings, and the autonomist slogans were perceived as signals of a desire for an act of *fitna*. The suspicions of the existence of the Kurds' hidden agenda were also raised by the Christian communities of Jazira.

For Christians, the Kurdish revolt in northern Syria was unexpected since they perceived the Kurds as "backward, rural and rough," and, consequently, they underestimated Kurdish potential for collective political action concerning local and concrete politics in the region. Given that the economic and political power of the Christians in Jazira had already diminished at the end of the French Mandate, the Qamishli revolt exacerbated the distress of the local Christians as they realized that they were losing social, cultural, and economic distinction and elite status in local affairs: "The challenge of the Kurds to Christian economic, political and social supremacy reached its peak during the revolt, which resulted in significant feelings of insecurity among the Christians in general."[88] Indeed, many Christians, particularly the Syriacs, feared that the Qamishli revolt would develop into a recurrence of the anti-Christian massacres perpetrated by the Kurds with the collaboration of the Committee of Union and Progress at the end of World War I.

The Yekîtî and its allies attempted to place their actions under a more universal framework (human rights) with limited success. According to the human rights lawyer Anwar al-Bunni, Kurds did not play a role in Syrian politics, since their participation in this area "was limited to demands placed upon authority. They did not engage with the rest of Syrian political society."[89] Most of the participants in the movements were Kurds and the majority of demands advanced by the Yekîtî came under the identity theme. However, the identity theme was a channel to vertical mobilization, which blocked horizontal collective actions to some degree, as well as the expansion of the movement to include other sectors of Syrian society. To put this another way, the identity repertoire limited the movement's available options for support and contributed to its isolation. The "identity repertoire" both permitted and restricted the movement.

Marwan 'Uthman recognized the phenomenon of isolation of the Kurdish movement. According to this leader, "[t]here is a problem with the Syrian left.[90] It has never said anything against the oppression of the Kurds." In spite of this,

> we need to overcome the division between the Kurds and the left, between the Kurds and the Arabs, so that the left and the democratic parties are able to build bases and bridges to resolve the Kurdish problem. For [t]he Kurds alone do not have the strength to democratize Syria

though " neither does the left alone." In the end "we need an alliance between the two" (Den Hond 2004).

*Ambiguous spaces, ambiguous strategies*

Paradoxically, while the lines separating the "moderates" (the Alliance and the Front) from the "radicals" (Yekîtî, Azadî, Kurdish Future Movement, and PYD) seemed to harden after the launching of the Declaration of Damascus, the efforts for a unified Kurdish movement in Syria had never been more present. At first, Shaykh Mashuk al-Khaznawi tried to play the role of unifier for the Kurdish parties between 2004 and 2005.[91] In December 2005, the boost given to the movement by al-Khaznawi found its response in Paris with the first international conference to resolve the "Kurdish problem" in Syria. The participants included the Kurdish parties, intellectuals, and Syrian opponents. In the text of the final resolution, the emphasis was put on the necessity of establishing a project to unify the Kurds and to maintain the collaboration of the Syrian opposition.[92]

Soon after, in March 2006, a similar conference held in Washington DC provided a 13-point document which provided an outline of the basic demands and strategies of the Syrian Kurdish movement. The final resolution confirmed the territorial nature of Kurdish claims in Syria stating that "the Kurdish people in Syria live on their historical lands and are an indigenous people of the country." The text also called for a "process of democratic change and the abolishing of the dictatorial regime in Syria."[93] In May of the same year, the organizers of this conference launched a new initiative in Brussels, the Kurdistan National Assembly of Syria (KNA-S). In theory, the goal of this assembly was to reunite all of the Kurdish political parties existing in Syria and in exile, including members of collectives and independents, under one umbrella. This platform was intended to become the mouthpiece for the Syrian Kurds and their representative to the Syrian opposition and third states/foreign countries. In reality, this assembly, created with the support of the United States was not attended by the Syrian parties at the last minute and ended up representing only the parties and personalities in exile, including Ismet Sharif Vanly and the president of the Assembly, Sharko Abbas.[94]

The motive behind the retreat of the Syrian parties is not clear. Before the conference, they had agreed to participate actively in this new common organization.[95] However, gradually, as the preparatory work advanced, the leaders of the Kurdish parties introduced new conditions (particularly the number of representatives) on their participation in the KNA-S.[96] The impossibility of controlling the activities of an assembly which functioned exclusively abroad and the fear of certain parties of being seen as pawns of the United States seemed to be the determining arguments which led to the withdrawal of certain parties.

This theory is supported by the fact that the Kurdish parties continued to work toward the creation of a common platform despite the fiasco of the KNA-S. When the second congress of Kurdish Political Movements in Syria was held in Paris on March 16, 2007, eleven parties – the Front, the Alliance, a coordinating committee which included Yekîtî, Azadî, the Kurdish Future Movement, and the PYD – convened in order to advance toward a unified political project. Despite the limits of the results,[97] this formal meeting between nearly all the Kurdish groups in Syria, with the exception of *Wifaq*, represented the greatest moment of unity for the Kurdish movement since the 1970s. However, the reticence of the parties to work together, the closeness of certain parties with the Syrian regime, and an opaque political culture turned out to be significant obstacles to the project of political unification.[98]

In addition, according to Reinoud Leenders, the military and political events in Iraq since 2003, seen through the prism of Syrian policy, had two contradictory effects. On the one hand, the Syrian opposition, particularly certain Kurdish parties, launched a more aggressive strategy toward the government of Bashar al-As'ad. On the other hand, the Syrian regime knew how to exploit the deteriorating situation in Iraq. Thus, the regime and the official media established explicit parallels between the riots of Qamishli and the deterioration of public order in Iraq. Playing on the fear of the possibility that Syria would plunge into a similar situation of ethnic and religious violence after a foreign intervention or a destabilization from the inside, the Syrian regime presented itself as the only "solution to safeguard Syria from falling into the same chaos as that experienced in Iraq" (Leenders 2007: 72).

This fear spread among a number of "progressive and secular" Kurds. For these Kurds, the Ba'ath regime, with its clear limits, became a preferable enemy to a regime dominated by the Muslim Brotherhood. Thus, despite conciliatory declarations of the leader of the Muslim Brotherhood (which was integrated into the NSF) with regards to the cultural demands of the Kurds, there was a strong distrust in certain Kurdish circles upon seeing the emergence of an Islamic power and an increase of the Sunni Arab majority in politics, to the detriment of ethnic and religious minorities.[99] Finally, the ambiguity of the Syrian political sphere impeded the emergence of clear strategies. Thus, the Ba'athist regime took note of this new era, marked by the "Kurdish problem" in Syria. For the first time, the Syrian government publicly raised the issue (although without concrete results) of the census of 1962 in the province of Hasaka and the necessity of resolving the problem posed by awarding Syrian citizenship to the more than 200,000 Kurds in Jazira.

On an economic level, the Ministry of Irrigation, led by Nader al-Buni, announced that Syria intended to use water from the Tigris River to irrigate 150,000 hectares in the Qamishli area in order to develop the region.[100] In keeping with the action, the government had committed in its tenth five-year plan (2006–10) to transform Jazira under a "development platform" such as those in Turkey and Iraq[101] (Ababsa et al. 2007: 57).

For its part, the Syrian opposition had established ties with the Kurdish parties, all the while maintaining their strong opposition to certain "identity" demands which had grown in importance among the Kurdish population. Some Kurds had maintained relations with the Syrian opposition, the regime, and the rest of the Kurdish groups.

*Toward a new balance*

In general, the goal of the Kurdish actors is to integrate themselves into the existing states in the Middle East, to gain access to economic and political resources and to create legitimate acceptance for the principle of sharing symbolic resources (language, culture, administration, representation, etc.). In this sense, it is predictable that the Syrian Kurdish parties seek increased visibility of their group in order to capitalize on their association with the Syrian state. Faced with the unlikely fall of the regime provoked by foreign intervention, their clandestine activities with the Syrian opposition and their steps toward creating political unity for the Kurdish movement could be seen as assets which could be used to negotiate their place in the Syrian political space and potentially be granted some concessions by the government, particularly on the cultural field.

Establishing a parallel with the development of the Islamic protest after the massacre in Hama in 1982, a hypothesis could be drawn that this is the time when a new equilibrium was put into place, a new accommodation between the regime and the Kurdish movement in Syria. In this middle space, situated between "dissimulation" and violence, the Syrian regime would be more likely to allow a flexible approach with respect to public expressions of Kurdish identity (language, music, cultural festivals, publications), while the Kurdish movement would abandon, at least for the moment, the goal of overturning the government of Bashar al-As'ad. Although it is too early to prove this hypothesis, there are numerous indications of its validity.

After the repression of March 2004, Bashar al-As'ad indicated the direction that the Kurdish movement must take. Thus the Syrian authorities commanded that the "illegal" Kurdish parties cease all political activities with a view to transforming themselves into "legal" cultural associations.[102] In addition, at the time of the tenth Regional Congress of the Ba'ath Party, from June 6 to 9, 2005, Minister Bouthaina Shaaban made a rare Syrian public statement, proclaiming that "ethnic diversity is a national wealth that should be maintained," though the recognition of diversity should take place under the "umbrella of national interest,"[103] which remains, of course, entirely defined by the regime.

Although the Kurdish parties consider that their culture is threatened by the Syrian regime, a cultural activist in Qamishli confided to the author that since 2004, he had noticed a great flexibility of the authorities with respect to Kurdish folklore and music.[104] Similarly, for the poet Lukman Derky, the Syrian government seems to be opening up to the Kurds. The writer recently called for a concert of Syrian Kurdish artists in Damascus. The provisional nod of approval he received from the Ministry of Culture was unexpected, leading him to comment that "[t]here is a clear and noticeable change." [105] Additionally, it is reported that the festivities of Newroz,[106] the commemoration of victims of the massacres at Halabja, and the commemorations of victims of the "Qamishli revolt" have not been forbidden by the authorities despite some obvious moments of high tension and "displays of [Kurdish] national identity."

Accommodation or new equilibrium between the regime and the Kurdish movement does not, however, imply an absence of conflict. The arrests of Kurdish leaders, often of short duration, continue,[107] as does the repression of certain gatherings organized by the PYD (notably in Aleppo) and by the Yekîtî.[108] Furthermore, a certain "routinization" of violence was observable between demonstrators and security forces during Newroz festivals and other gatherings.[109]

Nor does accommodation imply an absence of tension among the implicated political actors. Consider the fact that the fundamental ideological principle of the Ba'athist regime was Arab nationalism. If the regime had already made certain concessions to the Islamists with regard to Islamic presence in the public sphere in Syria, could it handle making new concessions, this time for a minority group such as the Kurds, without compromising the last remaining pillars of its ideological legitimacy?

## 132  The Qamishli revolt, 2004

Like the Ba'athist regime, the Syrian Kurdish parties now find themselves faced with important challenges. The Kurdish mobilizations between 2004 and 2005 created new dynamics in the movement including the emergence of new actors, particularly young people and women,[110] thereby creating a new brand of sympathy for the Kurdish parties.[111] However, the decline of collective action, the stabilization of the regime in the international arena since 2006, and the lengthy process of bringing political unity to the Kurdish movement have ended by inducing a certain lassitude within the movement. This "social fatigue" is manifested in reduced public participation in assemblies,[112] criticism directed at the Kurdish parties, increasing focus of individuals on personal projects (professional and economic futures),[113] and increased migration toward the large Arab cities and also abroad.

From that time on, many questions have arisen as to the future role of the Kurdish political parties. Can they continue to exploit the memory of the victims of March 2004 without succeeding in obtaining official recognition of the Kurds as the second national group of Syria? Can they pursue their meetings in foreign lands in search of political unity without concrete results? In other respects, if the Kurdish parties were to succeed in obtaining official recognition of Syria's plurality by the state or even the return of citizenship to the more than 200,000 Kurds for whom this was revoked, would these successes be sufficient to ensure the popular support necessary for them to present themselves as the undisputed representatives of the Kurds to the Syrian regime?

As we have attempted to illustrate, the violent mobilizations of March 2004 were a response to the intersection of several factors. The full integration of the Kurds into the Syrian state depends on the capacity of the regime, and that of the Syrian opposition, to meet economic and social expectations. For the time being, the regime does not seem ready to expand the redistribution of goods to include the Kurdish populations. In keeping with this assertion, the government announced an investment of 523 million dollars to be made between 2007 and 2010, particularly in a large refinery in Dayr al-Zur, an Arab town. Upper Jazira, where the Kurds are in the majority, seems to be newly forgotten in terms of the industrialization projects which could diversify the region's economy. Furthermore, the regime does not appear ready to allow the widespread integration of Kurds into the regional administration, which could result in a closer administration of citizens and a source of employment.

Finally, the development of the regional context, including the situation in Iraq, the strategic alliance between Iran and Syria, and the future of Lebanon, may all have important consequences for both Damascus and the Kurdish populations, particularly in Jazira. Taking into account these factors, the Kurdish parties are far from capable of mastering all of these dynamics which come to bear on the "Kurdish problem." Hence, it is pertinent to wonder who is going to channel the uncertainty of those politicized and radical Kurds who refused to end their resistance and who finally erupted on the occasion of the "revolt of Qamishli."

# Conclusion

The late development of the Kurdish opposition movement in Syria cannot be explained by simplistic reasoning relying on the absence of conflict, the power of group solidarity (*'asabiyya*), or even the weak popular attachment to essential characteristics of ethnic Kurdish identity, such as the language. The active Kurdish movements in Iran, Iraq, and Turkey are also riddled with infraethnic groupings which undermine the possibility of coordinating a revolt by the diverse groups which call themselves "Kurds." In Turkey, where a large part of the Kurdish population has been linguistically assimilated, in contrast to the case in Syria, we have seen the potential for a sustainable violent opposition movement against the state. Therefore, it is important, through observation and historical validation, to identify the diverse variables and correlative factors affecting mobilization of ethnic identity in the political field, including political space, the relative power of each group, cultural contact with other ethnic groups, and the role of the group's elites, among others.

When France was focused on acquiring the territories of the Levant as a mandatory power, the Kurdish population occupied three narrow and separate zones along the Turkish border. Until the advent of contemporary Syria, the spontaneous reference point was not expressed as ethnicity or language, but as "groups of solidarity" defined by relational terms. It could be a matter of a geographic (valley, village, quarter), parental, clan, tribal, or sect (Yazidi) origin. Thus, the "Kurds" of Hama and Damascus, for example, were recognized as such not because of their linguistic affiliation but in terms of their origin (the Barazi tribal confederation in Hama) or their function (military for the Kurds of Damascus). Non-Kurdish "neighbors" were also of many diverse origins, such as urban Christians in Jazira, urban Arabs in Damascus, Aleppo, or Hama, and nomadic Arabs in Jazira.

The politicization of Kurdish ethnicity, defined by linguistic terms and blood lines, originated in the 1920s (Chapter 1), following the settlement in the Levantine territories of intellectuals and tribal chiefs of Kurdish origin from Turkey. The French Mandate in Syria and Lebanon offered ideal sociopolitical conditions for the "ethnicizing intellectuals" (Smith 1981: 108) to pursue their political and cultural agendas, the most eloquent of which would be consolidation of the Kurdish nationalist doctrine in the Kurmanji dialect. The main objective of

## 134 Conclusion

the Kurdish intellectuals was to safeguard the Kurdish language in an Arab-speaking environment. This "differentiation movement" (Horowitz 1985: 72–3) was not appreciated by the Syrian nationalist leaders who considered it an attempt to divide the "Syrian citizens." As a result, the Kurdish language became politicized by Kurdish activists and by the National Bloc.

Arabism, which had evolved as a cultural renaissance movement during the course of the nineteenth century, was introduced as a new political angle to guide local resistance faced with French Mandatory power between the two World Wars. The French policy of dividing Syrian territories based on ethnic and religious differences served to strengthen the Syrian nationalist movement, which was identified with the majority of the Arab and Sunni populations and the cities. The Kurds, living in the Syrian peripheral countryside under the influence of tribal chiefs and landowners enlisted by the mandatory power, were perceived more and more as elements foreign to the Arab "nation."

Furthermore, at the beginning of the mandate, while some Syrian political elites defended a national/civic vision of citizenship, others turned progressively toward an "organicist" concept of the nation (Chapter 2), distancing themselves from all democratic models. For the Syrian intelligentsia and increasingly for young officials, the rejection of imperialism went hand in hand with the refusal to adopt "western" democracy.

Between 1946 and 1957, the Kurdish nationalist movement in Syria followed the same evolution as in other areas of the Middle East, which is to say that it fell into a state of paralysis. The Syrian government had finally been able to integrate the Kurdish enclaves economically and culturally, as well as politically. However, it was the survival of the small literary societies and clandestine groups of young people, indoctrinated by elders, which made the restructuring of the Kurdish nationalist movement possible around the Kurdistan Democratic Party in Syria (KDPS) in 1957. At that time, they were faced with growing Syrian nationalism, which was becoming progressively more aggressive toward non-Arabs. Spurred on by the alliance between the older and younger generations of Kurdish nationalists, and by the events in Iraq, particularly the agreement between 'Abd al-Karim Qasim and Mustafa Barzani to integrate the Kurdish nation into the definition of the Iraqi state, the KDPS succeeded in mobilizing a large number of Kurds around the issue of ethnic identity between 1958 and 1961.

At the same time as the ideological "one-upmanship" in the political debates of the moment, the political restructurings which were taking place in the Middle East between the 1950s and 1960s strengthened the power of the old and new *'asabiyya,* certain of which have been sometimes labeled by scholars as tribal oligarchies, ethnic or community groups (Chapter 3). In Syria, a small group of officers from the Alawite *'asabiyya* were steadily taking over the reins of power. To obscure the social basis for its power, the group used ideological platforms of Syrian nationalism, pan-Arabism, and socialism, authoritatively imposed, never hesitating to resort to coercion and violence. The internal struggles taking place within the Ba'athist party, and, as a consequence, the fragility of Syrian power, could have allowed the Kurdish movement to mount a certain political resistance despite the national state of emergency established in 1963. However, the leaders of the Kurdish movement were thrown into prison in 1960, and, after 1965, the KDPS felt the beginning of its first internal ruptures which weakened its ability to mobilize in Syria.

In spite of this, the rural exodus toward large Syrian cities, which began in the 1960s, increased both the levels of urban intelligentsia and the lower social classes in the older Kurdish communities in Damascus and Aleppo. In fact, the coming and going of people between urban and rural areas allowed the Kurdish parties to be present in both the urban and rural settings. Also, the transborder tribes sent their members to support Mustafa Barzani's Kurdish revolt, launched in Iraq in 1961 (Chapter 4). Even though the involvement of tribal members in the Iraqi conflict was a response mostly to the logic of "group solidarity," it also facilitated the establishment of a historic relationship of lineage between the Kurdish resistance in Iraq and Syria.

The recruitment of Syrian Kurds in the ranks of the guerilla movements of neighboring countries took on a special form with respect to the PKK. The intensity of this phenomenon is difficult to explain relying solely on an analysis focused on 'asabiyya. Field studies have indicated that there were multiple contributing factors, including a feeling of national solidarity, getting away from the social control of the elders, for women, freedom from the patriarchy, individual interests (access to material and symbolic resources), and the attraction of a movement advocating armed struggle as opposed to the Syrian Kurdish parties which were considered "too moderate."

The success of the PKK in Syria is also due in part to the complicity of the regime of Hafiz al-As'ad (Chapter 5). The PKK was endowed with many material resources thanks to the financial support of the government in Damascus. This was not true of the other parties. The PKK also had access to symbolic resources which the smaller organizations, with the exception of the KDPS, did not have.

Nevertheless, the activities of the "Iraqi" and "Turkish" Kurdish parties in Syria had significant repercussions for Kurds in Syria. While during the first two decades of Ba'athist power in Syria, the Kurds had adopted a strategy of "dissimulation," after 1984, more and more Kurds revealed their attachment to different features of Kurdish identity. Arabized Kurds could assert their distinctive ethnic identity through the revival and reinterpretation of their local and tribal origins as well as through participation in "national" festivals. The Yazidi, historically marginalized by the Sunni Kurds, could proclaim themselves the guardians of real Kurdish values thanks to their religion which was promoted by the PKK to the rank of "original" religion of the Kurds. The cooperation between the PKK and certain Sufi brotherhoods in northern Syria made possible a sort of Kurdish–Sufi synthesis, making Sufism a kind of Kurdish school of Islam. At the same time, the leftist discourse of the PKK, which advocated connecting the class struggle to the struggle for national liberation, drew members from the lower classes into its ranks.

Certain intellectual circles, which had become "abeyance structures," were reactivated and provided strong momentum for the revival of the Kurdish language. The

Syrian Kurdish parties were also reinvigorated by these changes. Thus, the demand for political autonomy for the Kurdish regions in Syria featured on the agenda of some Kurdish parties at the end of the 1990s. Finally, the return in force of the "national agenda" in the Middle East – Palestinian Intifada and Kurdish autonomy in Iraq since 1991 – and in other areas, such as the Balkans and Central Asia, meant that the mobilization of the Syrian Kurds on the subject of identity appeared to be more "universal."

Resistance taking place in an infrapolitical level (secret language courses, dissident memoirs, the survival and reinvention of folklore, etc.) is in no way a threat to the regime. Nevertheless, as James C. Scott suggests, the dominant elites and the subordinates are committed to a relationship in which both parties seek out each other's weaknesses and work to exploit these small advantages (Scott 1990: 184). For example, in the 1980s, the government disguised the popularity of the Newroz festival among the Kurds by making it a national celebration and integrating it into the official Syrian calendar.

With the death of Hafiz al-As'ad, the ethnicization process of Kurdish identity joined the overtures of Bashar al-As'ad between 2000 and 2001, and the emergence of a Syrian opposition. At this stage, a Syrian Kurdish party until then marginal, the Yekîtî (Kurd), chose to bring the Kurd's complaints to the public arena (Chapter 6). The new era of "visibility" of the Kurdish question in Syria was confirmed in March 2004 following the riots which occurred in the Kurdish enclaves. For the first time in contemporary Syria, the Kurdish question was at the heart of the political debates from 2004 to 2005, thanks to the overtures of Bashar al-As'ad's regime and the Syrian opposition.

However, the Kurdish opposition rapidly lost its force. No leader or political party emerged to take the role of leader of the movement which was quickly fragmented along partisan lines. Can it be assumed from all of this that the movement had reverted to the status quo prior to 2004? Rather than attempt to predict the future of the evolution of Kurdish populations in Syria, it is worthwhile examining a few tendencies, sometimes contradictory, which are revealing. To be sure, the Kurdish movement remains extremely fragmented, despite various initiatives aimed at establishing common strategies for confronting the Syrian regime. Nevertheless, in the absence of an active civil society, the Kurdish parties fulfill their role of culturally framing in the various Kurdish enclaves. This allows them to act as incontestable intermediaries between the regime, local security forces, and the Kurdish populations. Even if the relationship between the regime and the Kurdish parties clearly favors the former, some members of the regime have become aware, since March of 2004, of the Kurds' capacity for protest, so much so that the Kurdish movement is able to reclaim a certain legitimacy within its population.

In addition, the pacification of the protests led by the Kurdish parties themselves was a prelude to a new balance between the Kurdish movement and the regime. The former has gained a certain freedom of action to create space for protest where Kurdish ethnicity can be openly displayed. The latter seems to confirm the selective withdrawal of the state. After having betrayed its founding principles, socialism and

Arab nationalism, by favoring the privatization of a part of the Syrian economy, by creating an increasingly personalized power and by promoting an official Islam, Bashar al-Asʻad seems prepared to tolerate the consolidation of a Kurdish space (cultural and symbolic), at least for the time being.

In the short term, the return to a strategy of "assimilation" by those Kurds identifying with a separate ethnic identity seems improbable. It remains to be seen if the Kurdish population, which, up until now, had distanced itself from the process of (re)-ethnicization initiated during the 1980s and solidified during the mobilizations of 2004 and 2005, will become conscious of this cultural space, which is parallel, but not completely autonomous from the other existing cultural spaces.

It is also too soon to know if this new equation will satisfy sectors of the population which were radicalized at the time of the riots of 2004. It is true that the young "rebels" of today are often the good citizens of the political parties of tomorrow. Nevertheless, certain elements indicate that a sector of the Kurdish youth is no longer prepared to rejoin the "peaceful struggle" in Syria. In this sense, and as a hypothesis, we may expect that a small faction of radicalized young Kurds, acting under a regime of hope (encouraged by the experience of administrative autonomy of the Iraqi Kurds and the promises of the American administration to liberate "oppressed people") and, at the same time, of despair (incapacity of the Syrian regime to transform itself and of the Kurdish political parties to offer an alternative), would respond to this tension by using violent means in Syria to set themselves up as the last generation of "suffering and servitude."

The routinization of urban violence between 2004 and 2007 and the involvement of the young Syrian Kurds in the ranks of the guerrillas of the PKK at Mont Qandil in Iraqi Kurdistan[1] seem to confirm this hypothesis. As for the PYD (ex-PKK), the struggle between the partisans who supported a confrontation with the regime and those who advocated a new strategic alliance with Damascus came to an end in January 2007 with the victory of the latter after the nomination of Dr Bahoz (Fehman Husayn) to the head of the People's Defense Forces, based in Mont Qandil. The outcome of this confrontation could be the breaking away of the youngest and most radical sector to form a rival group in Syria with the aim of taking violent action against the Damascus regime (Brandon 2007: 4–6). If this new direction of action against the Syrian regime were to come to fruition, it would give greater "visibility" to the Kurdish cause, but would also give rise to more dismal prospects.

Finally, the Kurdish issue in Syria is evolving in the tense context of the Middle-Eastern Kurdish space. Turkey and Iran are experiencing an upsurge in the armed Kurdish struggle within their borders. At the same time, Ankara and Teheran both aspire to play an important role, albeit occasionally a destabilizing role, in the region and most notably in Iraq. Thus, the Turkish government's threats of intervention in Iraqi Kurdistan with a view to clear out the PKK provoked a serious diplomatic crisis during the autumn of 2007. Iran and Syria made ambiguous remarks with regard to such an intervention which would threaten the principal achievement of the Kurdish nationalist movement in the Middle East since 1991: this achievement being the existence of an autonomous Iraqi Kurdistan as a political, territorial, and symbolic reference. The demonstrations in northern Syria on November 2, 2007, finishing with one death in Qamishli and ten arrests in Kobane, as a sign of protest against such a military intervention have served as a reminder to Damascus that a new chapter of Kurdish opposition could have dramatic and unforeseen consequences for the fragile Syrian equilibrium.

# Appendix

## Kurdish political parties in Syria

1 Partiya Yekîtî ya Demokrat a Kurdî li Suriyê
  Hizb al-Wahda al-Dimuqrati al-Kurdi fi Suriya
  Kurdish Democratic Union Party in Syria
  Head: Isma'il Amo

2 Partiya Demokrat a Pêshverû ya Kurdî li Suriyê
  Hizb al-Dimuqrati al-Taqadumi al-Kurdi fi Suriya
  Kurdish Democratic Progressive Party in Syria
  Head: 'Abd al-Hamid Hajj Darwish

3 Partiya Yekitî ya Kurdî li Suriyê
  al-Hizb al-Wahida al-Kurdi fi Suriya
  Kurdish Union Party in Syria
  Head: Fuad Aliko

4 Partiya Azadî ya Kurd li Sûriyê (union since May 2005 between Hevgirtina Gelê Kurd li Sûriyê and Partiya Çep a Kurdî li Sûriyê)
  Hizb Azadi al-Kurdi fi Suriya
  Kurdih Freedom Party in Syria
  Head: Khayr al-Din Murad

5 Partiya Demokrat a Kurdî li Suriyê
  Hizb al-Dimuqrati al-Kurdi fi Suriya
  Kurdish Democratic Party in Syria
  Head: Dr 'Abd al-Hakim Bashar

6 Partiya Demokrat a Kurdî li Suriyê (el-Partî)
  Hizb al-Dimuqrati al-Kurdi fi Suriya (al-Parti)
  Kurdish Democratic Party in Syria (The Party)
  Head: Nasr al-Din Ibrahim

7 Partiya Çep a Kurdî li Suriyê
  Hizb al-Yasari al-Kurdi fi Suriya

Kurdish Left Party in Syria
Head: Muhammad Musa Muhammad

8  Partiya Demokrat a Pêshverû ya Kurdî li Suriyê
   Hizb al-Dimuqrati al-Taqadumi al-Kurdi fi Suriya
   Kurdish Democratic Progressive Party in Syria
   Head: Aziz Da'ud

9  Partiya Demokrat a Welatparêz a Kurdî li Suriyê
   Hizb al-Watani al-Dimuqrati al-Kurdi fi Suriya
   Kurdish Democratic Patriotic Party in Syria
   Head: Tahir Sadun Sifuk

10 Partiya Demokrat a Kurdî ya Surî
   Hizb al-Dimuqrati al-Kurdi al-Suri
   The Syrian Kurdish Democratic Party
   Head: Jamal M. Baqi

11 Partiya Yekîtiya Demokrat (PKK)
   Hizb al-Itihad al-Dimuqrati
   Democratic Union Party
   Head: Fuad 'Umer

12 Rêkeftina Demokrat a Kurdî ya Surî (party of ex-members of PKK)
   Hizb al-Wifaq al-Dimuqrati al-Kurdi al-Suri
   Syrian Kurdish Democratic Concord Party
   Head: Fawzi Shengal

13 Shepêla Pêsherojê ya Kurdî li Suriyê
   Tayar al-Mustaqbal al-Kurdi fi Suriya
   Kurdish Future Movement in Syria
   Head: Mashal Tamu

*Coalitions*

1  Hevbendiya Demoqrat a Kurdî li Suriyê
   Al-Tahaluf al-Demokrati al-Kurdi fi Suriya
   Party nos. 1, 2, 6, 7

2  Eniya Demoqrat a Kurdî li Suriyê
   Al-Jabha al-Demokratiye al-Kurdiye fi Suriya
   Party nos. 5, 8, 9

3  Komîta Tensîqê ya Kurdî
   Lajnat al-Tansiq al-Kurdiye
   Party nos. 3, 4, 13

# Notes

**Introduction**

1 It is impossible for us to cite here all of the works which are dedicated to the Kurdish question, Kurdish identity, and nationalism in these three countries. We can, however, mention the contributions of C.J. Edmonds (1957), Chris Kutschera (1979), Elizabeth Picard (1991), Martin van Bruinessen (1992), Amir Hassanpour (1992), David McDowall (1996), Philip Kreyenbroek and Christine Allison (1996), Hamit Bozarslan (1997), and Martin Strohmeier (2003).
2 The determining role of two "Arabized" Kurds (Husni Za'im and Adib al-Shishakli) in the first *coups d'état* of contemporary Syria had been offered as proof of the successful integration of Kurds into Syrian society.
3 On this subject, see the *European Journal of Turkish Studies*, Thematic Issue no. 5, http://www.ejts.org.
4 We have conducted two field studies (April 2001, February–March 2007) in Syria. Unfortunately, the two visits were interrupted by security forces which "requested" us to leave Northern Syria. Aside from the sources cited, we wish to thank all of the people who bear witness anonymously.
5 In 1936, the High French Commissioner in Syria and Lebanon issued a decree which accorded legal recognition to the religious communities already recognized in the heart of the Ottoman Empire and assimilated their law of personal status into the constitution in 1930 (Hourani 1947: 74–7, 92–5).
6 We shall define an *ethnic group* as a set of local groups (tribes, village communities, urban populations) that "lay claim to a common origin, lifestyle, social principles of organization and mind set, which, although not necessarily similar, demonstrate through their very differences that they belong to a common tradition" (Dawod 2006: 87).
7 Interview with the author. Rajo, March 2007.
8 As a result of the political and military alliance negotiated between the Ottoman Empire and France in 1534, the capitulations brought the judicial foundations of the French presence into the Levant. Originally, it was a unilateral act, conceded by the sovereign of an empire by the strength of his personal power, to an ally country, which henceforth resulted in a certain number of benefits, including greater religious and commercial freedom, and judicial immunity. Rapidly extending to other commercial powers (particularly England), the capitulations changed the nature of the decline of the Ottoman Empire. The ambassadors and consultants gained local clientele recruited from the heart of the Jewish, Armenian, Greek, and oriental Christian communities, which little by little undermined imperial authority. During the nineteenth century,

traditional threads of economic and judicial management were transformed into a veritable system of cultural and political influence (thanks to the work of missionaries and the internal evolution of non-Muslim communities), henceforth supported by an enlarged foundation of community affirmation.
9 James C. Scott defines the "public transcript" as the open interaction between subordinates and those who dominate (Scott 1990: 2).
10 For more on the hypothetical existence of a "civil society" and the pertinence of this concept in Syria, see Hinnebusch (1995: 214–42).
11 By "minorities," we mean groups "judicially and sociologically minor" which live a reality of qualitative and differential order and a condition of dependence or subjugation, as it were.
12 The gap between official identity "space" and real identity "space" is found not only in the political positioning of the Syrian Kurds, but also among the Druzes, divided between Lebanon and Syria (Méouchy 2007: 306–7).

## 1 The Kurds during the French Mandate

1 The Gulkhane imperial rescript, promulgated on November 3, 1839, represented the greatest effort to avoid the collapse of the Ottoman Empire. Known by the name of *Tanzimat* ("reorganization"), this text constitutes the point of departure of a vast program of reforms, which shook the country institutionally, economically, and socially.
2 Of Arab origin (*milla*, "word" referring to a group of people who accept a "revealed book"), the term *millet* took, in the Ottoman Empire, the meaning of "community organized on a religious foundation," recognized as such by the imperial administration. With the *Tanzimat* reforms, the word took on a political connotation. Paradoxically, in 1839, the imperial rescript spoke of *millet* Ottoman, grouping together all the citizens of the empire without religious distinction, but still set Islam in opposition against the other *millets* (Planhol 1993: 22–4; Karpat 1982: 141–69).
3 By definition all the Yazidis are ethnically Kurdish. Their religion is a synthesis of pre-Islamic beliefs (Zoroastrianism, Manicheanism, Judaism, Christianity) and Muslim elements.
4 Despite rumors of a possible assassination, according to Commandant Victor Müller, Ibrahim Pasha died of congestion after having drunk water without taking precautions (Müller 1931: 138).
5 Sa'id Shamdin Pasha, for instance, used the capital that he had accumulated as *Amir al-Hajj* (commander of the pilgrimage) to purchase a series of farms and villages in the Ghuta, which he established as a valuable family endowment, and extensive property in Hawran and in Qunaytra. By the 1980s, he was reputed to own more land than any other individual in the Damascus province.
6 At the start of the mandate, the French had envisaged creating a center of anti-Arab resistance, indeed the establishment of a separate political and administrative entity from where the mandatory agents could diffuse their pro-French propaganda not only in northern Syria but also in the vilayat in Mosul. This project would, however, have been abandoned after the Druze revolt (1925–27) which forced the mandatory power to reconsider its policy toward minorities (Fuccaro 2003: 218).
7 The heterogeneous nature of the rebels, mobilized around the legendary Ibrahim Hananu, must be emphasized. In effect, besides Hananu, whose background was Kurdish, early field commanders included Ahmad bin 'Umar (also a Kurd), Najib 'Uwaid (another Kurd), 'Umar Bihar (an Arab), and Sha'ban Agha (a Turk) (Lawson 2004: 261).

8 The Murud movement (1933–40), led by Shaykh Ibrahim Khalil, was launched initially against the Kurdish aghas of the region, later becoming an anti-French movement. Supported in different ways by Turkey and, to a lesser degree by the National Bloc, the movement born in Kurd Dagh had, at the same time, social and religious connotations. The Murud leaders never established contact with the Kurdish movement.
9 *SHAT, 4H 319, Dossier no. 3*. The Director of Army General Security, Police Inspector General, to the Head of Press Services and of French Forces Propaganda in the Levant, no. 465/C.E/R. Beirut, January 19, 1943.
10 With the entry of the Ottoman Empire into the Great War, the British made contact with Arab representatives in order to guarantee access in Arabia, Palestine, Syria, and Iraq in the event of any direct military action against the government in Istanbul. In exchange, the British representatives seemed disposed to give their blessing to the creation of a large Arab state (the Arab peninsula, Iraq, and Syria) after the war, under the leadership of Sharif Husayn of Mecca.
11 The agreement of May 16, 1916 established two zones in which Great Britain and France recognized each other's right to establish direct control. France allocated itself the coastal region of Syria and northern Iraq, while Great Britain aspired to control the Basra region and Baghdad. Finally, an international zone would cover Palestine.
12 For a detailed analysis of the mandatory architecture, see Mizrahi 2003a: 76–88.
13 The "Lyautey system" did not seek to assimilate the population placed under French protectorate but to "associate" them, which is to say, to encourage participation of the local populations in the government of the country while respecting the local religions, customs, and traditions. But the knowledge and respect for the local languages and the social structures of the country were taken advantage of by the protectorate power.
14 Certain sectors of the mandatory apparatus, however, did not share this vision, advocating a better understanding of contemporary Syrian society through, in particular, sociological studies. In this sense, Robert Montagne, director of the French Institute in Damascus (1930–38), looked elsewhere for scientific know-how from colonial know-how (Métral 2004; Trégan 2004).
15 Certain Kurdish intellectuals, however, identified themselves with other nationalisms. Hence, Ziya Gökalp or Abdullah Javdat after having flirted with the Kurdist committees embraced Turkish nationalism. Similarly, the Kurds in Damascus or Aleppo participated in the awakening Arab cultural nationalism: 'Abd al-Rahman al-Kawakibi, originating in Aleppo, and Muhammad Kurd 'Ali of Damascus.
16 The most important of the Kurdish clubs in Istanbul was the *Kurdistan Teali Cemiyeti* ("Committee for the recovery of Kurdistan"; KTC), founded on December 17, 1918. The committee's leaders tried in their writings, particularly in the notes sent to the representatives of the Great Powers, to demonstrate the originality of the Kurdish nation and to confer on it a historicity in order to justify the necessity of, and the right to, an autonomous entity for the Kurds. The association also endowed itself in 1919 with a journalistic voice, which played a predominant role in the formulation of Kurdish nationalism, the journal *Jîn* ("Life").
17 The Shaykh Sa'id revolt was the fruit of an alliance between sectors of traditional Kurdish society (shaykhs and tribal leaders) and the nationalist organization Azadî ("Liberty"). Despite the committee's instigating role, the rebels' armed branch was made up of Sunni tribes and others loyal to Shaykh Sa'id from the Zazaphone regions situated to the north of Diyarbakir. The rebels obliged the Turkish authorities to mobilize thousands of soldiers to subdue the revolt.

18 The mandatory authority's attitude toward Kurdish refugees evolved from one of rejection in 1925 to one of encouragement to settle in Jazira, and to a lesser degree in Kurd Dagh. If before 1927 there were at most 45 Kurdish villages in this region, by 1939, they numbered between 700 and 800 agglomerations of Kurdish majority. According to an official census, in 1939 Jazira counted a total population of 158,550 habitants of which 81,450 were Kurdish Muslims and 2,150 were Yazidi Kurds. *CADN, Fonds Beyrouth, Cabinet Politique*, no. 1367. Distribution of population in Upper Jazira. Beirut, April 1939.

19 According to various lists elaborated by the Intelligence Services, we can confirm that the nucleus of the Khoybun at the time of its creation was made up of Jaladat Badirkhan (1893–1951), Kamuran Badirkhan (1895–1978), Sureya Badirkhan (1883–1938), Memduh Selim (1897–1976), Mehmed Chukru Sekban (1881–1960), Ihsan Nouri (1893–1976), Amin Raman (Amin Perikhane, ?–1928), Bozan (1895–1968) and Mustafa Shahin (?–1953), Shaykh 'Abd al-Rahman Garisi (1869–1932), and Rifat Mevlazande (?–1930). The arrival of new Kurdish refugees in 1929 gave new energy to the nationalist organization. Among them were Akram Jamil Pasha (1891–1974), Qadri Jamil Pasha (1892–1973), 'Uthman Sabri (1905–93), Ahmad Nafiz Zaza (1902–68), Arif Abbas (1900–84), and Shewket Zulfi (1899–?).

20 *AIR 23/416*. Special Service Officer Mosul to Air Staff Intelligence. "Form of oath. Khoybun Society." Baghdad, February 26, 1930.

21 *AIR 23/414*. Memo from Air Headquarters Baghdad to D.I.G. of Police. "List of Kurdo-Armenian nationalists." Baghdad, December 4, 1928.

22 *FO 371/13827/E 2122*. Memo from the British Consulate in Detroit, April 18, 1928.

23 In 1927, while the refugee Kurdish intelligentsia in the Levant prepared for the emergence of the Khoybun, Ihsan Nouri, ex-Ottoman army officer, visited Ararat, a rebellious region of Turkey situated in the extreme northeast of the country. Ihsan Nouri was named by the Khoybun central committee "Commander in General of the Kurdish forces" assuring a certain military discipline among the men of the Jelali tribe. However, the Turkish offensive of 1930, added to the hostile attitude adopted by the Soviet Union and Persia, drove Ihsan Nouri to surrender. Confronted by the gravity of the situation, the Khoybun leaders decided to undertake military action along the line of demarcation of the Turko-Syrian border in order to divert the Turkish troops. This action was, however, doomed to fail.

24 The struggle between the Milli clan and the Badirkhan brothers for the representative monopoly of the Kurdish nationalist movement to the mandatory authorities further weakened the movement. In effect, Kahlil and Mahmud bin Ibrahim Pasha brought very limited support to both the Khoybun nationalist committee and the Kurdish cultural movement between 1930 and 1940, each of them marked by the shapes of Jaladat and Kamuran Badirkhan. Faced with their loss of influence in the Kurdist movement, the Millis concentrated progressively on the reconstruction of their traditional position in the Syrian interior. While the larger part of the Milli tribe eventually settled on the Syrian side of the border at Ras al-'Ayn, it is paradoxically the refounding of the city of Raqqa by the French authorities that really cemented the Millis' role within republican Syrian society. Owing to their long presence in the region and especially their close association with several of the most prominent local Bedouin groups, the Millis emerged as one of the leading notable families of the city. I thank Stefan Winter for his additional information on the Millis and their installation in the town of Raqqa.

25 *FONDS RONDOT, Dossier Kurdes de Syrie*. Captain Azziz, Inspector of Special Services in the Levant. Muhafazat of Jazira, no. 254/HA/28. Hasaka, February 5, 1941.

26 *SHAT, 4H 387, Dossier* no. 3. Free France General Delegation in the Levant. Inspection of Special Services of Aleppo, no. 406/S.P. Aleppo, August 1, 1942.
27 The delegation received by D. Solod in Damascus consisted of Jaladat Badirkhan as well as Kurdish deputies (probably Hasan Hajo and the Shahin Bey brothers). The second Kurdish delegation was received in Beirut and consisted of Cigerxwîn, Nur al-Din Zaza, and Memduh Selim. Soon afterward the Soviet legation in Beirut received another visit from Dr Nafiz, Akram Cemil Pasha, and Cigerxwîn. This last delegation again delivered a memorandum to D. Solod for the San Francisco Conference and some documents on the subject of the Kurdish question. *CADN, Fonds Beyrouth, Cabinet Politique*, no. 802. Délégation Général de France au Levant, no. 853/D.B. Beirut, May 8, 1945.
28 *CADN, Fonds Beyrouth, Cabinet Politique*, no. 802. Délégation Général de France au Levant, no. 1766/D.B. Beirut, September 5, 1945.
29 *Hawar* boasted an illustrated supplement, *Ronahî*, which was above all a French propaganda tool in favor of France and the Allies.
30 *Roja Nû* included an illustrated supplement, *Stêr* ("The Star"). The four-page supplement was published exclusively in the Kurdish language and with numerous illustrations.
31 Born in 1904, Pierre Rondot entered the military school at St-Cyr in 1922 and joined the Foreign Legion in 1926. Accepted in 1928 into the *Service de Renseignements* (Intelligence Service), he was transferred to *La Section d'études du Levant* in Beirut, where he was in charge of relations with the patriarchs of the institution. He met Robert Montagne who directed him toward the study of the Kurds in the framework of the French Institute of Damascus. He got to know Jaladat and Kamuran Badirkhan who soon became "loyal friends" (Rondot 1993: 98–9). He learned Kurdish, led inquiries into the social life of Kurds in Syria and worked, albeit unofficially, in collaboration with the Badirkhan brothers on the correction and supervision of the revue *Hawar*, in particularly with regard to the French part.
32 Born in 1914, Roger Lescot earned a Bachelor of Arts degree and a diploma in Arab literature in 1935. He then earned diplomas in Turkish and Persian. In 1935, Lescot started to study Kurdish following the footsteps of Rondot and envisaged the edition of a thesis on the Kurds. He twice visited the Yazidis in Northern Syria in 1936. Lescot is also the author of a Kurdish grammar book which appeared in the collections of *L'Ecole Supérieure d'Arabe* in Damascus (Lescot 1991). He collaborated with Kamuran Badirkhan in the drafting of a Kurdish/French dictionary, to this day unpublished. During the World War II, Lescot participated actively in the Kurdish cultural movement, publishing numerous articles in French in the revues *Hawar*, *Ronahî*, and *Roja Nû*, translating proverbs, stories, and legends, including the epic *Mamê Alan*, origin of *Mem û Zîn* by Ahmad Khani.
33 As Pierre Rondot confessed in 1940 in his private journal, "I played their game, I kept their secrets, I was their accomplice. Their testimony today is my reward" (Blau 2000: 101).
34 Born in 1900, Father Thomas Bois came to join the new generation of Kurdish specialists in France between the Wars. In 1936, he was chosen to host the new Dominican mission in Jazira. His duty was to draw up a study of the Nestorians and the Kurds with a view to initiating a ministry for this community. He came into contact with Pierre Rondot and Roger Lescot and in 1940, left Jazira where he collaborated momentarily with Memduh Selim, eminent member of the Khoybun League. Bois wrote, from 1947, many works in all the disciplines of Kurdology: language, religion, folklore, history, and sociology.
35 Elaboration implies the broadening of the language's functions. In other words, the proposed norm had to adapt to all registers of communication and to all modern needs

146  *Notes*

through the creation of new words and neologisms or the borrowing of foreign words in order to refer, for example, to new techniques. Implementation assumes in turn the acceptance of the norm by governmental agencies, institutions, writers, and journalists. Activities such as the publication of journals, educational manuals, books, and the use of the norm by the *mass media* are all part of the process of implementation.

36  *CADN, Fonds Beyrouth, Cabinet Politique*, no. 1055. The Plenipotentiary Minister, High Commission Delegate to the Councilor of the High Commission. Beirut, July 25, 1933.

37  Kamuran Badirkhan was responsible for night classes in Beirut. The offer widened in 1938 with the foundation of a school in Damascus under the direction of 'Uthman Sabri and another school in Amuda. However, all these private initiatives failed in the long term.

38  Certain Koranic schools in Northern Syria eventually became "Kurdish schools" where the Kurdish classics (epic poems and mystical works) found a place. In 1932, Kurdish was the language of choice in a dozen schools of the mullahs in Jazira. *FONDS RONDOT, Dossier Kurdes de Syrie.* Report manuscript by Pierre Rondot on Kurdish school rights for the attention of the French Minister for Foreign Affairs, s.l., 1932.

39  Each literate Kurd (agha, shaykh, intellectual) was supposed to exercise the role of teacher for the others.

40  Nur al-Din Zaza (Usif 1941: 851–2) left us one of the rare accounts of the economic consequences of this crisis on the lives of Kurdish peasants in Jazira:

> It's the monsoon season [...]. Women have left their children and babies on the ground among the dust and dirt [...]. Children between 10 and 12 years old help them. They are half naked, barefoot and with shaven heads [...]. Most have already sold their worthless houses because they were starving and naked, perhaps also in debt. What remains will be taken in autumn by the hands of unscrupulous traders. Oppression by officers and the police is also their lot. There are still the shaykhs; after the monsoon and the beatings, their remains the belief of the shaykhs.

41  *CADN, Fonds Beyrouth, Cabinet Politique*, no. 1054. Petition addressed to General Billotte, High Commission Delegate in Syria. Aleppo, May 9, 1924; *CADN, Fonds Beyrouth, Cabinet Politique*, no. 1054. Petition addressed to General Billotte, High Commission Delegate in Syria. Aleppo, April 1, 1924; *CADN, Fonds Beyrouth, Cabinet Politique*, no. 569. Petition addressed to the High Commissioner, from the leaders of the Kurdish tribes in Jazira. Beirut, May 17, 1924.

42  *MAE, Quai d'Orsay, série Levant 1918–40, sous série Syrie-Liban*, no. 181. Memorandum presented by Sureya Badirkhan to Philippe Berthelot, general secretary to the Ministry for Foreign Affairs. Paris, August 7, 1928.

43  *CADN, Fonds Beyrouth, Cabinet Politique*, no. 1055. The Minister for French Foreign Affairs to M. Gaston Maugras, French High Commissioner. Paris, November 3, 1928.

44  *SHAT, 4H 319, Dossier* no. 3. The Director of Army General Security, to the Head of Press Services and of French Forces Propaganda in the Levant, no. 465/C.E/R. Beirut, January 19, 1943.

45  Ibid.

46  The development of small towns in Jazira, the colonization, economic development, and pacification of the extreme northeast of Syria was the result of the political will of the mandatory power. With the development of small towns and villages, France hoped to force the settling of the nomad tribes of the region in order to rid itself of the numerous conflicts linked to the pasture ownership. France, relying on the policy already

initiated by the Porte, chose to address the leaders directly, making them privileged interlocutors in order to assure security and to restrain their nomadic wanderings in the steppe. Apart from the official character of their rights of possession, the great tribal leaders became "sedentary" and received other advantages in the form of indemnities as well as legislative and property-linked measures that were in their best interests. In exchange, the mandatory power encouraged the leaders to develop their arable land, on the condition sine qua non that it be conceded. Having little interest in agriculture, the tribal leaders called on the help of Kurdish and Christian peasants to work their land.

47 Among the Kurdish tribe partisan to the Syrian nationalists, we can name the Tchitie clan of Hajji 'Ali, the Pinar 'Ali tribe of Husayn 'Ali, and the Dakkuri tribe of Sa'id Agha and Shukri Bey.

48 Other "autonomist" leaders were: Nayef Bey Mustafa Pasha (Miran), 'Abd al-Meri (Alian), 'Abd al-Agha Khalo (Mersinie), Nayef Hasan (Milli), Hajji Darwish (Kikie), Ahmad Agha Ayo (Yazidi), 'Abd al-Aziz Husayn (Tchitie). In the Jarablus caza, the Shahin Bey brothers represented the autonomist option.

49 The figure of shaykh Daham al-Hadi was central to the development of events in Jazira between 1936 and 1939. Although defeated in the legislative elections of 1936 by the autonomist's candidate, he harvested fruit in the middle term. In fact, some of the Arab and Kurdish tribes changed sides joining the partisans of Damascus. The key to success for shaykh Daham al-Hadi was the use of religious propaganda against the Christians.

50 *CADN, Fonds Beyrouth, Cabinet Politique,* no. 494. French Ambassador, Damien de Martel, to His Excellency the Minister for Foreign Affairs. Beirut, May 3, 1938.

51 *SAULCHOIR, Haute Djézireh, Dossier 45, Vol. II.* "The Manifesto from Jazira", April 1938.

52 *FONDS RONDOT, Dossier Presse Orientale.* Extract from the newspaper *Al-Ayam,* July 11, 1932.

53 *SAULCHOIR, Haute Djézireh, Dossier 45, Vol. II.* Declaration by Michel Dome, President of the Qamishli municipality to His Excellency the Count of Martel, High Commissioner, July 23, 1937.

54 For Goffman the concept of "framework" refers to schemas of interpretation to "localize, perceive, identify and label" events and situations with a view to organizing and directing action. The "mandatory framework" applies here to the mandatory authorities' discourse on the Syrian "Mosaic, which legitimizes the creation of local autonomies for the Druzes and the Alawites (Goffman 1974).

55 According to the British Consul at Aleppo, the autonomist flag is made up of two small French tricolors, a cross, a crescent, and two sheaves of wheat on a white background. *PRO, FO 371/23276/E1894.* Letter from Sir Davis, British Consul in Aleppo to the Foreign Office. Aleppo, March 6, 1939.

56 *SAULCHOIR, Haute Djézireh, Dossier 45, Vol. II.* "My Diary" by Father Thomas Bois, July 1937.

57 Since the preparation of legislative elections in 1936, a group of Syrian nationalist partisans was formed in Amuda and in the surrounding villages. The Kurdish leader Sa'id Agha of the Dakkuri tribe and leaders of Milan and Kikie tribal factions sided with Damascus, rallying behind the National Bloc candidate Daham al-Hadi. The revolt of 1937 which erupted in Hasaka and Qamishli prepared the ground for revenge by the partisans of Damascus. On August 9, 1937, about 500 men from the Dakkuri, Milan, and Kikie tribes attacked the Christian quarter in Amuda.

58 Chronicle from the newspaper *Al-Bashir,* August 18, 1938.

59 *SAULCHOIR, Haute Djézireh, Dossier 45, Vol. II.* Letter from Thomas Bois dated August 4, 1937; *PRO, FO 371/20849/E6059.* Letter from Sir Davis, British Consul to the Foreign Office. Aleppo, March 17, 1937.
60 Quoting Msgr Hebbé, "the trouble is that there are now differences of opinion between the French officers of the Special Services and those of the Bedouin Control. Daham al-Hadi would have said that it is the French Officer of the Bedouin Control who led him in that direction [anti-autonomist propaganda]". *SAULCHOIR, Haute Djézireh, Dossier 45, Vol. I.* Letter from Msgr Hebbé, Syriac Catholic Bishop, to Cardinal Tappouni. Hasaka, May 2, 1936.
61 *CADN, Fonds Beyrouth, Services Spéciaux*, no. 2202. Frontier Post at 'Ayn Diwar, no. 3/AN/29. 'Ayn Diwar, January 25, 1945.
62 The Kurdish deputies' texts underline the problems of corruption among Arab functionaries, the lack of schools, hospitals, and roads in Jazira, and finally, the privileges of the Bedouin tribes before tribunals in cases of conflict with Kurdish tribes. *CADN, Fonds Beyrouth, Services Spéciaux*, no. 2202. Army Security. Damascus, January 15, 1945.

## 2 Syria in transition, 1946–63

1 Initially the region of Ras al-'Ayn belonged to Khalil Bey Ibrahim Pasha, chief of the Kurdish tribe of Millis. After World War II, the area was divided into half between Khalil Bey and the two brothers, Asfar and Najjar, who were Christians from Diyarbakir, the latter taking up the costs. A similar arrangement brought the two brothers together with the Shaykh 'Abd al-Rahman, chief of the Arab tribe of Tay, who formed a partnership to work the land in Amri, to the southeast of Qamishli (Gibert and Fevret 1953: 94).
2 During the Ottoman Period, the territory of Jazira, like most of Syria, was governed under land laws called "amiria." Under these laws, undeveloped lands belonged to the state and could be conceded to occupants who could increase their value. The mandatory departments preserved this system. They were happy to conduct brief examinations to grant the authorizations as required, often granting petitioners control over much larger pieces of land than they were capable of using effectively. Usually, the mandatory administration did not know the farmer or *fellah* any better than the previous administration had. Only the large landowners, sedentary or nomadic, were able to argue their rights or solicit concessions. The first agrarian reforms did not take place in Jazira until 1958 (Rabo 1984: 217–22).
3 According to Albert Hourani, the "politics of notables" was contingent upon three factors: a cultural context that encouraged hierarchical relationships which bound clients to their patrons, the domination of urban society by important families who had access to both economic resources and higher political authority, and a degree of autonomy for local notables that allowed them to exercise variable degrees of authority in local affairs (Hourani 1968: 41–68). In other words, the political society of Syria was characterized, according to this model, by vertical and parochial ties of dependency.
4 The Syrian Communist Party (SCP) was founded in 1931. During the 1930s, dominated by minorities (most notably the Armenians), the SCP experienced a process of "Arabization" in its structural cells. However, the SCP always remained dominated by minorities.
5 The Syrian Popular Party (SPP) founded in 1932 by Antoun Sa'da, son of a Greek Orthodox Lebanese, managed to unite a large number of minorities under a Syrian nationalist project. Syrian nationalism, competing with Arab nationalism, and the

secular aspects of the program of the SPP attracted, above all, non-Arab Christians, Druzes, and Alawites, in addition to Kurds.
6 The Ba'ath Party (the Arab Renaissance Party) was officially founded in 1946 under the direction of Michel Aflaq, son of a family from the large Christian bourgeoisie, and Salah Bitar, a Sunni Muslim. The Ba'ath was first developed as a national liberation movement in opposition to the French. It later called itself an organized response to what its founders referred to as the ideological insufficiencies of the older generation of Syrian nationalists.
7 Although some Damascene Islamist populist groups developed autonomously during the French Mandate, the Syrian Muslim Brotherhood headquarters was established by Mustafa Sibai, born in Homs to a prominent family of *'ulama* in 1945. Under Sibai's leadership, the Syrian Muslim Brotherhood developed differently from its Egyptian counterpart, created in 1928. It was not so much an underground revolutionary movement (unlike the latter), but functioned to a great extent within the mainstream Syrian political framework, in the public sphere and in parliamentary life.
8 Arab nationalism spread across the Middle East in the mid-1950s, especially following the Suez War in 1955 and the Iraqi Revolution in 1958. In 1952, Gamal Nasser's Free Officers had staged a coup and gained control in Egypt, and on February 22, 1959, Syria, led by the then ruling National Front and Nasser's Egypt, formed the United Arab Republic.
9 In 1941, Great Britain and the United States committed themselves to promoting the right of all people to choose the form of government under which they wished to live and wished to see sovereign rights and self-government re-established for those from whom it had been taken by force. The principles and ideas proclaimed by the charter applied, in theory, to the entire world.
10 According to Sinemxan Badirkhan (daughter of Jaladat Badirkhan), the movements of her father were controlled by police. Otherwise, it was feared that he would have attempted to stand as an independent candidate in the Syrian elections of 1949. Arrested at Aleppo by Syrian authorities, Jaladat was sent back to Damascus and placed under house arrest. Interview with the author, Irbil, September 2006.
11. When Syria became embroiled in the first Arab–Israeli war in 1948, Kamuran Badirkhan was working for Israeli intelligence. According to some sources, Kamuran was sent to Transjordan, Syria, and Lebanon with a view to examining how the Arab state's war effort could be disrupted. He reported back proposing that Israel should help organize an uprising of discontented minorities, including the Kurds (Randal 1997: 188; McDowall 1998: 15).
12 Other young Kurdish nationalists, including Nur al-Din Zaza, members of the Hajo family, or Ismet Sharif Vanly, opted to study in Beirut in foreign universities and colleges. After the defeat of all military and diplomatic attempts to create an independent Kurdistan, they dreamed first of raising the level of teaching of the new "elites" who would go on to provide better service to the country. Vanly claimed to have "studied law with the objective of nullifying the Treaty of Lausana and its clauses which were unfavorable to the Kurds." After leaving Beirut, Vanly went to Lausana to pursue his studies and begin his "mission." Interview with the author, Lausana, December 2006.
13 *CADN, Fonds Ankara, Ambassade*, no. 104. Minister of the Interior. Direction of general information. Paris, December 22, 1949.
14 *CADN, Fonds Beyrouth, Cabinet Politique*, no. 802. French General Delegation in Levant. Army Security. Beirut, May 6, 1946.
15 Although Khalid Bakdash is often cited as an example of an "Arabized Kurd," it seems that his attitude towards Kurdish ethnicity was complex. Certainly Bakdash battled against Kurdish nationalism. But Maxime Rodinson deplored that fact that he began to

## 150  Notes

forget his role as an Arab chief [...] his innate pride and his desire for power causing Khalid to put his "Kurdism" in the forefront when his self-control slipped under the influence of alcohol. At these times, he would brag of his Aryanism as compared with the Semitic Arabs who surrounded him." (Rodinson 1972: 420)

Furthermore, Bakdash held on to his relationships with Kurdish nationalist representatives. For example, he visited certain people who were engaged in the Kurdish movement like Rewshen Badirkhan, the wife of Jaladat Badirkhan. Sinemxan Badirkhan recalled that "with us, he (Khalid Bakdash) spoke in Kurdish, and his wife, too." Interview with the author, Irbil, September 2006.

16 Traditional Kurdish notables negotiated pragmatic allegiances during the French Mandate and maintained these same ties during the first years after independence. Thus, Kurdish notables in Damascus, like 'Ali Agha Zilfu, a wealthy landowner, maintained relations with both the Kurdish nationalists and the communists, especially with his *protégé*, Khalid Bakdash.

17 In Iraq, the same logic explains the large presence of Kurds, Jews, and Shi'is in the Iraqi Communist Party.

18 *FO 195/2650/1827/6/509*. Information no. 7885. Damascus, September 25, 1950.

19 The minister of interior, Rashid Barmada; the director of police and security, Major Shawkat; and the director of police of Aleppo, Captain Bakri Kotrash, were all Kurds. Ibid.

20 'Abd al-Baki Nizam al-Din was allied with the National Bloc against the autonomist candidate, Hasan Hajo, since the time of the legislative elections of 1943. At the time, his candidacy in Jazira benefited from the support of certain clans of the Arabic tribe Tay and some Kurdish tribes, such as the Tchities, the Millis, and the Dakkuris.

21 The sympathy Husni Za'im may have felt for Antoun Sa'da did not stop him from betraying him. In fact, after the flight of the leader of the SPP of Lebanon, Za'im offered him asylum in Syria and promised to protect him. Once he was in Syria, Za'im delivered Antoun Sa'da to the Lebanese authorities, and after a brief trial, he was executed on July 8, 1949. Colonel Sami al-Hinnawi, a member of the SPP, wanted to avenge the death of Sa'da and proceeded with a *coup d'état*. He proceeded to have Husni Za'im arrested and had him executed.

22 Fawzi Selo studied at the military school in Homs where he was a member of the Special Forces. He participated in the Arab–Israeli war of 1948, where he was very close to Husni Za'im. When Za'im acceded to power in 1949, Selo became the military attaché at the Syrian–Israeli peace negotiations. With the *coup d'état* of Adib al-Shishakli, Selo approached him and became his confidant. In July 1953, Selo became the president of the republic. In spite of this nomination, al-Shishakli had effective control of Syrian politics.

23 Despite the cultural, social, and political integration of the Barazi family in the Arab environment of the town of Hama, Muhsen Barazi worked during the 1930s with Jaladat Badirkhan on the project of latinizing the Kurdish alphabet. Interview with Ismet Sharif Vanly, December 2006.

24 *CADN, Ankara, Ambassade*, no. 104. M. Jacques-Emile, Minister of France in Damascus to His Excellence the Minister of Foreign Affairs (Africa – Levant). Damascus, December 5, 1951.

25 Ghaleb Mirzo was Muhafiz of Hawran, Muhammad Sa'id al-Yusuf (descendant of the Kurdish notability of the Syrian capital), was appointed acting-Muhafiz of Damascus, whilst 'Abd al-Hamid Sarraj, a young officer, was placed by Husni Za'im in the Military Intelligence Office.

26 Interview with Sinemxan Badirkhan. Irbil, September 2006.
27 Neither Sabri nor Cigerxwîn give the exact names.
28 At the time of the signing of the Turko-Syrian border protocol concluded in Ankara on June 2, 1929, Turkey and mandatory Syria created a permanent border commission to address the question of security. During these meetings, Turkey demanded several times that the mandatory authorities deliver the Kurdish chiefs of Khoybun to the Ankara government. The French representatives never gave in to these Turkish demands, well aware that the "Kurdish card" could be used, if necessary, against Turkey.
29 When questioned regarding this hypothesis, Sinemkhan Badirkhan responded with conviction that Za'im had attempted to mobilize a kind of Kurdish *asabiyya* in order to remain in power after the fashion of As'ad clan among the Alawites starting in 1970. Interview with the author. Berlin, April 2007.
30 On February 5, 1958 the proclamation was ratified by the Egyptian and Syrian parliaments, the sole dissenting vote belonging to the communist leader, Khalid Bakdash.
31 The new policies were only slowly applied due to technical problems and deceptive devices used by landowners who manipulated the definition of irrigated or nonirrigated land by removing pumps or dividing their lands among family, while respecting the fixed rules of the law. It was, however, implemented in the Ghuta of Damascus, as a form of punishment for the Damascene political class, and also implemented in parts of Jazira.
32 According to the local version of events, the projectionist and other administrators of the cinema had left when the fire broke out, and all exits had been blocked from the outside. When the residents of Amuda tried to save the lives of the children, the police came between them and the fire claiming that it was "too dangerous."
33 The founding of the KDPS took place in Damascus, at the home of Rewshen Badirkhan, widow of Jaladat Badirkhan. This choice illustrates that, in spite of the desire of the directors to create a new movement with a "progressive" program, the ties between the "old" and the "new" generations persisted. Interview with Sinemxan Badirkhan, Irbil, September 2006.
34 The power grab of General 'Abd al-Karim Qasim, on July 14, 1958, put an end to the monarchy in Iraq. It inspired hope among the Kurds, insofar as the provisionary constitution of July 7 recognized, for the first time, that the Arabs and Kurds were tied to each other. Barzani, the legendary leader of the KDP, came back to Iraq after a long period of exile. At this time, General Barzani was engaged in pro-Soviet posturing and, as a result of his close relation with Iraqi Communist Party, became allied to Qasim. This coalition was disapproved of by Damascus, because it relied on two undesirable allies, both for the Ba'ath and the Nasserists. However, between the end of 1960 and the beginning of 1961, relations with Qasim diminished. Kurdish language newspapers were forbidden and General Barzani sought refuge in Barzan, his fiefdom. Soon after, Qasim unleashed a war against the KDP that lasted 9 years.
35 The prosecutor demanded a death sentence for Nur al-Din Zaza, 'Uthman Sabri, and Rashid Hamo and imprisonment of 2–6 years for the other detainees. Thanks to an international campaign, their death penalties were reduced to a year and a half and prison sentences to 1 year and 7 months.
36 At the time of the elections of 1961, Nur al-Din Zaza ran as a candidate for the town of Qamishli with a group of candidates that consisted mostly of Kurds. According to Zaza, before the first favorable election results with the Kurdish nationalist group, the local authorities proceeded with diverse measures of intimidation against the voters and representatives of the KDPS in the voter's office. They would also stuff the ballot boxes with the names of the government candidates (Zaza 1982: 181–2).

37 Despite the attempts at reconciliation of the KDP during the year 1961, Qasim chose to launch himself into ultranationalist politics. He raised the question of Kuwait by proclaiming the "Iraqness" of this territory, "stolen" by the British. On July 1, 1961, at the request of the Amir of Kuwait, British troops were sent to dissuade Iraq from interfering with this new independent state.
38 It seems that the Syrian authorities exaggerated the extent of the phenomena as a way of justifying the 1962 census. *FO 371/164413/E41821/1.* "Report on the census taken in the province of al Hassakeh." From T.E. Bromley (Damascus) to G.F. Hiller (London), November 8, 1962.

## 3 The Ba'athist system and the Kurds

1 The struggle evolved between the National Command of the Revolutionary Council (NCRC; dominated by Aflaq and Bitar) and the National Command of the Party, on the one side, and the Military Committee and the Regional Command (the latter dominated by the military and young marxists), on the other. These four groups were in competition with one another.
2 Besides the Ba'ath, the other members of the front were the Communist Party, the Arab Socialist Union (pro-Nasser), the Arab Socialist Movement (partisans of Akram Hourani's orientation), and the Organization of Socialist Unionists (ex-Ba'athist Nasserists).
3 Intellectuals (journalists and professors) were among the Arab nationalists of the first generation which defended the Arab culture including Shukri al-Quwwatli, Shukri al-Asali, 'Ali Rida al-Rikabi, Lutfi al-Haffar, Ahmad, and Muhammad Kurd 'Ali.
4 It is important to note, however, that the ideologies of Arab nationalism were aware of obstacles to the formation of a western-style nation. They considered that there were two dynamic constituent elements of their social reality: the *'asabiyya* (group solidarity) and religion. In order to condemn the divisive aspects of the *'asabiyya,* the western elites wanted to preserve the esprit de corps but to change the object: it was necessary to replace it with the community or the national community. In other words, it was necessary to create a nationalist *'asabiyya* (Méouchy 1995: 121).
5 Participants in the populist organizations came from a wide range of social backgrounds: wealthy grain merchants and the local "petty bourgeoisie," landowning notables and merchant *'ulama,* Bedouin shaykhs and local bullies.
6 Certain Arab nationalist ideologies cite some explicit sources of inspiration. Such is the case for Sati' al-Husri (1882–1963), for example, who was influenced in his concept of the nation by the German philosophers Herder and above all Fichte, most notably in what concerns the nation as understood by *Stamme* (clan or tribe). But, it is intellectually problematic to establish direct connections between ideas and their creators and their concrete application in the Middle-Eastern political scene, without taking into account the effects of these having been adopted into a local setting.
7 In spite of Aflaq's "overtures" to integrate the Kurds into the "Arab fatherland," he would have refused to allow the Kurdish members of the Arab Socialist Party led by Akram Hourani into the new Ba'ath Arab Socialist Party, even though it was a fusion of these two parties (Seida 2005: 181).
8 In reality, the ambitions of the Ba'ath were more modest. Thus, from 1966 to 1975, the Syrian Ba'ath seemed to be regionalist, limited to Syria. Next, it more or less adopted the views of Greater Syria which had already been formulated by the Syrian Populist

Party in 1930. The concept of "Grand Syria" comprised the nations of Syria, Lebanon, Jordan, and Palestine.
9 Oliver Roy's definition of *'asabiyya* (1997) is suitable to the Syrian regime. *'Asabiyya*, according to Roy, was defined as a particular social network, in which the relationships are largely predetermined by membership in a family, clan, or community. Contrary to other social networks – like political parties or unions – the solidarity of its members precedes the existence of an objective justifying the creation of a group.
10 The over-representation of minorities (Druzes, Alawites, and Isma'ilis) in the Syrian army during the postmandatory period cannot be explained simply by its French heritage. According to Hanna Batatu, there were two more significant causal factors. The depressed economic condition of the Alawites can be used to explain their large numbers in the army. The army was seen as a secure job. In addition, prior to 1964, Syrians were permitted to buy exemptions from military service (*badal*) for the sum of 500 pounds. In the following years, the practice was discouraged and the *badal* raised significantly. For the peasants, *badal* was simply too expensive, and they could not avoid the military service. Ultimately, however, it was the rise of the Alawite's dominance in the officer corps that assured their decisive control of the armed forces (Batatu 1999: 158).
11 According to the organization Human Rights Watch, there were, in the beginning of the 1990s, up to fifteen departments dedicated to security and information gathering in Syria. All were relatively independent, possessing separate administrative departments and heads who reported directly to the president. The security agencies had counteracted one another in coup attempts or for influence and power, creating trends of competition within the state, even with al-As'ad's family (HRW 1991: 40–3).
12 According to Charles Tilly, in such a regime, warlords, bandits, and other political predators typically work their ways in collusion with or in defiance of rulers (Tilly 2003).
13 In 1960, 34,000 people were employed in the public sector, and by 1974 331,000 people were employed in it.
14 In 1964, the author of this 160-page study was promised a government post at Hama and was employed as minister of supplies from 1964 to 1970.
15 When in February 1963 the Ba'ath seized power in Baghdad, its first action as to attack the Communists. But after this had been done, it was feared that the communists had escaped to the Kurdistan region where the Kurdish leader, Mullah Mustafa Barzani, had been in revolt since 1961. So the new cabinet went to war against Barzani in June 1963. In a show of "Arab solidarity," Syria sent a brigade (6,000 men) to the Iraqi Kurdistan, "but in the unfamiliar terrain it suffered many casualties" (Seale 1988: 91). The soldiers were withdrawn from the area by January 1964, having achieved little. Nevertheless, at a military parade in Damascus described as "the most glorious day in the life of the Syrian Arab people," Colonel al-Shair was hailed as a hero by the chief of state, General Amin al-Hafi (Vanly 1992: 152).
16 Muhammad Talab al-Hilal admitted that he was inspired by certain measures taken in Turkey regarding the Kurds, most notably the massive deportations.
17 Beyond the political objective of warding off the "Kurdish danger," the government had planned to displace the Kurdish populations of that region since discovering oil wells at Qarachok and Remilan.
18 The model farms were conceived as avant-garde approaches to agriculture which allowed agricultural workers to familiarize themselves with modern techniques of production, all the while also serving as venues where Ba'athist principles could be cultivated in Jazira.
19 According to diverse sources, 30 years after the settlement of these Arab families, relations with these colonies and the Kurds remained unstable. When one part of the

154  *Notes*

colonies had learned Kurdish and been fully integrated into their physical and cultural environment, for others poor or nonexistent relationship with the Kurds persisted. Interviews conducted in Amuda and Qamishli, April 2001.

20 The Syrian Constitution does not recognize any non-Arab inhabitants in the Syrian Arab Republic. Article 1 states that "[t]he people of the Syrian Arab Region are part of the Arab Nation, who work and struggle to achieve all-embracing unity." Thus Armenians, Assyrians, Circassians, Kurds, and Turkmans are not taken into consideration except in terms of cultural absorption.

21 As for the Armenians, the other significant ethnic minority in Syria, Hafiz al-As'ad also brought about a kind of nonwritten pact: the practice of state control over the communal activities of the Armenians would be relaxed in return for the Armenian's support, or acquiescence. Among the various restrictions imposed on them, foremost of these was the prohibition of open displays of activism (Migliorino 2006: 108).

22 Interview conducted in Qamishli, April 2001.

23 Interview with Mano Khalil (born in Qamishli, 1964), Kurdish film-maker exiled in Switzerland. Bern, March 2007.

24 Decree numbers 1865/S/25 and /24 respectively, December 1989.

25 Qamishli.com (accessed January 8, 2004).

26 In effect, a good number of the author's interviewees – in both Kurd Dagh and Jazira – had Kurdish names inscribed in the Civil Register, after the payment of a bribe.

27 The government retained the results of research realized by numerous foreign archeological teams, many of whom conducted digs in Kurdish regions like Tall Lilan, Shagar Bazaar, Tall Birak, Tall Halaf in the region of Ras al-'Ayn, Shiran in the region of Jarablus, and other sites in the Afrin region. Only findings that supported the official ideology were published.

28 Among the Kurds, Newroz commemorates the mythic rebellion during which Kawa, the blacksmith had saved the nation by killing Dohak, the evil tyrant, who habitually attempted to alleviate the pain of his own wounds by violently sacrificing young men.

29 The Turkish government adopted a similar strategy when faced with the strong Kurdish mobilizations at the time of Newroz (Massicard 2005a: 143–4).

30 In addition to his official function of *mufti*, Shaykh Kuftaru was the director of a private center for the training of Islamic preachers, imams, and teachers at the mosque. This center, which was called Abu al-Nur, also organized sessions for students from other countries.

31 Buti never denied his Kurdish origins and maintained his interest in the Kurdish language and literature. In 1982, Shaykh al-Buti published in Damascus a Kurdish edition of the epic *Mem û Zîn* by the author Ahmad Khani.

32 As a result of this new development, a letter that tackled the issue of the stateless Kurds, signed by forty-seven members of Parliament (comprising both Kurds and Arabs), was addressed to the president of the Parliament on June 8, 1991. However, the prime minister and the Ba'ath Party representative, Abdallah al-Ahmar, refused to open a debate on this issue. Further initiatives met with the same response.

33 As an example, in July of 1956, the arrest of thirty-eight smugglers between Nusaybin and Qamishli by Turkish agents provoked mounting diplomatic tension between the two countries. FO 371/121868. From Sir J. Bowker (Ankara) to Foreign Office (London), July 13, 1956.

34 None of the author's interviewees agreed to give the names of these "lords" for fear of possible reprisals.

35 Interviews conducted in Qamishli and Aleppo, March 2007.

## 4 The Kurdish issue and its transnational dimension

1 The oil-producing states, Saudi Arabia in particular, had subsidized the Syrian economy since the 1970s by way of credit and private investments. In exchange, Riyadh had been able to sanction the initiatives of Damascus in Lebanon and in the Arab–Israeli conflict.
2 By a "regional middle power," Ehtershami and Hinnebusch mean states which may rank as no more than middle powers in the global system but which are key factors in their regional systems. They are distinguishable from lesser regional powers by their assertion of regional leadership in the name of more general regional interests, by their centrality to the regional power balance, their regional spheres of influence, and their ability to resist a coalition of other regional states against them. Finally, such powers generally have leaders enjoying more than local stature and some extra-regional influence. Syria under Hafiz al-As'ad would qualify on all these grounds (Ehteshami and Hinnebusch 1997: 6–7).
3 The pipeline dispute (1972) concerned the amount of royalties to be paid by Iraq for oil exports via Syria, whereas the second dispute (1976) arose when in reaction Iraq decided to build alternative pipelines enabling it to discontinue oil exports via Syria.
4 In early 1975, Syria and Iraq clashed over the sharing of the Euphrates' waters. Damascus decided to raise the Tabqa Dam to its full capacity temporarily depriving Iraq of part of the water it previously received. On April 7, Iraq asked for the Arab League Council to discuss the matter. Syria, according to the Iraqi complaint, stored even more water in the lake than was actually necessary for irrigation and the generation of electricity.
5 The Iranian government had supported Mustafa Barzani with a view to putting pressure on the Iraqi government to revise the Shatt al-Arab Treaty of 1937 and, moreover, it hoped for a weakening of Iraqi power. However, beginning in 1975, the Shah of Iran changed his position and, at the time of the OPEC Summit in March 1975 at Alger, he arrived at an agreement with the Iraqi negotiator, Saddam Husayn. He planned on a strict and efficient control of the border between the two countries, in exchange for which the land and river borders between Iran and Iraq were redrawn to profit Iran. The same day that the agreement was reached, Iran's artillery was evacuated from Iraqi Kurdistan, opening the door to the collapse of the Kurdish resistance in the wake of massive Iraqi air bombardments.
6 From 1963, at the time of the cease-fire negotiations between Barzani and the Iraqi government, tensions between Jalal Talabani and Ibrahim Ahmad on the one side and Barzani on the other turned into an open crisis. The first two, representing a sector of left-leaning intellectuals, took the way of exile and stayed in Iran until 1965. In the beginning of 1966, Jalal Talabani, in the company of other former leaders of the Kurdish Democratic Party, rejoined the government of Baghdad and formed militias to confront Barzani's men. The defeat of Barzani in 1975 and his earlier exile, first in Iran and later in the United States, left the door open for the return, in force, of Talabani to the Kurdish political scene.
7 In November 1980 the PUK started to operate a radio station in Syria, the Voice of Revolutionary Kurdistan, broadcasting to Iraq.
8 About a Kurd of Derik. Interview conducted in Aleppo, March 2007.
9 Interview with a Kurdish journalist. Qamishli, February 2007.
10 However, the democratic Kurdish experiment turned into a checkmate because the two main parties mirrored each other according to the principle of a policy of

dividing the Kurdish institutions, but not on that of resources. Smothered by the double embargo and torn by old differences, a conflict about the sharing of customs resources degenerated, in May 1994, into armed confrontations between the KDP and the PUK. Unable to resolve their differences, goaded by neighboring countries which had little desire to see a consolidated Kurdish state, the two parties led the region into a civil war that lasted until 1997 and was responsible for nearly 3,000 deaths and tens of thousands of displaced persons.
11 The other port of entry in Iraqi Kurdistan was found and is still found, in the vicinity of the town of Zakho, on the Turkish–Iraqi border.
12 These charges were confirmed to the author by different sources in Aleppo and Berlin, March–April 2007.
13 Azadî Diwanî, representative of the Yekîtî (Kurd) party in Iraqi Kurdistan. Irbil, September 2006.
14 Individuals interviewed in Syria confirmed the use of these practices though they refused to give any examples.
15 After attempting to take refuge in Greece, he was driven to Kenya where he took refuge in the Greek embassy there. Thanks to Abdullah Öcalan's carelessness and collaboration between the Turkish and American intelligence services, the Kurdish leader was detected after only a few days. As a result of international pressure, Öcalan was delivered to the authorities and sent to Istanbul in a Turkish aircraft. The PKK leader was subsequently sent to the island prison of Imrali.
16 There are currently 170 PKK members in Syrian prisons. Interview with a Kurdish journalist. Qamishli, March 2007.
17 Despite the discourse adopted by PKK leaders regarding the importance of the democratization of the party, Kamal Shahin, the founder of *Wifaq* and former leader of the PYD, was assassinated on February 17, 2005 by PKK militants – who were then arrested and sentenced – in Sulaymaniyya, in Iraqi Kurdistan. Other members of *Wifaq* were subsequently assassinated – Kamuran Muhammad in August 2005 – or subject to assassination attempts, as was the case for Nadeem Yusif in September 2005. The PYD accused *Wifaq* members of working for the Syrian regime against their cause.
18 Even if the Kurdish peshmergas officially withdrew from the city in response to protests from Turkey, Kurdish fighters came with American soldiers who were in charge of security in Kirkuk. This Kurdish military presence allowed the KDP and PUK to organize the return to Kirkuk of thousands of Kurds who had been deported by the Iraqi regime during the 1970s in an effort to arabize the region.
19 AFP, June 8, 2005.
20 Kurdistanobserver.com (accessed February 8, 2007).

## 5 The Kurdish response and its margins: "dissimulation" of a hidden conflict

1 In reality, most Kurds tend to navigate between Kurdish and Arab cultures.
2 Although there are no official statistics relating to the Kurdish population, we estimate that around 600,000 Kurds out of a total of 1.5 million live in either Damascus or Aleppo.
3 *CADN, Fonds Ankara, Ambassade, 2ème série*, no. 104. M. Jacques Emile, the French Minister in Damascus to his Excellency the Minister of Foreign Affairs (Africa-Levant), no. 1434/ AL, Damascus, December 5, 1951.

4 Advocated not only by Shi'i religious authorities, but also by other minority denominations, "dissimulation" is a strategy of group survival used to avoid repression.
5 It is important to differentiate between these various modes of action, in the sense that these can be employed, either as explicit means of resistance or as survival strategies with varying degrees of intentiality.
6 This unanimist fiction nevertheless had some very real consequences. Even though the majority of Syrians claimed not to believe in the cult of their leader or the principles of the Ba'ath party, their participation in the story contributed to its legitimization. In addition, while their practical understanding of the rules of this cult allowed them to simulate their belonging while incurring minimal risks, at the same time, those who sought to mount an opposition would find their transgression of limited utility in this context (Wedeen 1999: 152–60).
7 Of course, there are many different forms of daily resistance. For example, the act of smuggling on the Turkish–Syrian and Syrian–Iraqi border can be interpreted as a means of protecting transnational social groups in resistance to government pressures to integrate Kurdish regions into the national market.
8 The principal reason is that the terms of the community equation tied the Kurds and local power structures to the Alawites, reducing the prospects of Kurdish Islamist groups.
9 *CADN, Fonds Beyrouth, Cabinet Politique*, no. 802. Stanislas Ostrorog (Beirut) to Georges Bidault (Paris). Beirut, December 10, 1945.
10 Interview with Hoshang Sabri, son of 'Uthman Sabri. Berlin, April 2007.
11 On one side was the camp organized around Izmet Sa'ida and another led by Salah Badr al-Din. Certain members of the Badr al-Din's wing went to fight for Talabani's PUK in Iraqi Kurdistan.
12 Interviews conducted between 2001 and 2007 in Switzerland, Germany, France, Syria, and Iraq.
13 Repertoire of actions is the term used here to describe a pre-existing palette of codified modes of action utilized to varying degrees, depending on group access, by different movements (Tilly 1984: 89–108, 1995: 30).
14 The incorporation of opposition parties translates into a willingness on the part of the incumbent power to negotiate the rules of the game and to take into account their opinions (Baduel 1996: 32).
15 'Abd al-Hamid Hajj Darwish was not arrested between 1960 and 1965 though he was suspected of having sabotaged 'Uthman Sabri's efforts to give new impetus to the KDPS in 1965 in collusion with the Syrian authorities (Gambill 2004: 3). He was arrested in 1965 and released ten months later. In spite of his time in prison, he was accused of collaboration with Damascus.
16 Salah Badr al-Din often changed camps and alliances during his political career. He was accused by the Iraqi KDP of collaborating with Baghdad and pro-Baghdad Palestinian groups, but more importantly, he was accused by Syrian Kurds of having served Damascus during the time he was in Lebanon in the 1970s and 1980s. These suspicions were confirmed in the written memoirs – *Le bîreweriyekanim* (1993) – of a militant of the Iranian KDP, Karim Husani. The passages dedicated to Badr al-Din's contact with the regime in 1981 were broadcast by various Kurdish websites including rizgari.com and amude.com.
17 The Ba'ath adopted a similar policy towards the end of the 1960s regarding the Syrian communists – both the political party and the unions. That is to say, they used a mixture of reprisals and corruption by systematically co-opting a member of the PCS at the

## 158 Notes

head of the Ministry of Transport and a leader of the Arab Socialist Union at a post in State Department. The offer of Hafiz al-As'ad to integrate the communists into the Progressive National Front (PNF) in 1972 provoked a rift in the party in 1973 between those who were represented by Khaled Bakdash – who favored the party's integration – and those led by Riad al-Turk – who were against the party's entry into the PNF.

18 In the towns of Jazira, the regime relied in particular on the Syrians to enlist them in the progovernment militias against the Muslim Brotherhood in the 1980s. The Syrian "clients" also conducted surveillance of Kurdish activities in the region. Testimonies of Kurds in Qamishli. February–March 2007.

19 Testimonies of Kurdish intellectuals in Qamishli. March 2007.

20 According to our sources, this refers primarily to the Kurdish Democratic Progressive Party in Syria of Aziz Da'ud, the Kurdish Democratic Patriotic Party in Syria of Tahir Sadun Sifuk, and the Kurdish Democratic Party in Syria (The Syrian) led by Jamal M. Baqi.

21 "Reticular action" describes actions taken by an individual to play upon their social network in order to launch an initiative (Fliche 2005: 149).

22 The Kurdish Union Party in Syria (Yekîtî-Kurd) is the only party to require the head of the party to alternate every three years. Interview with Husayn Muhammad, Yekîtî's representative in Berlin. April 2007.

23 Interviews conducted in Jazira in 2001 and 2007.

24 Besides traditional portraits of Mustafa Barzani hanging in peoples' homes, there are other such displays of admiration, such as calendars displaying his face and tattoos on peoples' arms, all of which served to cultivate the political myth surrounding Barzani. Finally, television broadcasts via satellite by Kurdistan TV, a channel in support of Barzani, have participated since January 1999 in its enterprise.

25 Interview with the author. Berlin, April 2007.

26 "El Partî" (alparty.org), Kurdish Democratic Progressive Party in Syria (dimoqrati.com), Kurdish Democratic Union Party in Syria (yek-dem.com), Kurdish Union Party in Syria (Yekîtî-party.org), and Kurdish Left Party in Syria (armanc.org).

27 Interview with Muhammad Hamo, journalist and poet from Afrin. Irbil, September 2006.

28 The so-called honor killings are still practiced when a woman is accused of engaging in extramarital or premarital sexual relations. In this case, the family's honor must be redeemed by killing the "guilty" woman. According to various sources, the perpetrators of such crimes are condemned to prison sentences of only six months. Honor killing is defined in Article 548 of the Syrian Penal Code of 1949 (Danish Refugee Council 2007: 14–19).

29 According to inquests held in Syria and Europe, doctors, teachers, lawyers, and shopkeepers fill the ranks of the PKK's guerilla forces, in addition to young men from disadvantaged backgrounds. Therefore, it can be said that the first generation of the PKK were branded with an eminently ideological commitment.

30 View of the majority of Kurds interviewed on this subject in Syria and Germany, March–April 2007.

31 Views of several Kurds from the Afrin region. Interviews conducted in Afrin (April 2001) and Irbil (September 2006).

32 Interview with a Kurdish student from Darbasiya. Irbil, September 2006.

33 There are other parallels to this dynamic – for example, the engagement of young Palestinian militants during the first infitada (1987–93) in the Occupied Territories (Larzillière 2004: 18–19).

34 It is interesting to note that the discourse regarding equality for Kurdish women in the revolutionary utopia of the PKK would draw a good number of women into the ranks

of their guerilla movement. As in Turkey, some women joined the PKK in order to "serve the nation" but also to escape from the pressures of the traditional organization, which was profoundly patriarchal.
35 For this analysis resulting from field studies in Syria the author has drawn on discussions, articles, and lectures by two specialists in Kurdish brotherhoods in Syria: Annabelle Böttcher and Paulo G. Pinto.
36 Sufism is the mystical branch of Islam. It represents the spiritual struggle which demands spiritual purification through asceticism, contemplation, and the invocation of God. Mystical ascension is achieved by passing a series of difficult tests, through which one must be guided by one who has already proven himself (shaykh) and, in the majority of cases, belonging to a group or brotherhood (*tariqa*) whose members have been trained under this individual. A Sufi brotherhood is like an informal school offering a standardized package of spiritual exercises and mystical techniques. These also play an important social and sometimes political role.
37 Khani wrote two texts for use in elementary teaching: an Arabic–Kurdish dictionary in verse form and a catechism in Kurdish.
38 Kurdish shaykhs were already settled in Damascus before the abolition of Sufi orders in Turkey. Such is the case of Isa al-Kurdî who settled in Damascus in 1877, after having studied in Diyarbakir, Mecca, and in Egypt becoming one of the great Sufi shaykhs, and Musa Kuftaru, grandfather of the future *Mufti* of the Syrian republic, Ahmad Kuftaru, who immigrated to Damascus around 1894.
39 *FONDS RONDOT, Dossier Kurdes de Syrie*. A handwritten report by Pierre Rondot on the student rights of Kurds for the French Minister of Foreign Affairs, s.l., 1932.
40 In Kurd Dagh, Shaykh Darwish, a Khoybun member and religious head of the Yazidi, directed a Kurdish school between 1927 and 1928 in the village of Qibar, with the tacit approval of the French officers posted there. Interview with Muhammad Hamo, journalist and poet from Afrin. Irbil, September 2006.
41 The system known by the name *Waqf* (pious endowments) was the principal source of revenue for the religious institutions in the Muslim world until the twentieth century. It allowed the *'ulamas* a certain degree of independence from the authorities.
42 Paulo G. Pinto defines this "official Islam" more as a "field" or a "universe of possible discourses" than a coherent body of doctrines and opinions. Official Islam established therefore discursive limits within which different actors can present their rival visions (Pinto 2007: 340).
43 Testimony of Annabelle Böttcher during the conference "The Kurds in Syria," held in Berlin in March 2003.
44 The principle Sufi religious orders among the Kurds of Syria are the Qadiriyya and the Naqshbandiyya. In Kurd Dagh and in the Kurdish communities in Aleppo and Damascus, the Rifa'iyya is also present.
45 Thus Abdullah Öcalan, leader of the PKK, had himself sanctioned the moves to bring Kurdish nationalism and Sunnism closer together, by explaining several times that "the PKK is more Islamist than the Islamists" (Bozarslan 1998: 843). The Democratic Union Party (PYD), heir to the PKK, had also included in its program an explicit reference to religion being the core element of (Kurdish) social organization. Kurdishmedia.com (accessed January 3, 2007).
46 Peter Van der Veer defines "religious nationalism" as the articulation between discourses and practices grounded in religious communities and the processes of imagining the nation. For religious nationalists in India, for instance, the existence of the nation is given by the sharing of a "common religion" among its members (Van der

Veer 1994: 25–77). However, while for the Hindu and Muslim religious nationalisms in India, religion and ethnicity constituted two separate spheres of social insertion and symbolic representation, the carriers of Kurdish religious nationalism combine ethnic and religious identities in their discourses about Kurdish identity (Pinto 2007: 4–5).
47 The music and dances are accompanied by traditional Kurdish instruments such as the *daf* (drums), the *zurna* (flute), and the Kurdish lute.
48 Peter Van der Veer nevertheless emphasizes that while secular nationalism deals with an abstract concept of the nation that is envisioned before it can be lived as a social reality, religious nationalism builds on a previous construction of religious communities that are experienced as the framework for supralocal identities before they can be imagined as a nation (Van der Veer 1994: xiii).
49 Statements reported by the *Christian Science Monitor*, June 16, 2005.
50 Various Kurdish interviewees attest that, in effect, al-Khaznawi could have become the "new Barzani" for the Syrian Kurds. Interviews conducted in Switzerland, Germany, and Syria, February–April 2007.
51 See the poems and articles dedicated to Mashuk al-Khaznawi on the website khaznawi.com.
52 Various Kurds interviewed from the Kurd Dagh region attest, in effect, that like children they lived their Kurdish identity without problems. The politicization of Kurdish identity came in two ways, the establishment of the PKK in this region and the rural exodus of the inhabitants of Kurd Dagh towards Arab towns and cities like Aleppo and Damascus. Interviews conducted between February and March 2007.
53 However, in Damascus as in Aleppo, an interest in the salvaging of the Kurdish language by the "Arabized" Kurdish communities is perceptible. Kurdish language courses have thus been organized as much for the young as for adults.
54 By way of an example, we have chosen articles published in different reviews: "Xwendevan" ("Reader"), *Stêr*, no. 2; "Kumandc kenc in lê nezan in" ("The Kurds are good but ignorant"), *Hawar*, no. 7, 1932; "Merhele" ("Step"), *Roja Nû*, no. 1, 1943.
55 Thus, for example, Jaladat Badirkhan made a plea to convince Kurdish women not to marry "foreign" men. Moreover, Kurdish women, the children's educators, were called upon to play a "national role" in the transmission of their language to the children given the impossibility of teaching Kurdish in public and private schools (Badirkhan 1941: 770–1).
56 The expression does not intend to suggest the nonpolitical character of the private sphere and in particular of the family. On the contrary, the private sphere has a political dimension as has been demonstrated, for example, in gender studies.
57 The privatization of Kurdish culture is particularly significant as far as the Kurdish language is concerned. In effect, many writers, artists and Kurdish intellectuals are recognized as having learned by themselves to write in Kurd. Interviews conducted in Europe and in Syria between 2006 and 2007. See also the interview with Muhammad 'Ali, a Kurdish writer and grammarian, in efrin.net (accessed June 7, 2007).
58 The Kurdish language remains the language of reference in primary communications in northern Syria as confirmed by a number of testimonies taken from scholarly Kurds during the 1970s, not knowing the Arab language at the time of their entry into obligatory schooling.
59 This open window through which they could express themselves was nonetheless at the mercy of the vagaries of relations and the mood, of the local *mukhabarat*. The payment of bribes to the police agents could also open the door to a certain "normality." Interviews with families from Qamishli (2001) and Kobane (2007).

60 *FO 371/132747E1821/6.* Note from the Direction of Political Affairs. Direction of Africa-Levant. Minute F.D.W. Brown, October 9, 1958.
61 Interview with a Kurdish family from Kobane. Geneva, May 2007.
62 Although the Badirkhan brothers had already called the Yazidis "real Kurds" and referred to Yazidism as the "religion of all Kurds" before the Islamization of the Kurds, this discourse had been largely forgotten by Kurdish nationalism until the PKK found in Yazidism a means of proclaiming pre-Islamic Kurdish unity and the ethnoreligious particularity of the Kurds, compared to their neighbors, in particular, Turks and Arabs (Badirkhan 1932: 289, 1935: 675).
63 According to Malmîsanij, other factors were important for the "spring" of the Kurdish culture: communications development, TV programs in Kurdish, and the return to Syria of some Kurds educated abroad who paid more attention to the importance of the Kurdish language (Malmîsanij 2007: 108).
64 The number of books that can freely be sold in bookshops is very limited with the few books in Kurdish having official permission for publication. Therefore, distribution of books is carried out in alternative ways. Authors tend to distribute and sell themselves their books. Some authors distribute their books with the help of Kurdish folk groups and political parties.
65 Among the most prolific writers of Kurdish reviews edited from the 1980s, we can name 'Abd al-Majid Shakho, Berzo Mahmud, Konê Rash, Helim Yusif, Jan Dost, Keça Kurd, Muhammad Hamo, and Nazir Palo.
66 Interview with an independent journalist in Qamishli, March 2007.
67 A Kurdish intellectual estimated at between 500 and 1,000 the number of people in Qamishli able to read Kurdish. Qamishli has a population of about 200,000 inhabitants. Qamishli, March 2007.
68 I would like to thank Rustum Mahmud, Kurdish journalist and correspondent for the *al-Hayat* newspaper, in Syria, for having sent his paper on the Kurdish press in Syria, which was to be presented during the fourth Badirkhan conference in Berlin in April 2007. Unfortunately, Rustum Mahmud was unable to attend.
69 Interview with the author. Bern, March 2007.
70 The other co-owner was 'Ali Ja'far who, faced with constant police pressure, left Syria to settle in Germany in 1994. After 'Ali Ja'far's departure, Muhammad Hamo changed the name of his bookshop to "Badirkhan Bookshop."
71 Unless indicated, all information has been supplied by Muhammad Hamo to the author. Irbil, September 2006.
72 While being held in jail in Aleppo in 1999, officials told Muhammad Hamo that his crime was very serious: "There are ten illegal Kurdish parties in Syria which demand cultural rights but you actually practice your rights. You are applying in practice what they want in theory!" (Malmîsanij 2007: 142).
73 Interview with Muhammad Hamo. Irbil, September 2006.

## 6 The Qamishli revolt, 2004: the marker of a new era for the Kurds in Syria

1 European, North American, and Arab television and newspapers provided important media coverage to the events in Qamishli. Furthermore, the Internet (amude.com; qamislo.com; and YouTube) played an important role in distributing images of the March 2004 revolt, and occasionally of demonstrations (e.g. the funeral of Muhammad Mashuk al-Khaznawi in 2005).

2 For instance, on April 6, 2005, when the Iraqi Kurdish leader Jalal Talabani was chosen as president of Iraq, Kurds living in Damascus played the Kurdish anthem, *Ey reqib*, in a street celebration. *The New York Times*, April 28, 2005.
3 The categorization "identity" made sense to the actors and designated a category of mobilization in which the demands were tied to issues of ethnic identity or *national* status – which occupied a central place. To analyze this categorization by the actors does not imply acceptance of the existence of an ontological difference between the categories of mobilizations, but rather indicates an "understanding of the logistics and consequences of such a classification" (Massicard 2005b: 89).
4 Collective action here means "all concerted actions of one or several groups searching to accomplish shared goals" (Fillieule 1993: 9). This definition also includes short-lived informal actions originating from improvised groups.
5 Shivan Perwer, a renowned Kurdish singer from Turkey and author of a song dedicated to the martyred village of Halabja, composed another song in honor of Qamishli.
6 The National Salvation Front was led by the former vice-president, 'Abd al-Halim Khaddam (after his defection in the fall of 2005), and the leader of the Muslim Brotherhood, 'Ali Sadr al-Din al-Bayanuni, exiled in Europe. For the first time since its foundation, the Muslim Brotherhood recognized in 2005 the legitimacy of Kurdish grievances.
7 The Reform Party of Syria was founded in 2001 and was integrated into the platform of the Syrian Democratic Coalition. This party presented itself as a secular, liberal alternative to the SNF.
8 The president of the Kurdish Regional Authority of Iraq, Masud Barzani, openly petitioned the Damascus regime to desist in its coercive measures towards the Kurds and to initiate reforms before the Kurdish problem degenerated still further in Syria. AFP, June 8, 2005.
9 The "old guard," Hafiz al-As'ad's influential barons, still play an important role, but they did not constitute a threat to the president's position. Bashar al-As'ad's power derived from various sources: the presidency, being his father's heir regarding the Alawite sect, and the party, the "generational" factor (differences between generations, old and new), and his ability to consolidate his power by systematically appointing trusted people to important positions (Perthes 2004: 8–9).
10 Several authors have questioned the existence of "civil society" in the Middle East (Gellner 1991: 495–510; Krämer 1992: 22–3; Waterbury 1994: 23–47), particularly in Syria (Hinnebusch 1995: 214–42). It is well known that the separation of the state and society is an artificial intellectual argument. In Syria, large parts of society have been placed under guardianship in the guise of corporatism, by means of the creation or takeover of unions and professional associations affiliated with Ba'ath. Today the field of associations remains strongly marked by the power relationships dictated by a regime which, furthermore, has condemned to extensive divisions (Le Saux 2006: 195). We are going to use this operational concept although the "civil society" in Syria remains a composite of associations, of economic interest groups which have neither the same rapport with the state nor the same demands.
11 There are also aid associations for rural development by the granting of micro credit (*Fund for Integral Rural Development of Syria*, founded in 2001), associations for the development of women's economic status (*Modernizing and Activating Women's Role in Economic Development*, founded in 2001), associations devoted to the environmental domain (*Syrian Environmental Association*, founded in 2002), human rights groups (*Human Rights Association in Syria*, founded in 2002), and groups dedicated to fostering a greater civic awareness in the broader Middle East (*Tharwa Project*, founded in 2004).

12 This is not the first time that Syrian associations had tried to intervene in the political debate. In the late 1970s, the Bar Association and Engineers Association called for the release of political detainees, and in 1980, the latter called for freedom of expression and an end to the state of emergency. In March 1980, these organizations and the Pharmacists Association called for a nationwide strike to protest against the lack of reforms. Nevertheless, these initiatives were a one-time occurrence and limited in terms of their effectiveness in accomplishing the depth of the changes demanded.
13 Like the Kurdish movement in Syria, the Syrian (Arab) opposition is fragmented by polar oppositions between secular and religious parties, groups active in Syria and in exile, and finally, reformists and those favoring a more radical change (e.g. regime change).
14 Basically the Committees of Defense of Democratic Freedoms and Human Rights in Syria (CDF), founded in 1989, and a newcomer, the Syrian Human Rights Association (SHRA), formed in July 2000.
15 In spite of this official restriction, and encouraged by massive movements which took place between March 2004 and June 2005, independent activists in Qamishli presented demands to found associations to the Minister of Social Affairs. None of these demands ever came to fruition. According to various sources in Qamishli, February–March 2007.
16 Interview with Azadî Diwanî, Yekîtî representative at Irbil. September 2006.
17 Ibid.
18 Marwan 'Uthman, for instance, has contributed to different Arabic reviews and has been a member of the General Secretariat of the AODEPF (Arab Organisation for the Defense of Expression and Press Freedom).
19 Interview with Azadî Diwanî, Yekîtî representative in Irbil. September 2006.
20 Ibid.
21 The political program submitted to the third convention of the Yekîtî Party in Syria. Available online: http://www.home.c2i.net/Yekîtî/program.htm.
22 Ibid.
23 *Akhbar al-Sharq*, December 14, 2002.
24 They appeared before a military court on January 15, 2003, at which they were referred to the Supreme State Security Court on charges of "inciting religious and ethnic discord." They were released on February 22, 2004.
25 It was not as if this was the first public demonstration organized by the Kurds. However, before, the demonstrations had a spontaneous character and did not involve large numbers of participants. On the other hand, since 2002, a variety of involved areas could be confirmed and a considerable increase in public action, as well as participation in action planned by the established Kurdish organizations.
26 A Damascus-based analyst, reported by Nicholas Blandford. *The Christian Science Monitor*, November 20, 2002.
27 *Le Monde*, March 14, 2004.
28 According to an eyewitness, a first match between the two teams was played in Dayr al-Zur two weeks earlier. On that occasion, some Kurdish fans had expressed sympathy for the Kurdish autonomous region in Iraq and cursed Saddam, which provoked the fans from Dayr al-Zur. As a consequence, clashes between the supporters broke out (Danish Refugee Council 2007: 5).
29 *Sharq al-Awsat*, March 13, 2004.
30 According to several participants, mobile phones were a major source of information and rapid mobilization for Kurds during demonstrations in Qamishli from March 13 to 16, 2004. Qamishli, February–March 2007.

31 Author interview with an eyewitness in Qamishli, February 2007.
32 Ibid.
33 These incidents are reminiscent of the riots which occurred in certain quarters of Hama and Aleppo, but also in Damascus, Homs, and Latakia during the 1970s. Groups of demonstrators had run through the streets shouting slogans attacking the political regime; official headquarters of the Ba'ath Party were pillaged and burned and popular organization officials attacked (Picard 1980: 7).
34 In the Syrian capital, Kurds blocked the principal road to Dummar, a suburb of Damascus, and they damaged several cars before being dispersed by the antiriot police. *Le Monde*, March 14, 2004.
35 Among the signatories of the communiqué were the Association of Human Rights in Syria, the Democratic National Assembly, the Communist Party, and several Kurdish parties. AFP, March 16, 2004.
36 Some 150 decided to leave Syria for refuge in Iraq. Most of these families did not return. Initially settled in a temporary camp in Moqbeli, they were finally provided with housing constructed by the regional Kurdish government. *The Kurdish Globe*, August 20, 2006.
37 The presence of these special forces which came to put down the riots in Qamishli was, at the time of the writing of this book, still visible. In effect, on the main road between Qamishli and Amuda, a public building is still occupied by the army.
38 The *Gamar* (literally "the drowned") are descendants of Arab groups, originally from Raqqa, who lost their lands when dams were constructed nearby during the 1970s. Afterwards they were relocated in Upper Jazira during the implementation of the "Arab Belt" policies.
39 Some of these students were admitted afterwards into Iraqi Kurdish universities. In 2006, there were sixty Syrian Kurdish students in Irbil and eighteen in Sulaymaniyya.
40 According to the Association of the Human Rights in Syria, thirteen Syrians, eleven of whom were Kurds, died under torture in 2004. AFP, April 7, 2005.
41 Author interview with Fadi 'Ali Muhammad, Ferhad's brother. Geneva, October 2005.
42 Although Salah al-Din Kuftaru, the son of the *Mufti* of Syria Ahmad Kuftaru of Kurdish origin, called for "respect for the Kurds" and did not view the Kurds as a "trouble factor," he supported the official version of the "plot" against Syria. AFP, March 19, 2004.
43 AFP, March 16, 2004.
44 At the time of this brief interview, the representatives of Damascus had not offered a single important political concession. The Kurdish delegation had to contend themselves with promises which had been made before concerning the ruling on the case of the 30,000 undocumented Kurds.
45 KurdishMedia.com (accessed August 4, 2006).
46 Idea held by various representatives of the political parties and the Kurds close to this cultural and political arena.
47 Curiously, this opinion had been expressed by all Kurds who had been in exile in Iraqi Kurdistan since 2004. Author interviews in Irbil, September 2006.
48 Interview with the author. Berlin, April 2007.
49 Yekîtî and the PYD kept up the traditional activities expected to commemorate Newroz. The crowd was, however, less impressive than in preceding years. AFP, March 21, 2004.
50 Instigators of nihilistic violence have no faith in the possibility of transforming the existing order, nor in the possibility of creating a new era. Self-suppression becomes the

only solution by which to remove oneself from the existing order so as to avoid any role in its decline.
51 This term describes a form of violence (suicide attempts, immolation by fire, hunger strikes) which relies on the destruction of the actor's body. In the context of these actions, the body becomes a site of self-destruction. These acts share a common willingness of individual expression for a cause that is undesired or under threat.
52 This form of violence stems from a conviction of the imminence of violence or at least of the necessity of deliverance by way of this violence. This violence substitutes fear of death with the belief in the absolute immunity of their god, and in the divine deliverance afforded to his soldiers.
53 Author interviews with several Kurds from Qamishli and Kobane. By the same token, Marwan 'Uthman, leader of the Yekîtî party, stated that the Kurds were "sick of the Syrian oppression and rose up against the Syrian regime." KurdishMedia.com (accessed March 27, 2006).
54 The Kurdish middle-class of Aleppo tend to live in neighborhoods with a large Kurdish population, such as Hamdaniyya, and in traditionally Christian quarters such as the Maydan.
55 The most important are among others Ush al-Warwar (Sunni Muslim from Dayr al-Zur), Tishrin and Mezze 86 (Alawites), Tadammun (Druzes), Dweila dn Tabala (Christians), Jaramana, Falastin, and Yarmuk (Palestinians), Wadi al-Mashari or Zorava and Jabal al-Rizz (Kurds).
56 This new order touched all of the middle class of Qamishli, without making distinctions based on ethnic origin, as well as other Arab towns having welcomed a large number of Iraqi refugees. Author interview with a schoolmaster. Qamishli, March 2007.
57 In Turkey and in Iran, the Kurds are more prolific than the rest of the population. As in Syria, the Kurdish regions in these countries are equally economically undeveloped.
58 Author interview with a Kurdish lawyer from Damascus. Berlin, March 2007.
59 Author interviews with Azadî Diwanî, representative of Yekîtî in Irbil (September 2006), a Kurdish intellectual and a schoolmaster (Qamishli, March 2007).
60 Author interview with Azadî Diwanî, representative of Yekîtî in Irbil. September 2006.
61 A member of this party commented that they thought like Syrian Kurds, but the Yekîtî and their allies thought more "like Kurds who happen to be in Syria" (Wikas 2007: 18). See also the interview with 'Ali Shamdin, member of the central committee of the KDPP, in dimoqrati.com (accessed May 8, 2007).
62 For an analysis of the self-sacrificing violence in the PKK, see Bozarslan (2003: 93–115).
63 For example, Hasan Salih, Yekîtî secretary general, visited all the families of the victims of the riots in Qamishli to express his condolences and to listen to their grievances. Author interview with Azadî Diwanî, Irbil, September 2006.
64 Several Yekîtî and PYD officials were arrested between March and April 2004, others were forced into exile in Europe and Iraqi Kurdistan.
65 Author interviews with Husayn Muhammad, Yekîtî representative in Berlin (April 2007) and with Muhammad Hamo, poet and journalist, in Irbil (September 2006).
66 AFP, March 21, 2004.
67 Amude.com (accessed March 6, 2006).
68 Author interviews with Kurdish students exiled in Iraqi Kurdistan. Irbil, September 2006.
69 Since 2003, the PUK and KDP welcomed exiled Kurdish activists from Syria and provided them with facilities to organize politically. After the approval on March 8, 2004

of the interim Iraqi constitution that recognized the Kurds as an autonomous group and gave Kurds veto power over the drafting of a permanent constitution, the leaders of PUK and KDP signaled that they would not disapprove of Kurdish political agitation in Syria (Gambill 2004: 4).
70 Author interviews with Kurds in Syria, Iraqi Kurdistan, and Europe, between 2005 and 2007.
71 Author interview with a participant in the demonstration on March 13, 2004. Qamishli, March 2007.
72 Author interview with Muhammad Hamo. Irbil, September 2006.
73 Banners with slogans such as "Intifada until the occupation ends" were reportedly seen during the Qamishli revolt. *The Daily Star*, May 6, 2005.
74 On the contrary, the repertoires of action of certain groups can remain unaware for a long time that structural conditions were evolving, suggesting as well that each group had their own temporalities and variable degrees of resistance and susceptibility to change (Filleiule and Bennani-Chraïbi 2003: 73).
75 It is important to recall, however, that the Syrian youth make up the majority of the population of the country. Furthermore, according to the statistics of the United Nations (2004), 60 percent of the population of Syria was less than 19 years old.
76 Between 2004 and 2007, forty-six minors had been tried in relation to the riots of March 2004.
77 The participation of young Kurds in the actions of March 2004 contrasts with the inhibitions of the young Arabs participating in the "Damascus Spring." Author interview with Hasan Abbas, Syrian cultural activist. Washington, November 2005.
78 Author interviews with Yekîtî representatives, statements "off the record."
79 The confrontations between young Kurds and the police at Aleppo occurred regularly between 2004 and 2006, creating a certain social tension particularly in the Kurdish quarter in Ashrafiyya. At the beginning of 2007, twelve youths, three of whom were minors, were condemned to prison for two and a half years after having thrown molotov cocktails at the security forces in 2005. AFP, February 4, 2007.
80 The Kurdo-Arab collaboration was followed up with a series of initiatives in 2005 including the formation of the National Coordination Committee for the Defense of Basic Freedoms and Human Rights and the Committee for the Revival of Civil Society.
81 English version available on-line, http://faculty-staff.ou.edu/L/Joshua.M.Landis-1/syriablog/.
82 Declarations on the Lebanese TV channel *al-Mustaqbal*, reproduced on the Kurdish site amude.com (accessed September 2, 2006).
83 Some oppositional leaders, such as Anwar al-Bunni and Damal al-Labwani, have expressed some openness to the idea of federalism. The former was arrested in May 2006 after having signed, together with 300 Syrian and Lebanese intellectuals, the Beirut–Damascus declaration. The text demanded that Syria improve its relations with Lebanon, first by setting up embassies in each country and by clearly demarcating the border between the two states.
84 Author interview with Husayn Muhammad, Yekîtî representative in Berlin, April 2007.
85 Joe Pace interview with Anwar al-Bunni, *Syria Coment*, August 7, 2005.
86 In 1958, the Iraqi Constitution recognized, for the first time, Kurdish "national rights."
87 Author interview with Faysal Badr, lawyer and member of the Yekîtî's political committee. Berlin, April 2007.
88 Seda Altug, scholar having done her academic field work in Jazira between 2004 and 2006. Email to author, August 2007.

Notes 167

89 Joe Pace interview with Anwar al-Bunni, *Syria Comment*, August 7, 2005.
90 Namely the Arab Socialist Union, the Syrian Communist Party (Riad al-Turk), the Workers' Revolutionary Party, the Movement of Arab Socialists, and the Democratic Socialist Arab Ba'ath Party.
91 See the interview with Shaykh Murshid al-Khanawi, son of Shaykh Mashuk al-Khaznawi, exiled in Norway in khaznawi.com (accessed February 21, 2007).
92 Ciwan Semo, co-organizer of the conference. Email to the author, August 2007.
93 See the full version in KurdishMedia.com (accessed March 20, 2006).
94 For the complete list of people elected and political parties represented in the KNA-S, see amude.com (accessed May 30, 2006).
95 The KNA-S is made up of a presidency (which rotates every six months), an executive committee (president plus two vice-presidents), and various working commissions (internal affairs, media, finances, projects…).
96 Author interview with Gengis Khan Haso, chairman of the KNA-S and representative of the Yazidi community. Berlin, April 2007.
97 The participants in the congress created a provisional committee of five members (four representatives of political parties and one independent). It was decided to reunite in Europe in September 2007 to expand the committee to eleven members, draw up a program together, and open a central office in Europe. Conversation by telephone with Alan Amouni, co-organizer of the congress, March 2007.
98 Author interview with Faysal Badr (member of the central committee of Yekîtî), Husayn Muhammad (Yekîtî representative in Berlin), Sa'id 'Abd al-Majid (representative of the Kurdish Progressive Party, 'Abd al-Hamid Hajj Darwish, in Berlin), Biha Muhammad (president of the Syrian Kurds Association in Berlin-Brandenburg), Berlin, April 2007.
99 Author interviews with Kurds in Europe and Syria.
100 *Syria Times*, June 12, 2005.
101 Apart from the fact that other promises of the state to invest in the region were never honored, the Kurdish parties feared that these irrigation projects would be accompanied by new measures of forced Arabization in Upper Jazira. In July 2007, six Kurdish parties had already denounced the decree of the Minister of Agriculture no. 12/16/MZ of the March 3, 2007 allowing 100 Arab families to settle in the region of Derik, in the heart of Kurdish country. See the protest manifesto in efrin.net (accessed July 6, 2007).
102 Reuters, June 3, 2004.
103 *The Syria Report*, June 16, 2005.
104 Author interview with a Kurdish editor in Qamishli, March 2007.
105 Reuters, July 2, 2007.
106 Some restrictions, particularly in the governorship in Aleppo, seemed to persist, however. Thus, in 2007, an official decree would have forbidden the sale and possession of *zurna* (flute) and *daf* (tambour) with a view to limiting the festivities of Newroz. Author interview with a family in Afrin, March 2007.
107 For instance, Muhi al-Din Shaykh 'Ali, Secretary of the Kurdish Democratic Unity Party, was arrested on December 20, 2006 in Aleppo. He was released two months later.
108 The assembly organized by Yekîtî in Qamishli on the occasion of International Human Rights Day on December 10, 2006 was interrupted by security forces and was ended by confrontations between the demonstrators and the police. Amude.com (accessed December 10, 2006).
109 In Raqqa, for example, authorities allowed Kurds to celebrate the Newroz festival on March 21, 2007. However, the following day, local authorities ordered the destruction of informal dwellings in the Kurdish suburbs.

168  *Notes*

110 According to Sirwan Hajji Husayn, creator of the site amude.com, women were the second group, along with the young, to emerge in an unexpected way at the time of the actions of March 2004. Email to the author, June 2007.
111 This point of view was clearly expressed by Murshid al-Khaznawi. "After the assassination of the shaykh, we have begun to support Kurdish movements from the bottom of our hearts." *The New York Times*, July 2, 2005.
112 Between 2004 and 2005, the demonstrations and marches in the city of Qamishli brought together 10,000–20,000 people, and, in 2007, the actions commemorating the "martyrs" of March 2004 mobilized between 2,000 and 3,000 participants.
113 Author interviews with Kurds in Jazira. February–March 2007. Julie Gauthier noted the same tendency in the region of Afrin at the time of her last field work in Syria in the summer of 2007. Thus, some ex-PKK militants had established relations with the local *mukhabarat* in order to continue with their "dubious" affairs, sometimes even becoming Ba'ath militants. Telephone conversation with Julie Gauthier, August 2007.

**Conclusion**

1 Mano Khalil, Kurdish film maker exiled in Europe, made a film about PKK guerillas in the camps of Iraqi Kurdistan, "David der Tolhildan" (2006). According to Khalil, Syrian Kurds continue to enlist in great numbers in the ranks of the PKK for the same reasons as in the 1980s and 1990s, that is to say, to fight for Kurdistan's independence, including the Kurdish regions of northern Syria. Author interview with Mano Khalil in Bern, March 2007. By the same token, according to James Brandon, 20 percent of the PKK's 4,000 troops stationed in Mount Qandil are of Syrian origin (Brandon 2007: 4).

# Bibliography

## Archival sources

Archives diplomatiques, Nantes, France
Archives dominicaines, Paris
Colonial Office, London
Foreign Office, London
Institut kurde de Paris, Paris
Ministère des Affaires Etrangères, Paris
Service Historique de l'Armée de Terre, Vincennes, France

## Newspapers and magazines

*Akhbar al-Sharq*
*Al-Hayat*
*Hawar* (new edition by Firat Cewerî, 2 vols., Stockholm, Nûdem, 1998)
*Le Monde*
*Roja Nû* (new edition by Jîna Nû, Uppsala, Jîna Nû, 1986)
*Ronahî* (new edition by Jîna Nû, Uppsala, Jîna Nû, 1985)
*Sharq al-Awsat*
*Stêr*
*The Christian Science Monitor*
*The Daily Star*
*The Kurdish Globe*
*The New York Times*
*The Syria Report*

## Books and unpublished manuscripts

Ababsa, M., Roussel, C., and al-Dbiyat, M. (2007) 'Le territoire syrien entre intégration nationale et métropolisation renforcée', in B. Dupret, Z. Ghazzal, Y. Courbage, and M. al-Dbiyat (eds) *La Syrie au présent. Reflets d'une société*, Paris: Actes Sud.

Abboud, C. (2007) 'Les quartiers informels de Damas: une ceinture de misère', in B. Dupret, Z. Ghazzal, Y. Courbage, and M. al-Dbiyat (eds) *La Syrie au présent. Reflets d'une société*, Paris: Actes Sud.

Aflaq, M. (1977) *Choix des textes de la pensée du fondateur du parti Ba'ath. Unité-Liberté-Socialisme*, Madrid: s.n.

Albert, J.-P. (1998) 'Du martyr à la star', in P. Centlivres, D. Fabre, and F. Zonabend (eds) *La fabrique des héros*, Paris: Editions de la maison des sciences de l'homme.
Anderson, B. (1983) *Imagined Communities: Reflections on the Origins and Spread of Nationalism*, New York: Verso.
Badie, B. (1987) *Les deux Etats. Pouvoir et société en Occident et en terre d'Islam*, Paris: Fayard.
—— (1995) *La fin des territoires. Essai sur le désordre international et sur l'utilité sociale du respect*, Paris: Fayard.
Badirkhan, C. (1973) *Gazi Mustafa Kemal Pasha Hazretlerine Açık Mektup*, Nuri Dersimi (ed.), s.l.
Balanche, F. (2006) *La région alaouite et le pouvoir syrien*, Paris: Karthala.
Barth, F. (ed.) (1969) *Ethnic Groups and Boundaries. The Social Organization of Culture Differences*, Oslo: University of Forlaget.
Batatu, H. (1988) 'Syria's Muslim brethren', in F. Halliday and H. Alavi (eds) *State and Ideology in the Middle East and Pakistan*, New York: Monthly Review Press.
—— (1999) *Syria's Peasantry, the Descendants of Its lesser Rural Notables, and Their Politics*, Princeton: Princeton University Press.
Bennani-Chraïbi, M. and Fillieule, O. (eds) (2003) *Résistances et protestations dans les sociétés musulmanes*, Paris: Presses de Science Po.
Berman, B. and Lonsdale, J. (1992) *Unhappy Valley: Conflict in Kenya and Africa*, London: James Currey.
Bokova, L. (1990) *La confrontation franco-syrienne à l'époque du mandat, 1925–7*, Paris: L'Harmattan.
Bozarslan, H. (1997) *La question kurde. Etats et minorités au Moyen-Orient*, Paris: Presses de Sciences Po.
—— (2003) 'Pouvoir et violence dans l'Irak de Saddam Hussein', in H. Dawod and H. Bozarslan (eds) *La société irakienne. Communautés, pouvoirs et violences*, Paris: Karthala.
—— (2004) *Violence in the Middle East. From Political Struggle to Self-Sacrifice*, Princeton: Markus Wiener Publishers.
—— (2005a) 'Persécution des Kurdes en Irak, Iran, Syrie et Turquie. Etude comparative', in C. Kutschera (ed.) *Le livre noir de Saddam Hussein*, Paris: Oh Editions.
—— (2005b) *100 mots pour dire la Violence dans le Monde Musulman*, Paris: Maisonneuve & Larose.
Breuilly, J. (1993) *Nationalism and the State*, 2nd edn, Manchester: Manchester University Press.
Bullock, J. and Darwish, A. (1993) *Water Wars*, London: Rowland.
Canfield, L.R. (1991) 'Introduction: the Turko-Persian tradition', in R.L. Canfield (ed.) *Turko-Persia in Historical Perspective*, Cambridge: Cambridge University Press.
Carré, O. (1996) *Le nationalisme arabe*, Paris: Payot.
Chabry, L. and Chabry, A. (1984) *Politique et minorités au Proche-Orient. Les raisons d'une explosion*, Paris: Maisonneuve.
Chaliand, G. (1992) *Le malheur kurde*, Paris: Seuil.
Chatterjee, P. (1986) *Nationalist Thought and the Colonial World: A Deliberative Discourse?*, Minneapolis: University of Minnesota Press.
Christmann, A. (1998) 'Islamic scholar and religious leader: Shaikh Muhammad Sa'id Ramadan al-Buti', in J. Cooper, R.L. Nettler, and M. Mahmoud (eds), *Islam and Modernity. Muslim Intellectuals Respond*, London and New York: I.B. Tauris.
—— (2007) 'Les cheikhs syriens et l'Internet', in B. Dupret, Z. Ghazzal, Y. Courbage, and M. al-Dbiyat (eds) *La Syrie au présent. Reflets d'une société*, Paris: Actes Sud.

Cigerxwîn (1995) *Jîneńigariya min*, Spanga: Apec.
Corm, G. (1989) *L'Europe et l'Orient de la balkanisation à la libanisation: histoire d'une modernité inaccomplie*, Paris: La Découverte.
Dawn, E. (1973) *From Ottomanism to Arabism*, Urbana: University of Illinois Press.
Dawod, H. (2006) 'Ethnicity and power: some reflections on ethnic definitions and boundaries', in F.A. Jabar and H. Dawod (eds) *The Kurds. Nationalism and Politics*, London: Saqi Books.
Deutsch, K.W. (1962) *Nationalism and Social Communication: An Inquiry into the foundations of Nationality*, Massachusetts: MIT Press.
Droz-Vincent, P. (2004) *Moyen-Orient: pouvoirs autoritaires, sociétés bloquées*, Paris: PUF.
Dupret, B., Ghazzal, Z., Courbage, Y., and al-Dbiyat, M. (eds) (2007) *La Syrie au présent. Reflets d'une société*, Paris: Actes Sud.
Dupret-Schepens C. (2007) 'Les populations syriennes sont-elles homogènes?', in B. Dupret, Z. Ghazzal, Y. Courbage, and M. al-Dbiyat (eds) *La Syrie au présent. Reflets d'une société*, Paris: Actes Sud.
Edmonds, C.J. (1957) *Kurds, Turks and Arabs: Politics, Travel and Research in Northeastern Iraq, 1919–25*, Londres: Oxford University Press.
Ehmed Namî, S. (2000) *Dîmenin ji dîroka winda*, Stockholm: APEC.
Ehteshami, A. and Hinnebusch, R.A. (1997) *Syria and Iran. Middle Powers in a Penetrated Regional System*, London and New York: Routledge.
Eickelman, D.F. (1981) *The Middle East. An Anthropological Approach*, Englewood Cliffs: Prentice Hall.
Fillieule, O. (1993) *Sociologie de la protestation: les formes de l'action collective dans la France contemporaine*, Paris: L'Harmattan.
—— (1997) *Stratégies de la rue. Les manifestations en France*, Paris: Presses de Sciences Po.
Fillieule, O. and Bennani-Chraibi, M. (2003) '*Exit, voice, loyalty* et bien d'autres choses encore…', in M. Bennani-Chraïbi and O. Fillieule (eds) *Résistances et protestations dans les sociétés musulmanes*, Paris: Presses de Sciences Po.
Fliche, B. (2005) 'De l'action réticulaire à la recherche du semblable, ou comment faire lien avec l'administration', in G. Dorronsoro (ed.) *La Turquie conteste. Mobilisations sociales et régime sécuritaire*, Paris: CNRS.
Fournié, P. and Riccioli, J.-L. (1996) *La France et le Proche-Orient, 1916–46. Une chronique photographique de la présence française en Syrie et au Liban, en Palestine, au Hedjaz et en Cilicie*, Tournai: Casterman.
Fuccaro, N. (2004) 'Minorities and ethnic mobilisation: the Kurds in Northern Iraq and Syria', in N. Méouchy and P. Sluglett (eds) *Les mandats français et anglais dans une perspective comparative*, Leiden and London: Brill.
Geertz, C. (1973) *The Interpretation of Cultures*, London: Hutchinson.
Gellner, E. (1999) *Nations et nationalisme*; trans. Bénédicte Pineau, Paris: Payot.
Gelvin, J.L. (1998) *Divided Loyalties: Nationalism and Mass Politics in Syria at the Close of Empire*, Berkeley and Los Angeles: University of California Press.
George, A. (2003) *Syria. Neither Bread nor Freedom*, London and New York: Zed Books.
Gershoni, I. and Jankowski, J. (1997) 'Introduction', in J. Jankowski and I. Gershoni (eds) *Rethinking Nationalism in the Arab Middle East*, New York: Columbia University Press.
Ghazzal, Z., Dupret, B., and Courbage, Y. (2007) 'Introduction', in B. Dupret, Z. Ghazzal, Y. Courbage, and M. al-Dbiyat (eds) *La Syrie au présent. Reflets d'une société*, Paris: Actes Sud.

Goffman, E. (1974) *Les rites d'interaction*, Paris: Ed. de Minuit.
Gurr, T.R. (1970) *Why Men Rebel?*, Princeton: Princeton University Press.
Hanna, A. (2007) 'The attitudes of the Syrian Communist Party and the Arab Socialist Party towards the peasant movement in Syria in the 1950s', in G.D. Khoury and N. Méouchy (eds) *Etats et sociétés en quête d'avenir (1945–2005): Dynamiques et enjeux*, Paris: Geuthner.
Hassanpour, A. (1992) *Nationalism and Language in Kurdistan, 1918–85*, San Francisco: Mellen Research University Press.
Haugen, E. (1983) 'The implementation of corpus planning: theory and practice', in J.A. Fishman and J. Cobarrubias (eds) *Progress in Language Planning. International Perspectives*, New York and Amsterdam: Mouton Publishers.
Hinnebusch, R.A. (1995) 'State, civil society, and political change in Syria', in R. Norton (ed.) *Civil Society in the Middle East*, vol. I, Leiden and New York: Brill.
Hopwood, D. (1988) *Syria, 1945–86. Politics and Society*, London, Sydney, and Wellington: Unwin Hyman.
Horowitz, D. (1985) *Ethnic Groups in Conflict*, Berkeley and Los Angeles: University of California Press.
Hourani, A. (1947) *Minorities in the Arab World*, London: Oxford University Press.
——(1962) *Arabic Thought in the Liberal Age, 1798–1939*, Oxford: Oxford University Press.
——(1968) 'Ottoman reform and the politics of notables', in W.R. Polk and R.L. Chambers (eds) *Beginnings of Modernization in the Middle East. The Nineteenth Century*, Chicago IL: University of Chicago Press.
Hroch, M. (1985) *Social Preconditions of National Revival in Europe. A Comparative Analysis of the Social Composition of Patriotic Groups Among the Smaller European Nations*, Cambridge: Cambridge University Press.
Human Rights Watch (1991) *Syria Unmasked*, New Haven: Yale University Press.
Jankowski, J. and Gershoni, I. (1997) *Rethinking Nationalism in the Arab Middle East*, New York: Columbia University Press.
Jemo, M. (1990) *Osman Sebrî, Apo. Analyse bio-bibliographique*, University of Sorbonne Nouvelle.
Karim, F. (1992) 'La lutte armée entre le mythe et la réalié', in H. Halkawt (ed.) *Les Kurdes par-delà l'exode*, Paris: L'Harmattan.
Karpat, K. (1982) '*Millet*s and nationality: the roots of the incongruity of nation and state in the post-Ottoman era', in B. Braude and B. Lewis (eds) *Christians and Jews in the Ottoman Empire. The Functioning of a Plural Society*, vol. I, New York and London: Holmes & Meier Publishers.
——(1988) 'The Ottoman ethnic and confessional legacy in the Middle East', in M. Esman and I. Rabinovich (eds) *Ethnicity, Pluralism and the State in the Middle East*, New York and London: Cornell University Press.
Kashani-Sabet, F. (1999) *Frontier Fictions. Shaping the Iranian Nation, 1804–1946*, Princeton: Princeton University Press.
Kazemi, F. (1980) *Poverty and Revolution in Iran. The Migrant Poor, Urban Marginality and Politics*, New York: New York University Press.
Kedourie, E. (1986) *Nationalism*, Londres, Melbourne, and Sydney: Hutchinson.
Khalaf, S. (1993) 'Cheikhs, paysans et membres du parti Ba'th: changements politiques en Syrie du Nord', in R. Bocco, R. Jaubert, and F. Métral (eds) *Steppes d'Arabie. Etats, pasteurs, agriculteurs et commerçants: le devenir des zones sèches*, Paris: PUF.
Khoury, G.D. and Méouchy, N. (eds) (2007) *Etats et sociétés en quête d'avenir (1945–2005): Dynamiques et enjeux*, Paris: Geuthner.

Bibliography 173

Khoury, P.S. (1983) *Urban Notables and Arab Nationalism. The Politics of Damascus 1860–1920*, Cambridge and New York: Cambridge University Press.

——— (1987) *Syria and the French Mandate. The Politics of Arab Nationalism, 1920–45*, Princeton: Princeton University Press.

——— (1997) 'The paradoxical in Arab nationalism: interwar Syria revisited', in J. Jankowski and I. Gershoni (eds) *Rethinking Nationalism in the Arab Middle East*, New York: Columbia University Press.

Kienle, E. (1990) *Ba'th versus Ba'th: The Conflict Between Syria and Iraq, 1968–89*, London: I.B. Tauris.

Klein, J. (2001) 'En-gendering nationalism: the *woman question* in Kurdish nationalist discourse of the late Ottoman period', in M. Shahrzad (ed.) *Women of a Non-state Nation: The Kurds*, Costa Mesa: Mazda.

Kreyenbroek, P.G. and Allison, C. (eds) (1996) *Kurdish Culture and Identity*, London and New Jersey: Zed Books.

Kutschera, C. (1979) *Le mouvement national kurde*, Paris: Flammarion.

Landis, J. (1998) 'Shishakli and the Druzes: integration and intransigence', in T. Philipp and B. Schäbler (eds) *The Syrian Land: Processes of Integration and Fragmentation*, Stuttgart: Franz Steiner Verlag.

Lapidus, I.M. (1990) 'Tribes and state formation in Islamic history', in P.S. Khoury and J. Kostiner (eds) *Tribes and State Formation in the Middle East*, Londres and New York: I.B. Tauris.

Larzillière, P. (2004) *Etre jeune en Palestine*, Paris: Editions Balland.

Laurens, H. (2004) *L'Orient arabe. Arabisme et islamisme de 1798 à 1945*, Paris: Armand Colin.

Lawson, F.H. (2004) 'The northern Syrian revolts of 1919–21 and the Sharifian regime: congruence or conflict of interests and ideologies?', in T. Philipp and C. Schumann (eds) *From the Syrian Land to the States of Syria and Lebanon*, Beirut: Orient-Insitut der DMG.

Le Gac, D. (1991) *La Syrie du général Assad*, Bruxelles: Editions Complexes.

Lescot, R. (1975) *Enquête sur les Yézidis de Syrie et du Djebel Sindjar*, Damas: Institut Français de Damas.

Lescot, R. and Badirkhan, C. (1991) *Grammaire kurde*, Paris: Librairie d'Amérique et d'Orient.

Lichbach, M.I. and Zuckerman A.S. (eds) (1997) *Comparative Politics: Rationality, Culture and Structure*, Cambridge: Cambridge University Press.

Longrigg, S.H. (1958) *Syria and Lebanon Under French Mandate*, Oxford: Oxford University Press.

Lynch, M. and Perveen, A. (2006) *Buried Alive. Stateless Kurds in Syria*, Washington: Refugees International.

McAdam, D., McCarthy, J.D., and Zald, M.N. (eds) (1996) *Comparative Perspectives on Social Movements: Political Opportunities, Mobilizing Structures, and Cultural Framings*, New York: Cambridge University Press.

McDowall, D. (1996) *A Modern History of the Kurds*, London and New York: I.B. Tauris.

——— (1998) *The Kurds of Syria*, London: KHRP.

Malmîsanij (2007) *The Past and the Present of Book Publishing in Kurdish Language in Turkey and Syria*, Istanbul: Vate.

Massicard, E. (2005a) *L'autre Turquie. Le mouvement aléviste et ses territoires*, Paris: PUF.

——— (2005b) 'Les mobilisations identitaires en Turquie après 1980: une libéralisation ambiguë', in G. Dorronsoro (ed.) *La Turquie conteste. Mobilisations sociales et régime sécuritaire*, Paris: CNRS.

## 174  Bibliography

Mela Ehmed, M. (2003) *Apo Osman Sebrî. Xebatkarê kurd ê mezin*, Berlin: Havîbûn.
Méouchy, N. (ed.) (2002) *France et Liban 1918–46. Les ambiguïtés et les dynamiques de la relation mandataire*, Damascus: Institut Français d'Etudes Arabes de Damas.
——— (2004) 'Rural resistance and the introduction of modern forms of consciousness in the Syrian countryside, 1918–26', in T. Philipp and C. Schumann (eds) *From the Syrian Land to the States of Syria and Lebanon*, Beirut: Orient-Insitut der DMG.
——— (2007) 'Comment interroger les mobilisations sociales de l'Orient arabe?', in G.D. Khoury and N. Méouchy (eds) *Etats et sociétés en quête d'avenir (1945–2005): Dynamiques et enjeux*, Paris: Geuthner.
Méouchy, N. and Sluglett, P. (eds) (2004) *Les mandats français et anglais dans une perspective comparative*, Leiden and London: Brill.
Métral, J. (2004) 'Robert Montagne et les études ethnographiques', in N. Méouchy and P. Sluglett (eds) *Les mandats français et anglais dans une perspective comparative*, Leiden and London: Brill.
Meyer, G. (1990) 'Rural development and migration in Northeast Syria', in M. Salem-Murdock and M.M. Horowitz (eds) *Anthropology and Development in North Africa and the Middle East*, Boulder, San Francisco, and London: Westview Press.
Mizrahi, J.-D. (2003) *Genèse de l'Etat mandataire. Service des Renseignements et bandes armées en Syrie et au Liban dans les années 1920*, Paris: Publications de la Sorbonne.
Montgomery, H. (2005) *The Kurds of Syria. An Existence denied*, Berlin: Europäisches Zentrum für Kurdische Studien.
More, C. (1984) *Les Kurdes aujourd'hui. Mouvement national et partis politiques*, Paris: L'Harmattan.
Müller, V. (1931) *En Syrie avec les Bédouins. Les tribus du désert*, Paris: Librairie Ernest Leroux.
Natali, D. (2005) *The Kurds and the State: Evolving National Identity in Iraq, Turkey, and Iran*, Syracuse: Syracuse University Press.
Nazdar, M. (1978) 'Les Kurdes en Syrie', in G. Chaliand (ed.) *Les Kurdes et le Kurdistan*, Paris: Maspero.
Nemir, F. (1992) 'La politique kurde de la Syrie', in H. Hakim (ed.) *Les Kurdes par-delà l'exode*, Paris: L'Harmattan.
Northedge, F.S. (1986) *The League of Nations: Its Life and Times, 1920–46*, New York: Leicester University Press.
Norton, R. (1995) 'Introduction', in R. Norton (ed.) *Civil Society in the Middle East*, vol. I, Leiden, New York, and Cologne: Brill.
Nouri Pacha, I. (1986) *La révolte de l'Agri Dagh*, Peresh (ed.), Geneva: Editions kurdes.
Obershall, A. (1973) *Social Conflicts and Social Movements*, Englewood Cliffs: Prentice Hall.
Olson, R. (2005) *The Goat and the Butcher: Nationalism and State Formation in Kurdistan-Iraq Since the Iraqi War*, Costa Mesa: Mazda.
Owen, R. (1991) 'Class and class politics in Iraq before 1958: the colonial and post-colonial state', in R.A. Fernea and L.W. Roger (eds) *The Iraqi Revolution of 1958. The Old Social Classes Revisited*, London and New York: I.B. Tauris.
Perthes, V. (1995) *The Political Economy of Syria Under Asad*, London and New York: I.B. Tauris.
——— (2002) 'La sécurité nationale et le développement de l'identité nationale en Syrie: de l'affrontement à la paix des braves?', in A. Dieckhoff and R. Kastoryano (eds) *Nationalismes en mutation en Méditerranée orientale*, Paris: CNRS.

―― (2004) *Syria Under Bashar al-Asad: Modernisation and the Limits of Change*, Adelphi Paper no. 366, Oxford and New York: Oxford University Press.
Picard, E. (1980) 'La Syrie de 1946 à 1979', in A. Raymond (ed.) *La Syrie d'aujourd'hui*, Paris: CNRS.
―― (ed.) (1991) *La question kurde*, Bruxelles: Complexes.
―― (1993) 'Arab military in politics: from revolutionary plot to authoritarian state', in A. Hourani, P.S. Khoury, and M.C. Wilson (eds) *The Modern Middle East. A Reader*, London and New York: I.B. Tauris.
Pinto, P.G. (2004) 'Performing *baraka*: sainthood and power in Syrian Sufism', in G. Stauth (ed.) *On Archaeology of Sainthood and Local Spirituality in Islam: Past and Present Crossroads of Events and Ideas*, Bielefeld: Transcript Verlag.
―― (2005) 'Bodily mediations: self, values and experience in Syrian Sufism', in J. Heiss (ed.) *Verämderung und Stabilität. Normen und Werte in islamischen Gesellschaften*, Wien: Verlag der Österreichischen Akademie der Wissenschaften.
―― (2007a) 'Les Kurdes de Syrie', in B. Dupret, Z. Ghazzal, Y. Courbage, and M. al-Dbiyat (eds) *La Syrie au présent. Reflets d'une société*, Paris: Actes Sud.
―― (2007b) 'Le soufisme en Syrie', in B. Dupret, Z. Ghazzal, Y. Courbage, and M. al-Dbiyat (eds) *La Syrie au présent. Reflets d'une société*, Paris: Actes Sud.
―― (2008) 'Sufism, ethnicity and religious nationalism in Northern Syria', in S. Hajo, C. Borck, E. Savelsberg, and B. Kemmerich (eds) *Syrien und die Kurden Vom Osmanischen Reich bis in die Gegenwart*, Münster: Unrast Verlag.
Planhol, X. (1993) *Les nations du prophète. Manuel de Géographie de politique musulmane*, Paris: Fayard.
Provence, M. (2005) *The Great Syrian Revolt and the Rise of Arab Nationalism*, Austin: University of Texas Press.
Randal, J.C. (1997) *After Such Knowledge, What Forgiveness. My Encounters with Kurdistan*, New York: Farrar, Straus and Giroux.
Raymond, A. (1980) 'La Syrie, du royaume arabe à l'indépendance (1914–46)', in A. Raymond (ed.) *La Syrie d'aujourd'hui*, Paris: CNRS.
Revel, J. (1996) *Jeux d'échelles. La micro-analyse à l'expérience*, Paris: Gallimard/Seuil.
Robinson, R., Gallagher, J., and Denny, A. (eds) (1981) *Africa and the Victorians: The Official Mind of Imperialism*, 2nd edn, London: Macmillan Press.
Rodinson, M. (1972) *Marxisme et monde musulman*, Paris: Seuil.
Romano, D. (2006) *The Kurdish Nationalist Movement. Opportunity, Mobilization and Identity*, New York: Cambridge University Press.
Rondot, P. (1993) 'Syrie 1929, itinéraire d'un officier', in A.-M. Bianquis (ed.) *Damas. Miroir brisé d'un Orient arabe*, Paris: Autrement.
Roussillon, A. and Ferrié, J.-N. (2006) 'Réforme et politique au Maroc de l'alternance', in J.-N. Ferrié and J.-C. Santucci (eds) *Dispositifs de démocratisation et dispositifs autoritaires en Afrique du Nord*, Paris: CNRS.
Roy, O. (1997) *La nouvelle Asie centrale ou la fabrication des nations*, Paris: Le Seuil.
―― (2004) 'Groupes de solidarité, territoires, réseaux et Etat dans le Moyen-Orient et l'Asie Centrale', in H. Dawod (ed.) *Tribus et pouvoirs en terre d'Islam*, Paris: Armand Colin.
Said, E.W. (1978) *Orientalism*, New York: Pantheon Books.
Schmitt, C. (1972) *La notion du politique. Théorie du partisan*, Paris: Calmann-Lévy.
Scott, J.C. (1990) *Domination and the Arts of Resistance. Hidden Transcripts*, New Haven and London: Yale University Press.
Seale, P. (1965) *The Struggle for Syria*, Oxford: Oxford University Press.

—— (1988) *Asad of Syria, The Struggle for the Middle East*, London: I.B. Taruris.
Seida, A. (2005) *La question kurde en Syrie. Chapitres oubliés d'une longue souffrance*, Paris: l'Harmattan.
Seurat, M. (1980) 'Les populations, l'Etat et la société', in A. Raymond (ed.) *La Syrie aujourd'hui*, Paris: CNRS.
—— (1989) *L'Etat de la barbarie*, Paris: Seuil.
Sluglett, P. (2004) 'Les Mandats/The Mandates: some reflections on the nature of the British presence in Iraq (1914–32) and the French presence in Syria (1918–46)', in N. Méouchy and P. Sluglett (eds) *Les mandats français et anglais dans une perspective comparative*, Leiden and London: Brill.
Smith, A.D. (1981) *The Ethnic Revival*, Cambridge and New York: Cambridge University Press.
Strohmeier, M. (2003) *Crucial Images in the Presentation of a Kurdish National Identity*, Leiden and Boston: Brill.
Suny, R.G. (1993) *Looking Toward Ararat. Armenia in Modern History*, Bloomington and Indianapolis: Indiana University Press.
Tarrow, S. (1994) *Power in Movement. Social Movements, Collective Action and Politics*, New York: Cambridge University Press.
Tatchjian, V. (2004) *La France en Cilicie et en Haute-Mésopotamie. Aux confins de la Turquie, de la Syrie et de l'Irak (1919–33)*, Paris: Karthala.
Tejel, J. (2007a) *Le mouvement kurde en exil. Continuités et discontinuités du nationalisme kurde sous le mandat français en Syrie et au Liban (1925–46)*, Bern: Peter Lang.
—— (2007b) 'Jeunesse kurde: entre rupture et engagement militant', in B. Dupret, Z. Ghazzal, Y. Courbage, and M. al-Dbiyat (eds) *La Syrie au présent. Reflets d'une société*, Paris: Actes Sud.
Ter Minassian, T. (1997) *Colporteurs du Komintern. L'Union Soviétique et les minorités au Moyen-Orient*, Paris: Presses de Sciences Po.
Tibi, B. (1991) *Arab Nationalism. A Critical Enquiry*, ed. and trans. by M. Farouk-Sluglett and P. Sluglett, New York: St Martin's Press.
Tilly, C. (1972) 'The modernization of political conflict in France', in E.B. Harvey (ed.) *Perspectives on Modernization: Essays in Memory of Ian Weinberg*, Toronto: University of Toronto Press.
—— (1991) *Coercion, Capital, and European States, AD 990–1990*, Oxford: Basil Blackwell.
—— (1995) 'Contentious repertoires in Great-Britain, 1758–1934', in M. Traugott (ed.) *Repertoire and Cycles of Collective Action*, Durham and London: Duke University Press.
—— (2003) *The Politics of Collective Violence*, Cambridge: Cambridge University Press.
Trégan, F.-X. (2004) 'Approche des savoirs de l'Institut français de Damas: à la recherche d'un temps mandataire', in N. Méouchy and P. Sluglett (eds) *Les mandats français et anglais dans une perspective comparative*, Leiden and London: Brill.
Vali, A. (2003) 'Genealogies of the Kurds: constructions of nation and national identity in Kurdish historical writing', in A. Vali (ed.) *Essays on the Origins of Kurdish Nationalism*, Costa Mesa: Mazda.
Van Bruinessen, M. (1978) *Agha, Shaikh and State. On the Social and Political Organization of Kurdistan*, Utrecht: University of Utrecht.
—— (1992) *Agha, Shaikh and State. The Social and Political Structures of Kurdistan*, London and New Jersey: Zed Books.

Van Dam, N. (1979) *The Struggle for Power in Syria: Sectarianism, Regionalism and Tribalism in Politics, 1961–78*, London: Croom Helm.
—— (1996) *The Struggle for Power in Syria. Politics and Society Under Asad and the Ba'th Party*, London: I.B. Tauris.
Van der Veer, P. (1994) *Religious Nationalism. Hindus and Muslims in India*, Berkeley: University of California.
Vanly, I.C. (1968) *Le problème kurde en Syrie*, Publication du Comité pour la défense des Droits du Peuple kurde: s.l.
—— (1978) 'Les Kurdes en Syrie', in G. Chaliand (ed.) *Les Kurdes et le Kurdistan*, Paris: Maspero.
—— (1992) 'The Kurds in Syria and Lebanon', in P.G. Kreyenbroek (ed.) *The Kurds. A Contemporary Overview*, London and New York: Routledge.
Velud, C. (1991) *Une expérience d'administration régionale en Syrie durant le mandat français: conquête, colonisation et mise en valeur de la Gazîra, 1920–36*, unpublished thesis, University of Lyon 2.
Waterbury, J. (1994) 'Democracy without democrats? The potential for political liberalization in the Middle East', in G. Salama (ed.) *Democracy Without Democrats?*, London and New York, I.B. Tauris.
Wedeen, L. (1999) *Ambiguities of Domination. Politics, Rhetoric and Symbols in Contemporary Syria*, Chicago and Londres: University of Chicago Press.
White, P.J. (2000) *Primitive Rebels or Revolutionary Modernizers? The Kurdish National Movement in Turkey*, London and New York: Zed Books.
Wieviorka, M. (1999) *La violence en France*, Paris: Seuil.
—— (2004) *La violence*, Paris: Balland.
Yildiz, K. (2005) *The Kurds in Syria. The Forgotten People*, London: Pluto Press.
Zaza, N. (1982) *Ma vie de Kurde ou le cri du peuple kurde*, Lausanne: Favre.
Zelter, M. (1969) 'Minorities in Iraq and Syria', in A. Shiloh (ed.) *Peoples and Cultures of the Middle East*, New York: Random House.
Zisser, E. (2001) *Asad's Legacy. Syria in Transition*, foreword by I. Rabinovich, New York: New York University Press.

## Articles

*Abbreviations*
AI          *Les Annales l'autre Islam*
ASR         *American Sociological Review*
BEO         *Bulletin d'études orientales*
CI          *Critique internationale*
EK          *Etudes Kurdes*
IJMES       *International Journal of Middle East Studies*
ISIM        *International Institute for the Study of Islam in the Modern World*
JKS         *The Journal of Kurdish Studies*
MERIP       *Middle East Report*
MMM         *Monde arabe Maghreb Machrek*
NN          *Nations and Nationalism*
REMMM       *Revue du Monde Musulman et de la Méditerranée*
VS          *Vingtième Siècle*

Ababsa, M. (2006) 'Contre-réforme agraire et conflits fonciers en Jazîra syrienne (2000–5)', *REMMM*, 115–16: 211–30.
Abdulhamid, A. (2005) 'Syria: another regimefall looming', *ISIM*, 16: 36–7.
Badirkhan, J. (1932a) 'Buts et caractères de la revue Hawar', *Hawar*, 1: 29–30.
——— (1932b) 'Shêx Evdirehmanê Garisî çû Rehmetê', *Hawar*, 11: 224.
——— (1941) 'Navên kurdmanci', *Hawar*, 31: 770–1.
——— (1942) 'Newrûz', *Hawar*, 42: 976–8.
——— (1943) 'Merhele', *Roja Nû*, 1: 1.
Badirkhan, K. (1932) 'Notice sur la Bible noir', *Hawar*, 12: 289.
——— (1933) 'La femme kurde', *Hawar*, 19: 390.
——— (1935) 'Zerdesht û rêya Zerdesht', *Hawar*, 26: 675.
Baduel, P.-R. (1996) 'Les partis politiques dans la gouvernementalisation de l'Etat des pays arabes', *REMMM*, 81–2: 9–51.
Blau, J. (2000) 'Pierre Rondot (2 juin 1904–6 avril 2000)', *EK*, 2: 101–2.
Bocco, R. (1995) 'Asabiyât tribales et États au Moyen-Orient', *MMM*, 147: 3–12.
Bois, T. (1962) 'La vie sociale des Kurdes', *Al-Machriq*, July–Oct.: 599–661.
Böttcher, A. (1998) 'L'élite féminine kurde de la Kaftariyya, une confrérie naqsbandi damascène', *AI*, 5: 125–40.
Bou-Nacklie, N.E. (1993) 'Les Troupes Spéciales: religious and ethnic recruitement, 1916–1946', *IJMES*, 25: 645–60.
Bozarslan, H. (1995) 'Remarques sur l'histoire des relations kurdo-arméniennes', *JKS*, I: 55–76.
——— (1998) 'Islam, islamisme et question minoritaire: le cas kurde', *AI*, 5: 333–50.
——— (2003) 'Le nationalisme kurde, de la violence politique au suicide sacrificiel', *CI*, 21: 93–115.
——— (2005) 'Le Kurdistan d'Irak aujourd'hui', *CI*, 29: 25–36.
Brandon, J. (2007) 'The PKK and Syria's Kurds', *Terrorism Monitor*, 5(3): 4–6.
Braud, P. (1993) 'La violence politique: repères et problèmes', *Culture et conflits*, 9–10: 13–42.
Chiffoleau, S. (2006) 'Présentation. La Syrie au quotidien: cultures et pratiques du changement', *REMMM*, 115–16: 9–18.
Chouet, A. (1995) 'L'espace tribal alaouite à l'épreuve du pouvoir. La désintégration par le politique', *MMM*, 147: 93–119.
Danish Refugee Council (2007) 'Syria: Kurds, honour-killings and illegal departure', *Danish Immigration Service*, 5: 1–23.
Dieckhoff, A. (1996) 'La déconstruction d'une illusion. L'introuvable opposition entre nationalisme politique et nationalisme culturel', *L'Année sociologique*, 46(1): 43–55.
Droz-Vincent, P. (2001) 'Syrie: la "nouvelle génération" au pouvoir', *MMM*, 173: 14–35.
Freitag, U. (1994) 'Writing Arab history: the search for the nation', *British Journal of Middle Eastern Studies*, 21(1): 19–37.
Fuccaro, N. (2003) 'Ethnicity and the city: the Kurdish quarter of Damascus between Ottoman and French rule, c. 1724–1946', *Urban History*, 30(2): 206–24.
Gambill, G.C. (2004) 'The Kurdish reawakening in Syria', *Middle East Intelligence Bulletin*, 6(4): 1–4.
Gauthier, J. (2005) 'Les événements de Qamichli: irruption de la question kurde en Syrie?', *EK*, 7: 97–114.
——— (2006) 'Syrie: le facteur kurde', *Outre-Terre. Revue française de géopolitique*, 14: 217–31.

Gellner, E. (1991) 'Civil society in historical context', *International Social Science Journal*, 129: 495–510.
Gelvin, J.L. (1994) 'The social origins of popular nationalism in Syria: evidence for a new framework', *IJMES*, 26(4): 645–61.
Gibert, A. and Fevret, M. (1953) 'La Djézireh syrienne et son réveil économique', *Revue de Géographie de Lyon*, 28: 1–15 and 83–100.
Grojean, O. and Küçük, B. (2006) 'Le PKK après la capture d'Öcalan', *EK*, 8: 63–84.
Human Rights Watch (1996) 'Syria: the silenced Kurds', 8(4): 1–57.
Kaylani, N.M. (1972) 'The rise of the Syrian Ba'th, 1940–58: political success, party failure', *IJMES*, 3(1): 3–23.
Khoury, P.S. (1984) 'Syrian urban politics in transition: the quarter of Damascus during the French Mandate', *IJMES*, 16(4): 507–40.
Kienle, E. (1992) 'Entre *jamâ'a* et classe: le pouvoir politique en Syrie contemporaine', *REMMM*, 59–60: 211–39.
Krämer, G. (1992) 'Liberalization and democracy in the Arab world', *MERIP*, 174: 22–5.
Landis, J. and Pace, J. (2006–7) 'The Syrian opposition', *The Washington Quarterly*, 30(1): 45–68.
Leenders, R. (2007) 'Au-delà du Pays des deux fleuves: une configuration conflictuelle régionale?', *CI*, 34: 61–78.
Le Saux, M. (2006) 'Les dynamiques contradictoires du champ associatif syrien', *REMMM*, 115–6: 193–209.
Lescot, R. (1940/1988) 'Le Kurd Dagh et le mouvement Mouroud', *Studia Kurdica*, 1–5: 101–26.
Lowe, R. (2006) 'The Syrian Kurds: a people discovered', *Middle East Programme Briefing Paper*, 6(1): 1–7.
McCarthy, J. and Zald, M.N. (1977) 'Resource mobilization and social movements: a partial theory', *The American Journal of Sociology*, 82(6): 1212–41.
Mardin, S. (1977) 'Youth and violence in Turkey', *International Social Science Journal*, 1(2): 229–54.
Méouchy, N. (1995) 'Les nationalistes arabes de la première génération en Syrie (1918–28). Une génération méconnue', *BEO*, 97: 109–28.
Migliorino, N. (2006) '*Kulna Suriyyin*? The Armenian community and the State in contemporary Syria', *REMMM*, 115–6: 97–115.
Mizrahi, J.-D. (2003a) 'Le nationalisme de la frontière turco-syrienne au début des années 1920', *VS*, 78: 19–34.
——— (2003b) 'La répression du banditisme sur les confins de la Syrie mandataire: nouveaux Etats et nouvelles frontières dans le Moyen-Orient des années 1920', *Relations internationales*, 114: 173–87.
Öktem, K. (2004) 'Incorporating the time and space of the ethnic "other": nationalism and space in Southeast Turkey in the nineteenth and twentieth centuries', *NN*, 10(4): 559–78.
Picard, E. (1980) 'Y a-t-il un problème communautaire en Syrie?', *MMM*, 87: 7–21.
——— (1996) 'Fin des partis en Syrie', *REMMM*, 81–2: 207–29.
Pinto, P.G. (2003) 'Dangerous liaisons: Sufism and the state in Syria', *IWM Junior Visiting Fellow's Conferences*, 14: 1–10.
——— (2006) 'Sufism, moral performance and the public sphere in Syria', *REMMM*, 115–6: 155–71.
Rabo, A. (1984) 'Great expectations: perceptions on development in Northeast Syria', *Ethnos*, 49(3–4): 211–25.

Resho, H. (1968) 'Nûçeyên Welêt', *Çiya*, 5: 14–6.
Rondot, P. (1937) 'Les tribus montagnardes de l'Asie antérieure. Quelques aspects sociaux des populations kurdes et assyriennes', *BEO*, 6: 1–49.
Roy, O. (1991) 'Ethnies et politique en Asie centrale', *REMMM*, 59–60: 17–36.
Snow, D., Rochford, B., Worden, S., and Benford, R. (1986) 'Frame alignment processes, micromobilization, and movement participation', *ASR*, 51(4): 464–81.
Stenberg, L. (2005) 'Young male and Sufi Muslims in the city of Damascus,' in J. B. Simonsen (ed.) *Youth and Youth Culture in the Contemporary Middle East,*" Aarhus: Aarhus University Press.
Taylor, V. (1989) 'Social movement continuity: the women's movement in abeyance', *ASR*, 54: 761–75.
Teitelbaum, J. (2004) 'The Muslim Brotherhood and struggle for Syria, 1947–58', *MES*, 40(3): 134–58.
Tejel Gorgas, J. (2006) 'Les Kurdes de Syrie, de la "dissimulation" à la "visibilité"?', *REMMM*, 115–6: 117–33.
Thomas, M.C. (2002) 'French intelligence-gathering in the Syrian mandate, 1920–40', *MES*, 38(1): 1–32.
Tilly, C. (1984) 'Les origines du répertoire de l'action collective contemporaine en France et en Grande-Bretagne', *VS*, 4: 89–108.
Usif, N. (1941) 'Perîshanî', *Hawar*, 35: 851–2.
Vali, A. (1998) 'The Kurds and their *others*: fragmented identity and fragmented politics', *Comparative Studies of South Asia, Africa and the Middle East*, 18: 82–95.
Van Bruinessen, M. (1988) 'Between guerrilla war and political murder: the PKK', *MERIP*, 153: 40–6.
——(1994) 'Nationalisme kurde et ethnicités intra-kurdes', *Peuples Méditerranéens*, 68–9: 15–37.
——(1998) 'The Kurds and Islam', *AI*, 5: 13–35.
Watenpaugh, K.D. (2003) 'Middle-class modernity and the persistence of the politics of notables in inter-war Syria', *IJMES*, 35(2): 257–86.
Wedeen, L. (1998) 'Acting "as if": symbolic politics and social control in Syria', *Comparative Studies in Society and History*, 40(3): 503–23.
Wikas, S. (2007) 'Battling the lion of Damascus: Syria's domestic opposition and the Asad regime', *Policy Focus*, 69: 1–34.
Wimmer, A. (1997) 'Who owns the state? Understanding ethnic conflict in post-colonial societies', *NN*, 3(4): 631–65.
Zarcone, T. (1992) 'Réseaux confrériques et guides charismatiques dans les relations turco-arabes (héritage de l'histoire et situation actuelle)', *Anatolia moderna*, 4: 99–107.
Zengi, D. (2000) 'Jiyanameya Helbestvan Qedrîcan', *Pirs*, 21: 16–25.

## Electronic references

Altug, S (2007) 'Qamishli revolt'. Email (August 10, 2007).
Amnesty International (2004) *Syria: Unfair Trial of Kurdish Prisoners of Conscience and Torture of Children Is Totally Unacceptable*. Available online: http://www.amnesty.org/en/report/info/MDE24/048/2004 (accessed June 12, 2004).
Amnesty International (2005) *Syria: Kurds in the Syrian Arab Republic One Year After the March 2004 Events*. Available online: http://web.amnesty.org/library/print/ENG-MDE240022005 (accessed March 15, 2005).

Den Hond, C. (2004) 'Interview with Marwan Othman', *IV Online magazine*, IV 360/1. Available online: http://www.internationalviewpoint.org (accessed December 10, 2004).

Hajji Husayn, S. (2007) 'Qamishli revolt'. Email (May 30, 2007).

Semo, C. (2007) 'Resolution text'. Email (August 10, 2007).

Tejel Gorgas, J. (2006) 'Les constructions de l'identité kurde sous l'influence de la connexion kurdo-française au Levant (1930–46)', *European Journal of Turkish Studies*, Thematic Issue no. 5, 'Power, ideology, knowledge – deconstructing Kurdish studies'. Available online: http//www.ejts.org/document751.html (accessed January 10, 2007).

United Nations (2005) *Civil and Political Rights, Including Questions of Freedom of Expression*, Economic and Social Council (United Nations), E/CN.4/2005/64/Add.1,29 March 2005. Available online: http://www.domino.un.org/UNISPAL.NSF (accessed July 21, 2005).

Yekîtî (1999) *The Political Program Submitted to the Third Convention of the Yekiti Party in Syria*. Available online: http://www.home.c2i.net/yekiti/program.htm (accessed July 30, 2006).

# Index

Abbas, Sharko 129
'Abd al-Karim Muhammad 31
abeyance structures 84, 135
Adib al-Shishakli Party (Arab Liberation Movement) 45
al-Afghani, Jamal al-Din 54
'Aflaq, Michel 56–7, 72, 149n6
Afrin, PKK offices 77
*ajanib* Kurds 51, 120
Alaedinan tribe 10
Aleppo: anti-French revolts (1919) 12; Kurdish army units used to suppress trouble 67; Kurdish quarter since the nineteenth century 11; PKK offices 77; use of Kurdish language 103
Alger Agreement 72
'Ali Agha Zilfu 43
Aliko, Fu'ad 67, 111
Amikan tribe 9
amiria 148n2
Amo, Isma'il 111
Amuda: children's deaths in movie house 48, 151n32; Qamishli revolt 115
Amuda affair 34
Apostolic Armenians 31
"Arab belt" 61, 65, 73
Arab Liberation Movement (Adib al-Shishakli Party) 45
Arab Renaissance Party *see* Ba'ath party/regime
Arab Republican Party 39
Arabism 134
Ararat revolt (1927–31) 4, 17–18, 20–2, 94
armed struggle: incorporation in Kurdish nationalist myth 94; Syrian Kurds non-use of 85

army: growth of 40; ideological debates within 47; Kurds in 44, 66–7; purges of Kurdish officers 46; suspicious deaths of Kurds in 117
*'asabiyya* 4, 46, 57, 153n9
al-As'ad, Bashar 80–1, 109–10, 113–14, 117
al-As'ad, Basil 107
al-As'ad, Hafiz 53–4, 57, 62–3, 66, 71, 73, 75–8, 94, 98, 107, 109
al-As'ad, Maher 117
al-As'ad, Rifat 67
Asfar 38, 148n1
*Aso* (literary magazine) 105
Atatürk dam 77
'Ayn Diwar, smuggling 68
Ayyubi, Mahmud 66
Azadî 127, 129

Ba'ath party/regime (Arab Renaissance Party): 2000 shift of "control" 109–10; favoring dissimulation 83–4; formation of 39–40, 149n6; led Syrian integration into UAR 47–8; overview 54; proposed autonomy for the Iraqi Kurds 72; public statement that ethnic diversity should be maintained 131; role in the election of Shaykh Kuftaru as Mufti of the Republic 97; tensions within 57–9; view of Arab nationalism 54–7; years of exploitation (1970–2000) 62–8; years of ideological purity (1963–70) 59–62
"Badirkhan" forum 110
Badirkhan, Jaladat 17, 19, 21–2, 30–2, 42, 45, 64, 103, 149n10, 160n55
Badirkhan, Kamuran 17, 20–1, 23, 26, 42, 103, 144n19, 144n24, 145n32, 146n37, 149n11

## Index

Badirkhan, Rewshen 104, 151n31
Badirkhan, Sureya 18
Bakdash, Khalid 43, 48, 149n15
Barazi Confederation 10, 28, 30
al-Barazi, Muhsen 45–6
Barudi, Fakhri 35
Barzani, Idris 72
Barzani, Masud 78, 80, 91
Barzani, Mustafa 72–3, 78, 87, 91, 102, 135
Barzanji, Mahmud 102
Bawalia clan 73
al-Bayanouni, 'Ali Sadr al-Din 101, 127
Birkî, Majid 68
Bitar, Salah 53
Biyan tribe 9
Bois, Thomas 24, 145n34
boundary activation 123
Bozarslan, Hamit 70, 85, 118
Braud, Philippe 119
al-Buni, Nader 130
al-Bunni, Anwar 128
al-Buti, Muhammad Sa'id Ramadan 66, 96

Camp David Agreements 72
census, 1962 Jazira 50–1, 73, 112
Center of Kurdish Studies 42
"Charter for the Construction of a Modern State in Syria" 109
*chawi* 60
children: punishment for speaking Kurdish 63; tortured 116
Cigerxwîn 23, 43
citizenship, loss of 50–1
civil society, in Kurdistan 111
*Ciwanên kurd* comity 23
"Communiqué of 185 Expatriated Syrians" 109
Corrective Movement 53–4, 71–2
cotton shaykhs 38–40
cultural framing: of the Kurdish community 92–3; of Syrian Kurds by PKK 104–5
cultural reviews 104–5
cultural tool kit 93

Dakkuri tribe 10
Damascene Kurds: history 10–11; loyalty to the French 11–13
Damascus: bombings 77; Damascus–PKK axis 75–7; guerilla factions invited to 75–6; woman beaten to death 120; *see also* Declaration of Damascus
"Damascus Spring" 107, 110–11
Darar, Riad 126
Darbasiya, PKK offices 77
Darwish, 'Abd al-Hamid Hajj 49, 67, 87, 89, 91, 157n15
*dawa* 57, 59
al-Dawalibi, Ma'ruf 50
Day of Kurdish Poetry 106
Day of the Martyred Kurd 123
Declaration of Damascus 126–7
Decree No. 50 110
*Delav* (journal) 105
Democratic Front 76
Democratic Party of Kurdistan in Syria 49
Democratic Party of Kurds in Syria 49; *see also* KDPS
Democratic Union of Kurdistan 72
Democratic Union Party 88
*Deng* (newspaper) 105
*Dengê Kurd* (newspaper) 104
Derik: Qamishli revolt 115, 116; smuggling 68
Derky, Lukman 131
Dersimi, Nuri 18
*Dev Genç* (political party) 75
*Dev Sol* (political party) 75
Dieckhoff, Alain 55–6
al-Din, 'Abd al-Baki Nizam 44, 48
al-Din, Salah Badr 87, 89, 127, 157n16
al-Din, Shaykh 'Ali Muhi 111
al-Din, Tawfiq Nizam 48, 51
dissimulation: definitions 83–4; strategy of 5
Dome, Michel 31, 33
Dominican Fathers *see* French Dominican missionaries
Dr Bahoz (Fehman Husayn) 137

ethnicity, as political tool 3–4
Euphrates' water 71–2, 75–8

Faysal I 13–14
films, in Kurdish language 106
*fitna* 2, 127
flags, autonomist 29, 34, 147n55
framing 92; *see also* cultural framing
France, policy toward the Kurds 4–5
Franco-Syrian Treaty (1936) 26, 29, 31, 34

## 184  Index

French Dominican missionaries 31–2
French Intelligence Service 5, 15, 18–19, 28; *see also* Special Services
French Mandate (1920–46): area covered 11; *civilizing mission* 15–16; as continuity and change 2–5; creation of 15; Kurdish populations under 8–11; Kurdish reactions to 11–13; overview 8; political policy 16
"Fundamental Document" 109

GAP project 75
Garisi, 'Abd al-Rahman 96
GCC (Gulf Cooperation Council) 117
*Gelawêj* (journal) 104
Gelvin, James L. 55
gender equality, promotion of, by PKK 94, 158n34
General Law on Printed Matter 110
"General National Accords" 109
Germany, propaganda to Kurdish leaders 20
Ghadri, Farid 108
groups of solidarity 133
Gulf Cooperation Council (GCC) 117
*Gulistan* (journal) 104
Gurr, Ted 118
*Gurzek Gul* (journal) 105

al-Hadi, Daham 31, 147n49, 147n57, 148n60
Hajo Agha 30–2
al-Halabi, Fuad Bey 43
Halabja 123, 125
Hama, revolt (1982) 98
*Hamidiyye* regiments 9
Hammud, 'Ali 113
Hamo, Muhammad 106–7, 125
Hamo, Rashid 4, 48–9, 86
Hananu, Ibrahim 142n7
Hariri, Rafiq 79
Hasaka, PKK offices 77
Hasaka census (1962) 50–1, 73, 112
al-Hasani, Bashir 96
Hasenan tribe 10, 73
*Hawar* (journal) 22–4, 26, 29
Hawatmeh, Nayif 76
*Hayy al-Akrad* 10
Hebbé, Hanna 31, 35–6
heroin 68

Heverkan tribe 10
*Hêvî* (journal) 105
al-Hilal, Muhammad Talab 60–1
al-Hinnawi, Sami 40, 44–5
history, rewriting of 64
honor killing 92, 158n28
Horowitz, Donald L. 119
Hroch, Miroslav 22
Husayn, Fehman (Dr Bahoz) 137
Husayn, Mahmud 100
Husayn, Saddam 72, 74, 79–81, 125, 155n5
Husayn, Sirwan Hajji 118

Ibesh, Nouri 45
Ibrahim, Habib 110
Ibrahim Khalil gate 81
Ibrahim Pasha 9–10, 142n4
ideational themes 93
"identity mobilizations" 108
Inönü, Ismet 43
Iran–Iraq War (1980–88) 73
Iraq, influence of events in 125
irrigation projects 62
Ishaq, Sa'id 30
Islamic Front 98

Jadid, Salah 58
Jamil Pasha, Akram 42
Jamil Pasha, Qadri 42
Jan, Qadri 23, 43
Jangir, Ubeydallah 96
Jarablus 8, 10, 28–9, 35, 68, 86, 94
Jazira: 1962 census 50–1, 73, 112; agricultural "miracle" 38–9; autonomist movement (Kurdish–Christian bloc) 29–37; *chawi* 60; Kurdish language marking boundaries defining Kurds 103; politics 27–9; renaming of towns 65
Jaziri, Mullah Ahmad 96
Jums tribe 9

Kabul, Salim 115
Kaddur Bey 30
Kandy, Nouri 27
KDP (Kurdistan Democratic Party in Syria) 86
KDP (Kurdistan Democratic Party of Iraq) 48–50, 72–4, 76, 78, 81

Index    185

KDPPS (Kurdish Democratic Progressive Party in Syria) 78, 91, 122; *see also* Darwish, 'Abd al-Hamid Hajj
KDPS (Kurdish Democratic Party of Syria, The Party) 48–9, 59, 76, 78, 86–7, 89, 92, 134–5; *see also* Miro, Daham
Kemal, Mustafa 43
Khaddam, 'Abd al-Halim 117, 127
Khalil ibn Ibrahim Pasha 20, 30
Khalil, Mano 106, 168n1
Khani, Ahmad 96, 106
Khani Book Store 106
Khani's Club 106
Kharzan tribe 9
Khastiyan tribe 9
al-Khaznawi, Ahmad 96, 97, 101
al-Khaznawi, Izz al-Din 101
al-Khaznawi, Muhammad Mashuk 101–2, 126, 128–9
Khoja, Muhammad 'Ali 48
Khoury, Philip S. 11
Khoybun League: formation in Lebanon 17–19; nucleus at the time of its creation 144n19; old members to beg for amnesty 46; program and doctrine 19–21; strategy of political participation 86; and Sufism 96; support to the Badirkhan brothers for cultural renaissance 22; withdrawal from political scene 42
Kienle, Eberhard 72
King–Crane commission 13–14
Kitkan tribe 10, 12
KNA-S (Kurdistan National Assembly of Syria) 129
Kobane, Qamishli revolt 116
Kochar tribe *see* Miran tribe
Komala 72
KRG (Kurdistan Regional Government) 91
Kuftariyya 65–6, 97, 99
Kuftaru, Ahmad 65–6, 97, 99
Kurd Dagh: candidates overtly declaring themselves as representatives of the PKK 77; French troops arrival 11; Kurdish language spoken "naturally" 102; PKK accommodating with Sufi shaykhs 99; PKK's militant's *de facto* control 77; religious authority of Sufi shaykhs 99; renaming of villages 65; tribes sharing 9
al-Kurdi, Mahmud 66
Kurdish community: delimitation of 82–3; policy of dissimulation 83–5
Kurdish cultural movement: Kurdish–French connection 23–5; Syria and Lebanon 21–3
Kurdish culture: defense of 102–4; militant "careers" in 106–7; politization of 104–6
Kurdish Democratic Alliance in Syria (*Hevbendiya, Al-Takhaluf*, the Alliance) 88
Kurdish Democratic Front in Syria (*Eniya, Al-Jabha*, the Front) 87–8
Kurdish Future Movement 127, 129
Kurdish identity: and Islam 95; and Sufism 95–6
Kurdish language: attempts to promote 21–3, 42–4; clandestine courses in 105; films in 106; legislation affecting 110; opportunities and constraints for standardization 25–7; politicization of 133–4; possession of books in, punishable by imprisonment 48, 63, 110; publication of books in 104–5, 161n64; as regular means of communication in Jazira 83; and Sufism 96–7; teaching prohibition 63; transmission via family 103–4; *see also* Kurdish culture; Kurmanji
Kurdish League 21, 86
Kurdish Leftist Democratic Party 87
Kurdish names, restrictions on registering 62–4
Kurdish Peasant Party 111
Kurdish political movement in Syria: cultural framing the community 92–3; dangers of being a member 91–2; evolution 86–8; future tendencies 136–8; late development of 133–6; opportunity structures 88–90; political participation 85–6; resource mobilization 90–1; theoretical framework of political parties 88, 93–5
Kurdish studies, omission of Syrian aspects 1–2
Kurdish–Christian bloc 29–37
Kurdistan: 1992 elections 74; history 69–71

Kurdistan Alliance 80
Kurdistan Regional Government (KRG) 91
*Kurdistan Teali Cemiyeti* (Committee for the recovery of Kurdistan, KTC) 143n16
Kurmanji 8, 99–101; *see also* Kurdish language

League of Nations 14–15, 70
Leenders, Reinoud 129
Lescot, Roger 23–4
Levonian, Ador 18
local festivals, invention of 29, 34
Lyautey system 16, 143n13

Mahmud ibn Ibrahim Pasha 10
Mahmud, Muhammad Isa 49, 86
*maktumin* Kurds 51
mandate system 14–15
al-Mansura, Muhammad 89
Mardam, Jamil 13, 35
martyrs 123
Masum Korkmaz training base 76
McDowall, David 77
*millet* system 8, 142n2
Millis tribe 9–10, 12
Ministry of Irrigation 130
"minorities," construction of concept under French Mandate 8
Miran tribe (Kochar) 9–10, 73, 76
Miro, Daham 63, 87, 89
Molotov, Mikhaylovich V. 21
Montagne, Robert 26, 143n14
Montgomery, Harriet 104
Movement for Social Peace 109
*muasasa* 58
Muhammad, Kamuran 156n17
Muhammad, Khalil 48
Murud movement (1933–40) 13, 143n8
Muslim Brotherhood 45, 47, 59, 97, 109; *see also* al-Bayanouni, 'Ali Sadr al-Din

Nahalawi, 'Abd al-Karim 50
Nasan, Ibrahim 110
Nasser, Gamal 47–8
National Bloc 35, 39, 134; *see also* Mardam, Jamil; "politics of notables"
National Party 39
National Progressive Front 67

National Salvation Front (NSF) 108, 127
"national" songs 34
Nayo, Mullah Muhammad 87
negative violence 124
"new man" discourse 83, 93
Newroz: 1986 incidents with the police 63; 1994 request not to celebrate 107; ban on festival 65, 131; founding myth of 64, 154n28; in official Syrian calendar 136; PKK promotion of open celebration of 104–5; political sponsorship of 105
*Newroz* (newspaper) 105
Nezan, Shewket 48
NSF (National Salvation Front) 108, 127
*nurca* 66
Nursi, Sa'id 66

Öcalan, Abdullah 76–9, 94, 119–23, 122–3, 156n15, 159n45
Orthodox Syriacs 31

Papazian, Vahan 18
patronization 59–60
People's Defense Forces 137
People's Party 39, 50
Perwer, Shivan 123
*peshmergas* 73
Picard, Elizabeth 40, 47, 54, 59, 141n1, 164n33
Pijan tribe 10
Pinto, Paulo G. 2, 82, 97–100, 103, 106, 159n42, 159n46
*Pirs* (journal) 105
PKK (Kurdistan Workers Party): analysis of, using theoretical framework 93–5; Assembly members open support for 67; cultural framing of the Syrian Kurds 104–5; Damascus–PKK axis 75–7; recruitment intensity 135; role in riots 122–3; structural dependence vis-à-vis Syria 77–9; Turkish threats against 137–8; *see also* PYD
*Place Where God Is Sleeping, The* (film) 106
PLAK (People's Liberation Army of Kurdistan) 76
PNF (Progressive National Front) 54, 109
political entrepreneurs, use of ethnicity 3–4
"politics of notables" 39–40

Index    187

positive violence 124–6
Provence, Michael 55
Puaux, Gabriel 35
PUK (Patriotic Union of Kurdistan) 72–4, 78, 81
PYD (Partiya Yekîtiya Demokratîc, Democratic Union Party) 79, 122–3, 126–7, 129, 131, 137

Qadurah, 'Abd al-Qadir 113
Qamishli: commitment to irrigate 130; expropriation of land 60; and Kaddur Bey 30; PKK offices 77; poor infrastructure of Kurdish suburbs 119; population growth 38, 120; smuggling 67–8; uprising on return of dead villager 63
Qamishli revolt of March 2004: as beginning of a new era 108–10; Christian and Arab involvement 115–16; events of March 2004 114–18; events preceding 110–14; making sense of the violence 118–21; prompting publications on Kurdish issue in Syria 1; as radicalizing ethnic divisions 126–31; as source of tension between Damascus and Kurdish parties of Iraq 80; subjectivity of the actors 124–6; violence as a "repertoire of action" 121–4
Qasim, 'Abd al-Karim 49
al-Qudsi, Nazim 50

radio broadcasts, in Kurdish 23, 104
Radio Levant 23
Ras al-'Ayn: historical ownership 148n1; PKK offices 77; Qamishli revolt 116; resurgence of economic activity 38
Reform Party of Syria 108
relative deprivation 118
relative frustration 120–1
religious nationalism 100–1, 159n46
renaming of towns/villages: Jazira 65; Kurd Dagh 65
resources mobilization 90, 121
reticular action 91, 158n21
"Revolt of 1937" 31, 35–6, 147n57
Robariya tribe 9
Roj (newspaper) 105
Roja Nû/Le Jour Nouveau (journal) 23–4

Rondot, Pierre 23, 97, 145n31, 145n33
Roy, Olivier 4

Sabri, 'Uthman 23, 46, 49, 86–7, 104
safe haven 74
Sa'id Agha 32
Sa'id Shamdin Pasha 142n5
Saif, Riad 126
Salah al-Din al-Ayyubi (Saladin) 10, 64
Salah al-Din Club 23
Salih, Hasan 111, 113, 122
San Francisco Conference 42
school books, removal of mention of Kurds from 62
Scott, James C. 136
SCP (Syrian Communist Party) 39, 43–4, 47–8, 86–7, 148n4
Second Gulf War (1991) 73
Seif, Riad 109
Selim, Memduh 19, 42, 144n19, 145n27, 145n34
Selo, Fawzi 45, 150n22
"separatist" movement (September 1961) 49
Serail 15, 19, 26
Seurat, Michel 104
Sevres, Treaty of 18
Shahin, Bozan 28, 144n19, 145n27, 147n48
Shahin, Kamal 156n17
Shahin, Mustafa 28, 43, 144n19, 145n27, 147n48
Shamdin family 11
Sharaf al-Din Bitlisi Club 23
Sharifians 13–14
Shaykh Sa'id Insurrection (1925) 17
Shedadan tribe 10
Sheikan tribe 9–10
Shibabi, Amir Bhajat 35
Shihaki, Hikmat 66
Shikakan tribe 9
al-Shishakli, Adib 40–1, 44–5
shu'ubiyyun 41, 57
SKDCP (Syrian Kurdish Democratic Concord Party, Wifaq) 79
smuggling: Kurdish pride in 83; as legitimate 70; as part of dissimulation 84; Qamishli 67–8
Society of Beneficence for the Poor of Jazira 110

Special Services 31–3, 35; see also French Intelligence Service
SPP (Syrian Popular Party) 39–40, 44–5, 47, 148n5
"Statement of 1,000" 109
"Statement of 99" 109
Steppe nationalism 33–4
Stêr (newspaper) 105
Sufism: cooperation with PKK 135; definitions 159n36; and Kurdish identity 95–6; reformation of the Kurdish Sufi brotherhoods in Syria 96–8; as synonymous with Kurdism 98–102
Sunni Islam: majority of Syrian Kurds as 8; political parties associated with 39
Sykes–Picot agreement 13–14
Syria: creation of 13–14; difficulty of conducting field work 2; impact of fall of Saddam Husayn 79–81; Kurdish dictators 44–6; open support of the PKK 75; post-Mandate upheavals 38–42; rise of Kurdish nationalism 16–17; "secessionist" period 49–52; Second Gulf War (1991) 73–4; stigmatization of minorities 40–2; tensions with Iraq 71–5
Syrian constitution: of 1973 54, 62; by the High Commission in 1930 27; inclusion of Arab nationalism 62; suspension in 1939 35
Syrian Kurdish movement, infrapolitics 5–6
Syrian Kurdistan, terminology 95, 112, 123
Syrian Kurds, lack of media attention 1
Syrian Muslim Brotherhood 39, 149n7
Syrian regime, relations with the Kurdish parties 89–90

Tabqa dam 61
Tachnak committee/party 18, 22
Talabani, Jalal 48–9, 72, 78, 81, 87, 115, 155n6, 162n2
Tamo, Mashal 125
Tanzimat 8, 10, 142n1
tariqa 65
Terrier, Pierre 28–9
Terrier Plan 5, 28–9
Tilly, Charles 58, 117–18, 121

Tlas, Mustafa 117
"traditional" dress 105
Turkish People's Liberation Army 75
Turkish–Israeli alliance (1996) 78

UAR (United Arab Republic) 47–8
UK, alienation of Kurdish leaders in Syria 20
UN Resolution 1559 79
UN Security Council Resolution 699 74
Unanimism 6, 83
"undocumented" Kurds 112; see also citizenship, loss of
United Arab Republic 41
United Front of Kurdistan 74
United Nations, Kurd's exclusion 42
Upper Jazira: lack of industrialization projects 132
US, need for "critical dialogue" with Syria 80–1
USSR, Kurdish nationalist sympathy for 20–1, 44
'Uthman, Marwan 111, 113, 122, 128

Vali, Abbas 111
van Bruinessen, Martin 3, 95
Van Dam, Nikolaos 58
Vanly, Ismet Sharif 1, 77, 129
Velud, Christian 30
violence: phenomenon of 118; as a "repertoire of action" 121–4; subjectivity of the actors 124–6
visibility, strategy of 6, 110, 112, 114, 119, 121, 130, 136–7
Von Hentig, W.O. 20

Waqf, Ministry of 97, 159n41
Washington DC 2006 conference 129
websites: dissemination of photos of Qamishli revolt 118; political parties 158n26; of Shaykh al-Khaznawi 101–2
Wieviorka, Michel 118
Wifaq see SKDCP
women: position of 25; see also gender equality, promotion of, by PKK
Writer's Union of Iraqi Kurdistan 107

Xunav (newspaper) 105
Xwendevan (journal) 105

Yasin, Shaykh 100
Yazidi: alienation of 100;
  geographic distribution of 8;
  inhabiting Sinjar 11; language 103;
  and PKK 135; population in
  Kurd Dagh 9
Yekîtî (Partiya Yekîtî ya Kurdî li Suriyê)
  110–14, 118, 121–4, 126–9, 131, 136
Yusif, Nadeem 156n17

al-Yusuf family 11
al-Yusuf, Muhammad Sa'id 46

Za'im, Husni 40, 44–6, 150n21
*Zanîn* (journal) 105
*zawiya(s)* 97, 99, 101
Zaza, Nur al-Din 49, 86–7
Zorava: deplorable state of Kurdish
  neighborhood 120; Qamishli revolt 116

 eBooks – at www.eBookstore.tandf.co.uk

# A library at your fingertips!

ebooks are electronic versions of printed books. You can store them on your PC/laptop or browse them online.

They have advantages for anyone needing rapid access to a wide variety of published, copyright information.

ebooks can help your research by enabling you to bookmark chapters, annotate text and use instant searches to find specific words or phrases. Several eBook files would fit on even a small laptop or PDA.

**NEW:** Save money by eSubscribing: cheap, online access to any eBook for as long as you need it.

### Annual subscription packages

We now offer special low-cost bulk subscriptions to packages of eBooks in certain subject areas. These are available to libraries or to individuals.

For more information please contact webmaster.ebooks@tandf.co.uk

We're continually developing the eBook concept, so keep up to date by visiting the website.

# www.eBookstore.tandf.co.uk

# Routledge Paperbacks Direct

**Routledge Paperbacks Direct** is an exciting initiative that makes the best of our hardback research publishing available in paperback format for authors and individual customers to purchase directly from the dedicated Routledge Paperbacks Direct Website

**Paperbacks direct** includes titles from our publishing programmes in Philosophy, Politics and International Relations, Military and Strategic Studies, Asian Studies, Economics, Business and Management.

www.routledgepaperbacksdirect.com

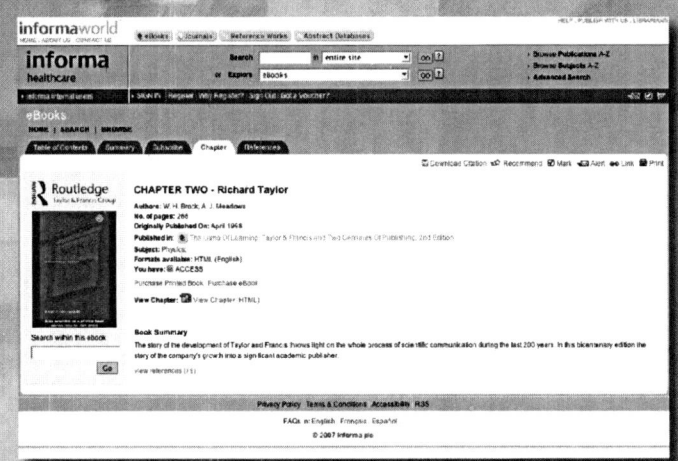

# Taylor & Francis eBooks

A flexible and dynamic resource for teaching, learning and research

**Provides quick and efficient access to the right material at the right time, where and when you want it**

- Over 17,500 eBook titles in the Humanities, Social Sciences, Behavioural Sciences, STM and Law from some of the world's leading imprints
- Quick search across all metadata, advanced search across full text
- Text Highlighting and Annotations: highlight text, annotate your observations, comment on sections of interest and edit, delete or print them

To find out more about the full range of eBooks available visit
**www.ebookstore.tandf.co.uk**

For further information on library subscriptions and purchases go to
**www.ebooksubscriptions.com**
or email **online.sales@tandf.co.uk**

**...reading will never be the same again**